WRITING AWARD WINNING ARTICLES

WRITING AWARD WINNING ARTICLES

Glenn F. Arnold,
Editor

Thomas Nelson Publishers
Nashville New York

 Published in Nashville, Tennessee, by Thomas Nelson Inc., Publishers and simultaneously in Don Mills, Ontario, by Thomas Nelson & Sons (Canada) Limited. Manufactured in the United States of America.

PUBLISHER'S NOTE

Concerning the sample articles reprinted in this volume, to preserve their uniqueness and their authenticity as teaching vehicles, the articles have not been reedited to match this publisher's house style. Except for any unintended and undetected mechanical errors, the articles appear exactly as they did when originally published.

Library of Congress Cataloging in Publication Data
Main entry under title:
Writing award winning articles.
Bibliography: p. 223.
1. Christian literature—Authorship. I. Arnold, Glenn F.
BR117.W7 1979 808'.066'2 79-10863
ISBN 0-8407-5682-8

This anthology is dedicated to the editors in the Evangelical Press Association. Throughout the past ten years, many of them have enriched my classroom and writing ministries. Much of what I teach in my journalism courses I first learned from empathetic EPA editors.

Some of these editor-friends have encouraged my journalism students by evaluating and later publishing their articles, by speaking to them in class, by giving advice, by sending them copies of their publications, and by becoming their friends.

The spiritual fellowship and the professional interaction at the EPA convention revive me each May and excite me for the next academic year.

Contents

Foreword—Joseph Bayly 11
Preface 13
Introduction: How to Use This Book 15
Chapter One: The History of Christian Journalism in America 17
Chapter Two: Tips on Writing for Evangelical Publications 29
Chapter Three: The First-Person Narrative 41
"Lord, I Believe You Want Me to Live," by Marilyn Henderson
"The Ones Who Are Left," by Elisabeth Elliot
Chapter Four: The How-to-do-it Article 61
"How to Produce a Children's Film Without Actually Crying," by Glenn F. Arnold
"The Mature Person Takes Inventory," by Jeanette Lockerbie
Chapter Five: The News Article
"The World of WIM," by Jerry Ballard
"A Minister Is Missing," by Edward E. Plowman
Chapter Six: The Interview Article 89
"Serving a Hungry World: A HIS Interview with Samuel Kamaleson"
"You Can Pray If You Want To: An Interview with Jesse Jackson," by Glenn F. Arnold
Chapter Seven: The Personality Article 115
"Don't Tell Mama," by Marinus M. Swets
"Solzhenitsyn—Whose Face in the Mirror?" by Cheryl Forbes
Chapter Eight: The General Expository Article 131
"The Price of Praise," by Virginia Stem Owens
"The Small Tribe Living Down By the Old Orchard," by Monte C. Unger
Chapter Nine: The Editorial 147
"Unmentionables," by Dr. John Stapert
"Climbing on Course," by Bernie May
Chapter Ten: The Critical Review 159
"Review of *The Late Great Planet Earth*," by Andrew Kuyvenhoven
"We Need the Eggs," by John Pott
"*The Omen*," by Dr. Thomas Howard

Chapter Eleven: The Column 183
"No Halo, Please, We're Human," by Gene Bertolet
"Rebirth," a review of Charles Colson's *Born Again*, by Wesley G. Pippert
Chapter Twelve: The Humorous Article 199
"Life Among the Nacirema," by Dr. F. F. Throckmorton with Steve Lawhead
"Ducking the Mailed Fist," by James D. Douglas
Appendix 213
Evangelical Press Association Doctrinal Statement and Code of Ethics
Glossary of Writing and Allied Terms 215
The Evangelical Free-Lancer's Library 223
Evangelical Press Association Market Guide 227

WRITING AWARD WINNING ARTICLES

Foreword

For more than a quarter of a century, the Evangelical Press Association has been bringing editors—who are often writers as well—and publishers together for an annual convention.

Men and women in this organization represent several hundred denominational, organizational, independent, and institutional American and Canadian periodicals and book publishing houses.

The highlight of the annual gathering is awards night, when the best writing is recognized. Both the writer and the periodical in which the piece was published are honored.

Over the years, this friendly competition has produced a standard of excellence that benefits and extends the mission of all of us in the evangelical community.

Through the involvement of EPA members in English and journalism departments of Christian institutions and in writers' conferences, the influence of this association has been extended still more.

For a number of years I have had the privilege of a rewarding professional relationship with Dr. Glenn Arnold, first at Moody Bible Institute, then more recently at the graduate school of Wheaton College.

Glenn Arnold is no ivory-tower professor; he possesses a keen awareness of the realities of Christian writing and publishing. That awareness enables him to help the aspiring writer, whether a student in the classroom or any reader of this book, to find an audience and communicate with it.

This book contains an exciting range of writing approaches and techniques from an exciting range of periodicals. With the cooperation of EPA's board of directors, Glenn Arnold has served us all well by bringing these pieces together—along with the article critiques and other instructional material.

Writing is a craft. We who exercise this craft for God must constantly try to improve and become better craftsmen.

This book will help.

Joseph Bayly
Past President (1960–62)
Evangelical Press Association

Preface

This anthology has been compiled to help journalism students in evangelical schools improve their writing by analyzing award-winning articles. This book has also been designed to assist Christian free-lance authors who want to write for evangelical periodicals.

In most cases the feature articles, editorials, and columns used in this book are the 1977 and 1978 first-place winners in the Higher Goals division of the annual Awards Contest of the Evangelical Press Association.

In general, the nonfiction categories of the Higher Goals competition have been used as the outline for this book. Poetry and graphics are not included. Three articles are used to illustrate article types that are not categories in the EPA contest: Jeanette Lockerbie's "The Mature Person Takes Inventory," my interview with the Reverend Jesse Jackson, and my "How to Produce a Children's Film Without Actually Crying."

Whenever attainable, the critiques that follow the illustrative articles have been written by the judges who selected them as first-place winners in the EPA contest. Contest judges are usually selected from practicing journalists in the secular media, professors of communications and journalism, and retired EPA editors.

Since 1954, the Awards Contest has been a feature of the annual EPA convention and has been a source of fellowship, stimulation, and encouragement for member editors and staff members.

I have appreciated support by the EPA Board of Directors, who originally proposed this book project. Jerry Jenkins, executive editor of *Moody Monthly* and an EPA board member, served as the liaison between the board and the editor. Peter Gillquist and Larry Stone, Thomas Nelson editors, gave me helpful insight as work on the anthology progressed. My beloved boss and chairman of the Graduate Communications Department here at Wheaton, James Engel, has provided counsel and guidance during this ten-month project.

Many thanks to good friend Wayne Stayskal, editorial cartoonist for the *Chicago Tribune*, who graciously permitted the use of his graphic insights to illustrate the subject areas of the main chapters.

My wife, Margaret Ann, typed all the correspondence with EPA editors, judges, and all three drafts of the manuscript. Without her typing and home office managing, this book would still be an idea.

Glenn F. Arnold, Ph.D.
Associate Professor of Journalism
Wheaton Graduate School
Wheaton, Illinois

Introduction: How to Use This Book

When this book is used as a journalism text, it is suggested that the instructor assign the chapters as preparation for the writing assignments.

In most academic semesters, quarters, or trimesters, time does not allow students to research and write all the article types presented in this anthology. Therefore, instructors will probably wish to concentrate on the chapters that coincide with the types of articles they want their students to practice.

Chapters 3–12 present and illustrate the following types of writing: first-person narrative, how-to-do-it, news feature, interview, personality sketch, general, editorial, review, column, and humorous. These categories of writing have been placed in an ascending order of difficulty. News writing is generally considered the foundation for all journalistic writing; the feature article presents increased challenges to the writer; the review, column, and editorial call for the most skill and experience. No one has yet been able to digest and adequately explain the quality or type called humor.

Each of these chapters is introduced with a definition and explanation of the type of writing being studied. These chapter introductions also include some suggestions for writing that type of article.

Each article is followed by a critique. Writers should find this helpful in determining why that particular piece was judged by an unbiased professional writer, editor, or educator to be a superior example of Christian journalism.

The critiques are followed by research assignments, practice suggestions, and discussion questions that can be done in conjunction with classroom assignments or independently by a free-lance writer.

It is recommended that when the student reaches chapter 3, he use the following internal sequence for each chapter: read the introduction to the article type, read the two articles and their critiques, and then read the articles a second time to study the bases for the critiques.

Many free-lancers collect examples of article types. These sample articles then serve as references and guides when an author is asked by an editor to write a certain type of article. The alert author will clip examples of the various kinds of writing from both secular and Christian publications. A careful study of these will enable a new writer to learn more quickly which techniques and structures are best received by editors and eventually by readers.

A starting writer should not go into "type trauma" upon seeing two or more article types within one article. For some subjects it is necessary to combine article types in order to present the material most effectively. A news feature may take the form of an interview; the column may be written in a satirical how-to-do-it form. Many exciting combinations exist for the creative writer, thereby multiplying the number of types illustrated in this text.

The Writer and *Writer's Digest* regularly publish how-to articles on the basic article types. These magazines give current listings for the religious or inspirational market, and they also contain advertisements for how-to books helpful to new writers.

The instructor may wish to use the discussion questions following each article as part of the classroom interaction or have the students write out their responses outside of class.

The research-practice-discussion questions have been designed as preliminary steps in the first attempt at writing the article type being studied.

Whenever possible, it is recommended that the student practice writing the article type being studied after reading the assigned chapter. No substitute exists for the actual process of writing and receiving feedback from fellow students, instructors, friends, and, if possible, editors.

The free-lance author may wish to use this book as a self-study guide or as a reference. On a self-tutorial basis, the free-lancer may wish to proceed through the book from the preface through the last chapter to gain an overview of the types of writing used most frequently in evangelical periodicals. Or, the individual writer may wish to use this text as a reference work, on a chapter-by-chapter basis, as part of the preparation for writing article types.

Writing Award-Winning Articles has been prayerfully written and compiled to help all who conscientiously will use this book.

1
The History of Christian Journalism in America

Christian journalism in North America came to life through an injection of English ink. The *Protestant Covenant* began publishing in England in 1682, nearly fifty years before the first similar effort in the American colonies.

During their infancy in the second half of the eighteenth century, all colonial magazines relied heavily on their journalistic forefathers in England. John Tebbel of New York University has noted that "the scissors and pastepot were indispensable tools of the first editors."[1]

Colonial Period

One century after Harvard University Press began printing Bibles, sermons, and hymnals, and thirty-three years before the Declaration of Independence, *Christian History* appeared in Boston on March 5, 1743. This first Christian magazine in the New World was published by Thomas Price, son of the pastor of Old South Church in Boston. *Christian History* served as the print arm of the Great Awakening in the American colonies and was really more a chronicle of events than a magazine. It began only two years after the first colonial periodical, *The American* (1741).

All colonial American periodicals faced the dual obstacles of low reader interest (because of the pioneer life-style) and poor distribution systems. Mail service was costly and inadequate. None of these magazines had any arrangement for receiving advance subscription payments.

Of the five religious magazines that existed between 1743 and 1794, not

[1]*The American Magazine: A Compact History* (New York: Hawthorn Books, 1969), p. 4.

one lasted more than ten years. A few church papers began publishing after the Revolutionary War. These Christian magazines were composed mostly of sermons in one form or another. Circulation for all early American publications averaged 500 and never exceeded 1,600.

Early Nationalistic Period

Many new Christian periodicals came down the birth canal of early American presses during the post-revolutionary period. They were nurtured in the climate of new missionary enthusiasm and revivals as Americans began moving into the Mississippi Valley. Controversies over Unitarianism, doctrinal infidelity, and free thinking filled many of these periodical pages.

The Theological Magazine (1795–1799) of New York typified Christian publications in the early years of the United States. With the subtitle, *A Synopsis of Modern Religious Sentiment on a New Plan,* this bimonthly published dull essays such as "The Effects of Skepticism in the Last Moments" and "On the Personality of Melchaesadec [*sic*]." Congregational and Presbyterian ministers wrote most of the articles, which discussed conversions and missionary activity. Poetry and reviews of new books filled the remaining pages of *The Theological Magazine.*

By the end of the first third of the nineteenth century, approximately one hundred religious newspapers and twenty-one monthly religious magazines were being published in this growing nation. Most of these publications were weekly papers that covered both religious and denominational news. Many competed favorably with the secular press. The most important of the denominational papers were the Congregational *Recorder* in Boston, the Episcopalian *Recorder* in Philadelphia, and the Methodist *Christian Advocate* and the Presbyterian *Observer* in New York.

These well-read, large-sheet newspapers often had correspondents in other cities who reported church and secular news. The religious news sometimes contained gossip and rumors from church leaders. All these papers remained politically neutral.

In 1819 the Baptists began publishing the *Christian Watchman,* which later became *The Watchman-Examiner.*

Several Christian weeklies begun in the first quarter of the nineteenth century continued well into the twentieth. These included the *Christian Index,* the *Universalist Leader,* and the *Unitarian Christian Reporter.*

Zion's Herald, which started in Boston in 1823, became the first weekly paper published by the Methodists. From the start it evidenced vitality and independence, advocating strong antislavery, temperance, and women's rights positions. The *Herald*'s copy often included debates on Calvinism and Universalism.

During the first half of the nineteenth century, mainline denominations committed large portions of budgets and staff to publishing newspapers and periodicals. The Congregationalists were publishing twenty-five periodicals and the Catholics nearly fifty. The United States census of 1850 showed 191 religious publications, about half of which were newspapers.

Pre-Civil War Period

As America rapidly approached conflict over slavery and as the population moved even farther west (1825–50), Christian newspapers, magazines, and journals continued to thrive. New publications appeared that also devoted much space to the slavery debate, the rise of the Campbellites, Unitarianism, and Universalism.

Before the start of the Civil War, the American Sunday School Union began publishing the *Sunday School Journal* (1831–58), which later became the *Sunday School Times*.

The American Tract Society published the *American Newspaper* (1843–1923), which had a monthly circulation of 190,000 in 1850, and *The Christian Banner and Tract Journal* (1858–72), a weekly paper. Before the United States split over slavery, each major Protestant denomination had at least twenty periodicals.

The rise of religious daily newspapers was a pre-Civil War phenomenon in Christian journalism. In 1839 a group of Philadelphia businessmen began publishing a daily paper called *The North American.*

From 1860 to 1861 the *New York Sun* was converted into a Christian newspaper. The principal backer, the Reverend Archibald Morrison of Philadelphia, lost nearly all his money in a futile attempt to make the *Sun* "a daily lay preacher to the poorer classes." *The World* was started in 1860 in New York City by another group of Christian businessmen from Philadelphia. As a one-cent religious daily, its format included church and Sunday school matters on the first page, and advertisements for sermon references appeared throughout. None of those religious dailies lasted more than two years.

During this period Christian publications began to receive increasing negative reaction from their secular counterparts. The following commentaries were typical:

> The religious newspapers "exploit" the religious sentiment of the community, and not infrequently, when manly and fair agreement is wanting, they have recourse to the most odious of all weapons in the discussion—appeals to sectarianism and superstition. (*Putnam's Monthly*, IX, 524, May, 1857.)

> In many parts of the United States conductors of sectarian journals permit themselves and their correspondents a license of language and personal allusion which they would both hesitate to employ were they amenable to the rules of men of the world. . . . Such editors may be Christians, but they certainly are not gentlemen. (*Russell's Magazine*, III, 376, July, 1858.)

Civil War Period

Even during the Civil War (1861–65), Christian periodicals in the North continued to expand as one of the largest specialized segments of American journalism, even surpassing the number of women's magazines.

As early as 1850, all Protestant denominations except the Episcopalians had already divided over the slavery issue. Many Southern publications, especially Methodist and Southern Baptist, were interrupted or killed by the war.

Post-Civil War Period

After the Civil War, church union became a principal topic in many of the Christian publications. One paper published at this time was called *Church Union* and two were called *Christian Union*. Also during this period, church periodicals began dropping the secular news coverage and became denominational reporters and opinion journals. One of the latter type was the *Christian Union*, founded in 1870 and edited by Henry Ward Beecher for twelve years.

After the war, several denominational weeklies designed for the Christian family appeared. One of these was *Christian at Work*, later *Christian Work* (1806–1866), which was edited for a while by Thomas de Witt Talmage. He also edited the monthly *Sunday Magazine* (1877–89) of New York. *Chicago Alliance* (1873–83) combined religious news with essays. None of these family weeklies was financially successful.

The *Christian Herald* began in 1878 as the New York edition of a London journal. Originally its main purpose was to reprint Spurgeon's sermons. The *Herald* later published Talmage's sermons and religious fiction.

Paradoxically, the number of Christian periodicals devoted to the publication of sermons increased in the 1870s and 1880s, while pulpit influence was decreasing in the lives of the people. The journals devoted to sermon reprinting included the *National Preacher* (1826–66), the *Boston Pulpit* (1872), *Chicago Pulpit* (1871–73), and the *New York Pulpit Treasury* (1883–1907).

Other evangelical post-war periodicals were *Missionary Review of the World* (1878–1939) from Princeton, New Jersey; the *National Sunday School Teacher* (1866–82) of Chicago; the YMCA's *Association News* (1879–91) from Philadelphia; and the *YMCA Watchman,* later *Association News* (1876–1932), published from Chicago, then from Cleveland, and finally from New York.

The Salvation Army began its *War Cry* in New York in 1882. Even while its *Christian Banner* was still being published, the American Tract Society started the more eye-appealing *Illustrated Christian Weekly* (1871–92), which competed favorably with general magazines. This new publication was edited in the early 1870s by Lyman Abbott and was illustrated by Timothy Cole's woodcuts.

These magazines discussed topics of the day such as the evolutionary theory and the question of future punishment in hell. Interest in the latter subject has been attributed to the preaching of Dwight L. Moody. His evangelistic meetings, which had peaked in 1881, followed a national financial panic. Moody began *The Record of Christian Work* in 1881 at Northfield, Massachusetts, and it lasted over fifty years. *The Institute Tie* (later *The Christian Worker* and now *Moody Monthly*) was started in 1900 at the Moody Bible Institute of Chicago.

At the close of the eighteenth century, several anti-Catholic periodicals emerged. The best known, even though it only had a circulation of 10,000, was the *Converted Catholic.* Others included the *American Protestant,* which lasted until 1898, and the *Protestant Standard,* which ran for twenty-two years until 1899.

The number of Christian magazines nearly doubled—from 350 to 650—between the end of the Civil War and the year 1885. About half of these were Sunday school papers, some with circulations exceeding 50,000. The best weeklies had 100,000 subscribers and the reviews 10,000 at the most. Journalistic quality did not improve correspondingly with the increasing number of new Christian periodicals. Monthly and quarterly journals and weeklies were filled with poorly written theological treatises and provincial controversies. These publications often attacked one another.

The following is an attack leveled by Theodore Tilton, editor of the *Independent*, against the editor of the *New York Evangelist:*

> Take a man who can neither write nor preach nor keep his temper nor mind his own business; thrill his bosom day by day with twenty years of dyspepsia; flesh his brain with the hallucination that his bookkeeping mind is competent to religious journalism; put a pen in his hand wherewith to write himself down a Peck-sniff, set him like a dog in his kennel, to make a pastime of snooping at the respectable people of the neighborhood, and then, gentle reader, you have a specimen copy of the *Evangelist.*[2]

During the last two decades of the nineteenth century, most Protestant periodicals in the United States decreased their coverage of secular news as secular daily newspapers grew and improved.

The products of the Catholic press had surpassed the Methodists by 1885. The most prominent Catholic publications were the *Catholic World* and *Ave Maria,* both beginning in 1865.

Black Periodicals

The African Methodist church began a quarterly in 1841 that became known as the *Christian Recorder* in 1852. By 1912 its circulation was 6,500. The magazine was viewed with suspicion by slaveholders and pro-slavery people of the North.

In the 1860s and 1870s came the *Southwestern Christian Advocate* (Methodist Episcopal), the *Christian Index* (Colored Methodist Episcopal), *The Star of Zion* (African Methodist Episcopal Zion), the *Afric-American Presbyterian,* the *American Baptist,* and *Georgia Baptist.*

In the early 1880s, the *Western Star* (Baptist), the *Baptist Vanguard,* and the *A.M.E. Church Review* emerged. Approximately four and a half million black Christians were members of the denominations that supported these publications.

In 1896 a former slave from Texas, Richard Henry Boyd, led the founding of the National Baptist Publishing Board in Nashville, Tennes-

[2]Frederic Hudson, *Journalism in the United States from 1690 to 1872* (New York: n.p., 1873), p. 298 as quoted in Frank Luther Mott, *A History of American Magazines* (Cambridge, Mass.: Harvard University Press, 1957), III, p. 64.

see, which sent out 100,000 copies of its Sunday school papers in the first year.

Twentieth Century

At the beginning of the 1900s, Christian periodicals reflected the tensions of the day. Articles were written about increases in Protestant church membership and attendance decline, the historical and literary criticism of the Bible, and new questions about man's origins and moral growth (triggered by new concepts of the universe provided by geological and anthropological studies).

Evolution was fully accepted by some of the larger Christian periodicals, including *Christian Union* and the *Independent*. The old *Bibliotheca Sacra* (1843–) held that the Genesis creation account was only allegorical.

Church heresy trials were reprinted thoroughly in Christian publications, which were facing competition from agnostic and free-thought magazines such as the *Ingersoll Memorial Beacon* (1904–1913) and *Lucifer* (1897–1906) of Chicago, and the *Humanitarian Review* (1903–1911) of Los Angeles.

Some of the Christian family weeklies such as the *New York Witness* and the *Christian Herald* conducted significant charitable work. A crusading weekly entitled *Ram's Horn* was published in Chicago from 1890–1910 by Frederick L. Chapman. It advocated prohibition, church union, positive Christianity, and equal suffrage. Featuring cover cartoons, the attractive *Ram's Horn* was sold on the streets and trains of Chicago and also by mail subscriptions, reaching a 50,000 circulation.

By the first quarter of the 1900s, most Christian periodicals stopped printing secular news and began publishing denominational news and articles for the family. Some Christian publications, such as *Outlook* and *Independent,* became secular magazines.

Format was also changing at the turn of the century. Most Christian periodicals switched from newspaper to magazine size and some to quarterly size. Advertising began to be moved up from the back sections to be interspersed with the main editorial content. While these innovations were introduced, Christian publications were experiencing a marked decline in prosperity and influence on American society.

Denominational magazines entered the new century vigorously, with the Methodists out in front with 150 publications. Three-fourths of the states had at least one Baptist publication, and Congregationalists,

Presbyterians, Episcopalians, Lutherans, Disciples of Christ, Quakers, and Unitarians all had their own periodicals.

As Christian journalism continued into the second half of the twentieth century, it was generally in good health. Loyal readerships had helped many publications survive the Depression and World War II.

Presbyterian Life had more than one million subscribers and the Methodist *Together* was close to that mark. In 1956 *Christianity Today* was founded as the voice of evangelical Christianity. The American Baptist *Crusader* news magazine reached 350,000 readers each month. The Roman Catholic church published 500 papers (weekly, monthly, and quarterly) with a total circulation of 25 million. The Protestant press also produced the same number of publications with a circulation of about 20 million.

However, Martin Marty in *The Religious Press in America* (1963) questioned whether the Protestant press in the second half of the twentieth century had even been noticed by the American people. He stated that it was too sharply focused on a small segment of the American public and dealt with minor issues that did not interest or affect the total culture. He felt that the institutions and denominations were placed before world concerns.[3] These judgments were made a decade and a half before the "year of the evangelical" (1976), which may now have developed into an ephemeral "Era of Evangelicalism."

Christian Magazine Associations

From the beginning of Christian journalism in America in the middle of the eighteenth century, Christian editors and publications in America had not fellowshipped together in any formal association. The temperament of some of the editors and the independent editorial stance of many of the publications during the first 150 years of Christian journalism hindered the formation of such organizations.

On December 6, 1916, in St. Louis, Missouri, twenty editors who were attending the quadrennial meetings of the Federal Council of Churches met for informal discussion. The editors decided that the group "should become a continuing body."

Thirty editors then met in Cleveland, Ohio, on May 6, 1919, to organize the Editorial Council of the Religious Press. This was essentially the

[3]*The Religious Press in America* (New York: Holt, Rinehart, and Winston, 1963), pp. 8–27.

founding of the Associated Church Press (ACP), that name being adopted in 1937.

The following are some of the church publications whose editors participated in the first council: *A.M.E. Zion Quarterly, A.M.E. Review, American Sunday School Union, The American Friend, The Arkansas Methodist* (three editors present), *The Baptist Herald, Christian Century, Christian Index, Christian Recorder, Christian Work, The Congregationalist, Evangelical Herald* (two editors), *Federal Council Bulletin, Indiana Federation of Churches, Methodist Recorder, Missionary Review of the World, Northwestern Christian Advocate, The Watchword,* and *Woman's Council of Home Missions.*

From 1916 to the present, ACP has grown from a fellowship of 30 editors to more than 160, mostly from mainline denominations. William B. Lipphard (ACP Executive Secretary, 1951–61) has evaluated the Associated Church Press this way:

> As a press organization or as a fellowship of editors and through its member publications, it has sought to guide humanity by the teachings of Christ. Like a guidepost welcomed by the anxious and weary traveler who has lost his way, the church press has pointed steadily toward the goal of a Christian world community. And it has tried to influence the world by the pen in spite of the fact that during its fifty years the world has three times, in the upheavals of war, been influenced and motivated by the machine-gun and its modern descendant, the atomic bomb.[4]

The Evangelical Press Association (EPA) was organized in Chicago, April 4–6, 1949. It held its first convention, adopted a constitution, and elected officers. Several evangelical editors felt that the ACP was too closely related to the National Council of Churches and had generally been led by theological liberals with a social gospel focus. The prime mover of EPA was James DeForest Murch, editor of the *United Evangelical Action,* organ of the National Association of Evangelicals (NAE).

The new journalism association adopted the NAE doctrinal statement as a membership requirement. The EPA's purposes were "to promote the cause of evangelical Christianity and to enhance the influence of Christian journalism." These objectives were to be reached "by providing Christian fellowship among the members of the association by rendering practical assistance and stimulating mutual and technical standards in the field of

[4]*The Associated Church Press: A Brief History: 1916-1961* (Chicago: The Associated Church Press, 1966), p. 50.

Christian journalism, and by suggesting concerted and timely emphasis upon important issues."

Membership was restricted to evangelical periodicals in the United States and Canada. Anticipated services to the members included information and inspiration, sectional conferences for editors and publishers, and distribution of news, photos, syndicated stories, and illustrations.

The first EPA convention in 1949 attracted 123 evangelical periodicals with a circulation of four million. Combined circulation of ACP members was over 21 million at that time.

The first officers were James Murch, president (*United Evangelical Action*); H. J. Kuiper, vice-president (*The Banner*); Robert Walker, secretary (*Christian Life*); and Martin Erickson, treasurer (*The Standard*).

A news service, called Evangelical Press Association Service, began in 1951. This became the EP News Service on a weekly basis in 1953. The EPA adopted a four-point code of ethics in 1954. The code begins with this statement of purpose: "The primary function of Christian publications is to advance the work and witness of Jesus Christ in all the world."

Increased circulation began to characterize evangelical periodicals. The most spectacular was 0 to 3,500,000 in the first five years for Billy Graham's *Decision* magazine. The sixties saw marked increases in subscriptions, circulation, and mailings. Some denominational publications used computers and other electronic equipment provided at the denominational headquarters.

An awards program, begun in 1954, originally had three categories: best editorial program, most thought-provoking editorial or article, and outstanding circulation campaign. *Christian Life* won the first two categories in 1954 and *Conquest* won the third. The contest now has two divisions: Awards of Excellence for types of publication (seven categories) and Higher Goals for the editorial and graphic components of the publications (seventeen categories).

The annual convention highlights the EPA year. Editors enjoy Christian fellowship and professional exchange, and they benefit from workshops that often take the form of short journalism courses conducted by EPA members and by outside experts, often from secular publications. The results of the annual Awards Contest are announced here also.

EPA gave birth to its own periodical, *Liaison*, in 1953. The bimonthly *Liaison* has become the official news organ of the association. The membership growth of EPA has been steady; 261 periodicals were listed in the 1978 EPA directory with a combined readership of over 16 million.

The Jesus People papers emerged in the sixties, providing a new chapter in religious journalism. Those specialized publications, located mainly on the West coast, included *The Hollywood Free Paper, The Los Angeles Free Press, Oracle,* and *Right On* in California; *Truth* in Spokane, Washington; and *Maranatha Free Press* in Vancouver, British Columbia.

Some of these monthly papers, which often featured testimonies of new Christians, reached circulations of over 100,000. The Jesus News Service International was formed to link these publications.

Into the mid-seventies, liberal periodicals continued to decline in circulation and merge while leading evangelical publications grew.

During the early seventies, reports were circulated that Time-Life Incorporated was discussing the possibility of publishing a magazine on religion and ethics entitled *Spirit*. The prototype for *Spirit* was suddenly shelved in favor of *People Weekly*.

Journalism education in evangelical schools of higher learning is beginning to have a positive effect on Protestant journalism. During the past fifteen years, journalism or communications majors have been established at Biola College, John Brown University, Grace College, Judson College, Moody Bible Institute, Multnomah School of the Bible, Olivet Nazarene College, St. Paul Bible College, Wheaton Graduate School, and others. Some graduates from these programs are now becoming EPA editors.

Religious News Service (RNS) was organized in 1933 as an independently managed operation of the Conference of Christians and Jews. A network of 900 news and photo correspondents around the world feed religious news stories to RNS headquarters in New York City.

RNS sends as many as seventy stories per day to more than 800 domestic and foreign clients. Photo service and radio scripts are also provided.[5]

Conclusion

Joseph Bayly, evangelical author and editor for over twenty-five years, observes that Christian periodicals are now attracting more qualified people as editors and art directors. He feels the quality of writing and the design of their publications have improved. Christian magazines have also made statements on social issues (such as race) that were not coming from America's pulpits.

[5]The main source for the historical data in this chapter is Frank Luther Mott's five-volume classic, *A History of American Magazines*.

Bayly notes that if there have been any losses in the last two decades it has been with the coverage given well-known personalities with odd experiences rather than speaking with the voice of God. He observes that evangelical periodicals may now be saying less important things better and also failing to criticize the status quo because so many of these publications are owned by leading evangelical organizations.

Wayne Christianson, *Moody Monthly* editor for thirty years, states that the functionality level has risen in Christian magazines. They are trying to write and edit to be as helpful as possible to the reader. Improved layout, photography, and other visual techniques have strengthened evangelical publications. He also has noted that the emphasis on horizontal relationships has crowded out articles on man's relationship to God over the last third of a century.

The history of Christian journalism in America can be divided into three main periods. The first was birth and vigorous growth from the mid-eighteenth century to the last quarter of the nineteenth century. A period of retrenchment followed, during which Christians spoke to other Christians through their publications and went almost totally unnoticed by the secular press. A resurgence of the evangelical press began after World World II. As part of the "Era of Evangelicalism," the secular media now seem to be taking an increasing interest in what is being written in Christian publications and are quoting more frequently from them as the Christian press moves into the last quarter of the twentieth century.

The future impact of Christian journalism on the church and all of American society will be determined largely by the dedication and professionalism of those who volunteer to serve Christ, His church, and mankind from behind an editor's desk. The influence of evangelical periodicals will depend on the significance and relevance of the articles these Christian editors choose to publish.[6]

[6]This chapter is an expanded version of the article "Christian Journalism" written by the editor for the *Tyndale Encyclopedia of Christian Knowledge* (Wheaton, Ill.: Tyndale House, forthcoming).

2

Tips on Writing for Evangelical Publications

Christian writing can change lives.

Hudson T. Armerding, president of Wheaton College, decided at an early age to commit his life to Jesus Christ. He tells how God used an article in a Sunday school take-home paper as one of several catalysts that brought him into a personal relationship with Christ that has deepened for more than fifty years:

"It was in Sunday school at age eight that I was confronted with the specific issue of making a commitment to Jesus Christ. I had a Sunday school paper that contained a story about a young man who had trusted Christ and signed a decision card.

"There was a facsimile of the decision card in the Sunday school paper. So I took the paper home and cut out the facsimile and put in my name and the date.

"As a result of that simple, straightforward commitment, I really believe that I became a Christian at that time."

This is one of the thrilling potentials of writing for the evangelical market. A writing gift that has been dedicated to God and then disciplined and developed can produce prayerfully prepared manuscripts that can serve as the midwife to spiritual births "from above" (John 3:3). Christian writing can also help people grow spiritually by warning them of dangers ahead and by encouraging them to higher levels of Christian maturity and service.

The Feature Article Defined

The feature article should live up to its name. It should feature or focus on a person, event, organization, movement, trend, or any subject that qualifies for specialized treatment. The most effective features often have a strong "people" element. Readers usually enjoy reading about other people and therefore are drawn to articles that have a strong human interest element.

The feature article can be written to inform, to explain, to encourage, to warn, to help, to analyze, or to entertain.

The feature article has many types. Several of these are discussed and illustrated in chapters 3 through 12 in this text. In addition, there are third-person narrative, expositional, and organizational (articles about organizations) types. In this book, these types will be considered subtypes of the general feature article.

The news story structure of listing facts in descending order of importance (the inverted pyramid) generally will not work in the feature article. The feature story must have a carefully planned structure that moves from the lead through the body and on to the conclusion. The most effective outlines flow from natural subdivisions of the article's subject, rather than from a predetermined structure into which the subject is forced.

Where to Get Article Ideas

Creative catalysts for articles lurk everywhere. The ardent author must be ready to pounce on them and retain them for future reference and use. Reading and personal observation provide a wealth of resource material for the alert writer.

News stories or feature articles in daily newspapers can spark an idea for a feature. There may be a feature story of human drama behind the news item, and there probably is at least one other major approach to any feature article subject. Books can also generate article suggestions. Sometimes even the titles and synopses of books listed in the best-seller list or book reviews can generate an idea.

Regular visits to a public or college library to peruse the periodical and new-book sections can produce rich results. Ed Eulenberg, veteran feature writer for the late *Chicago Daily News,* considered his library card the key to unlocking ideas and documentation.

All article ideas should be evaluated for significance. If the proposed subject is not important to prospective editors, readers, and the author, it should be dropped. People don't want to waste their time on the insignificant. Writers should cherish their time as a God-given gift, and they should write on subjects that are important enough to justify their efforts—and the time of their readers.

Research and Organization

After the material for an article has been gathered, it must then be organized. Some writers effectively use certain standard outlines for feature articles. Some of these are presented in subsequent chapters. However, before forcing new material into old outline molds, a writer should look for natural groupings within the data collected.

Many writers list all the topics covered in the research on as many pages as necessary. Then the natural groupings are noted under specific subheads, dropping the subtopics that are not relevant. This procedure often produces a three-, four-, or five-point outline with numerous subheadings. These then can be relisted in topic outline form, similar to the topic outline required for college research papers (Roman numerals for main points, capital letters for secondary points, and Arabic numerals for the third level).

Many professional feature writers recommend collecting three to ten times more information than will be used in the article. This gives the writer a broad spectrum of facts from which to choose. Theoretically, the article should be stronger using this method because only the most important and interesting points have been selected.

Other free-lancers feel that at this point in the writing process a thesis should be decided on. A thesis is simply a one-sentence statement of the article's main idea. Possibilities for the thesis often come to mind during the research, listing, and grouping processes.

Determining a thesis as early as possible in this article-writing sequence will give the subsequent outline creation and revision a much more forceful direction. Every idea for an anecdote, illustration, or quotation can be tested against the thesis. If an item fails the relevancy test, it should be discarded or filed for future use.

At an EPA convention workshop, William Peterson, editor of *Eternity* magazine, gave some practical tips on researching an article. He called the process, "Digging Out the Story." The following are some of his suggestions:

1. Find out enough to ask intelligent questions. (Read up on the subject in almanacs, encyclopedias, yearbooks, indices, *Current Biography,* and *Who's Who in America*.)
2. Make a friendly contact with a reliable, accurate source person, an authority in the field. (Call or write contributing editors to the key magazines in that subject area.)

3. Determine the value of source people in terms of time and money.
4. Get the word out to friends and associates that you're working on that subject. (Information often comes from unexpected sources.)
5. Accumulate as many sources of information from as many sources as possible. (Continue to ask, "Who else can give me information?")
6. Use your telephone, tape recorder, and published sources as much as possible. (Much time can be wasted traveling.)
7. Try to do the job as easily as possible but thoroughly. (Don't create unnecessary work.)
8. Try to avoid getting yourself obligated to a source. (Don't promise things that can't be delivered in order to get the story.)
9. Even while researching, try to visualize the way the article might take shape.
10. Believe in divine assistance.
11. Don't fail to get color along with the facts. (Strive to get the flavor, feel, and descriptions of the story.)
12. Prepare yourself and the interviewee for the interview session.
13. Find a cutoff point in the research. (If possible, do this at least a week before the article is due to give time for organizing, planning, writing, and rewriting.)
14. Work with realistic deadlines. (If you find you can't make a deadline, contact the editor right away to get advice and possibly negotiate a new due date.)

Benton P. Patterson, contributing editor of *Guideposts*, told the Wheaton Writers Conference in 1969 that research helps a writer gain factual knowledge and permits him to escape the walls of personal experience. He feels that thorough research gives the writer confidence and the writing an authoritative tone.

The Article-Writing Process

The challenge of the first draft involves getting the material on paper, following the outline as closely as possible. Whenever possible, this rough draft should be written in one sitting so that the momentum of the article is maintained. This will eliminate the warm-up and recall periods most writers need to get the mental, emotional, and spiritual juices flowing after breaks or interruptions. This can be a one-time process if the writer has done his homework—the research, thesis construction, and outlining.

The statement that the real writing is done in the rewriting still contains not merely a kernel but an entire earful of truth.

When weird-looking scratchings fill several pages of Ye Olde Legal Pad or hundreds of imprints have dented typing paper, the raw product is ready to be reshaped, refined, and polished. Satisfaction should come from the realization that the raw material is in place and the major creative hurdle has been cleared. Putting the rough draft aside for at least twenty-four hours will provide fresh insights for the revision task.

Display Window Concept

An effective feature must draw the reader into the article in a fraction of a second as the reader thumbs through the magazine. A reader can flip past an article faster than a television viewer can change channels.

The display window concept (title, subtitle, and lead) can be helpful in meeting this sliver-of-a-second challenge. The opening of a feature article can be thought of as the display window of a specialty shop. The title can be compared to the store's name, identifying the specialty on the plate glass window. The subtitle can be pictured as a sign in the window calling attention to a specific item of consumer interest. The lead or introduction may be viewed as the item on display that will cause the customer to wrap warm fingers around the metal doorknob and enter the store.

The display window of a magazine article must do the same for the reader. These three components (title, subtitle, and lead) must be so smoothly integrated that the reader will be drawn into the article before realizing what has happened.

A title should be concise (usually six words or less), attractive (with its creativity coming from the article subject), and relevant to the subject. Usually it should reflect the spirit and tone of the article rather than merely state the subject.

A subtitle usually is longer than a title (sometimes two or three sentences). It sometimes states the thesis (main idea), slant (specific focus or approach), purpose, or direction of the article. In general, the subtitle gives the reader a better idea of what is inside the article. Quite often the subtitle will expand on or help explain a title that has a question mark hook or a double meaning.

An editor does not necessarily agree to use the author's title and subtitle when accepting the manuscript. Space allocations or different tastes may result in a staff-written title and subtitle. However, the conscientious free-lancer should strive to compose such creative and compelling titles and subtitles that neither editor nor reader can resist.

The lead in a feature article can be the first sentence, the first paragraph, or the first three to five paragraphs. Basically, the lead is the introduction of the article. It should provide the reader with the article's thesis. If the lead isn't magnetic, the rest of the article will not be read. Some editors evaluate an entire article on the quality of the lead. They believe that usually a bad lead will be followed by an uninspiring article. The feature lead should not be longer than ten percent of the article.

A lethargic lead is a sin. It could be the sin of pride—when a writer assumes the reader is automatically interested in the article subject. It could be the sin of laziness—not taking the time to write a creative, compelling introduction. Closely related might be the sin of incompetence—not studying how others have written attractive leads and not practicing enough.

With supernatural subjects that have eternal dimensions, the Christian writer should pour his entire God-given creativity into every lead so that the reader will not miss something that may change his life.

Then comes the challenge of meeting reader expectations after he has entered the article. If the display window promises more than the article delivers, an irate reader will stomp out of the article. He will also be suspicious the next time he sees the same by-line. Christian writers should strive for satisfied, stimulated customers.

Article Conclusions

The feature article needs a conclusion. If the final paragraph or section is missing, the reader will put down the magazine feeling unsatisfied. A good conclusion gives a sense of completion.

In contrast, the straight news article begins by answering all the interrogatives (who, what, when, where, why, how) as soon as possible. It then proceeds to give the details in a descending order of importance. This enables the editor to cut the story almost any place layout dictates.

Not so with the feature article. It needs a summary section, generally not more than five percent of the entire article, to give the piece a sense of completeness.

Some of the most regularly used conclusions include a simple summary of the article, a restatement of thesis in fresh terminology, a recommended program of action for the reader, or the article in outline form. An anecdote, a direct quotation from an authority in the subject, or the second half of an anecdote begun in the lead can all be used as conclusions, depending on the appropriateness to the subject.

The conclusion should attempt to bring readers full circle. Some element in the conclusion should remind them of something said in the lead. The conclusion basically reminds the reader where he started from in the article. When this happens, the conclusion fulfills its purpose of article completeness.

Revision

Not many writers have the ability to achieve the mental picture of the article on the first try. Joe Bayly, vice-president of David C. Cook Publishing Company, says that after about twenty years of editing and writing, his writing began to emerge in acceptable form on the first effort. Others have estimated that it takes approximately a million words of experience to achieve this glorious plateau.

Therefore, new writers should not feel like manuscript martyrs if they need three or four drafts before they begin to feel slightly satisfied with their product. Hundreds and thousands of others are alumni of good old RU: Revisers Unlimited.

John McCandlish Phillips often wrote three to five different drafts of an article, as deadlines permitted, during his twenty-one years as a feature reporter on the *New York Times*.

Some authors use different-colored paper for each draft. Dr. Paul White, medical missionary and author of the *Jungle Doctor* parables, uses a different-colored pen for each reworking of the first draft. This method helps to remind him of the sequence of his mental interaction with his original draft. Then, he says, "When my manuscript looks like something akin to the Chinese flag, my lovely wife takes the horrible thing and types it into a beautiful piece that will gladden the heart of my editor." Color-blind writers may wish to devise their own approaches to the revision procedure.

When analyzing diction (word choice) during the revision process, verbs and nouns should be carefully evaluated. These are the writer's two most important parts of speech. Verbs function as the energy-package for sentences and nouns transport the content, like freight cars that contain the weight of what needs to be communicated.

A series of modifiers connected to verbs and nouns should be viewed with suspicion; the verb and noun choices are probably weak.

Forms of the verb "to be" should be avoided as much as possible unless "existence" is meant. If something more than a state of existence is intended, a more powerful verb should be used.

As another part of the revision process, certain barriers to effective communication should be eliminated: clichés, sobriquets, euphemisms, and tautologies.

A cliché is an overworked expression that has lost its vim and sparkle, sometimes several centuries ago. Deciding which expressions are clichés is somewhat subjective because what one person considers a trite expression could be a fresh, different way of saying something for the next person. Wide reading and frequent conversations with other people will help build sensitivity to expressions such as "crack of dawn," "apple of his eye," and "clear as crystal."

If an expression doesn't cause the reader to visualize the subject matter, it probably is a cliché. How many people see a gleaming crystal goblet when "clear as crystal" is used? Avoiding clichés indicates a high respect for the reader.

The sobriquet is the cliché's cousin. It is an overused nickname, such as "Old Glory" for the American flag or "Windy City" for Chicago. These also should be cleaned out of the copy.

The euphemism substitutes a diluted expression for a more direct and precise word or phrase. "Passed away" is often used to avoid the verb "died." A writer sometimes uses the euphemism to avoid hurting someone's feelings. (The funeral industry has compiled an entire lexicon of euphemisms.) Euphemisms often produce unclear prose.

Tautology is unnecessary repetition. An expression such as "endorse on the back" is redundant because the verb "endorse" contains the concept of "writing on the back." The first adjective in "hot water heater" is unnecessary. Repetition of ideas can be used effectively for emphasis.

Embarrassment and potential legal problems can be avoided by making distinctions between generic and specific (trademark) names. All trademark names must be capitalized: Kleenex, Coca-Cola, Frigidaire. These trade names should not be used as a substitute for the family name of an item: tissues, soft drink, or refrigerator.

Proofreading

Some writers have found that a fourfold proofreading process helps them achieve an excellent final draft.

The first reading is done aloud to check for matters such as smoothness (awkward word combinations), transitions, and logical progression. A second reading checks the punctuation, and a third the grammar. The final reading should focus on spelling. Reading the manuscript backwards, using a finger as the pacer, makes words stand out individually.

Author Intrusion

Except for the first-person article, the editorial, and the column, the feature writer should attempt to stay out of the article.

The feature should be enveloping a person, place, event, or movement in a brilliant floodlight. The author's shadow shouldn't fall across the subject; the subject should be the star. Readers and subjects will both appreciate this courtesy.

The Show, Don't Tell, Principle

Whenever possible, the reader should be allowed to see and hear the subject of the article. This is most effectively accomplished through anecdotes, direct quotations, and description. By using these techniques, a writer will not have to tell the reader about the subject. The reader will be able to view directly the person, place, or event.

An anecdote is merely a short narrative that shows the subject in action. Instead of telling the reader that the mayor was in a bad mood, let the reader see the tensions of the office as the mayor hurls a glass paperweight across the room. Usually, the shorter the time span of the anecdote, the more impact it has on the reader.

Style

The best advice about writing style is this: don't worry about it.

Writing style is really one's personality in print. Therefore, a new writer can't successfully copy anyone else's style. If a person has an orderly, logical approach to life, this should be evident in the structure of his writing. If he has a sense of humor, no matter how warped, his readers will see it squeezing through the syntax and will identify better with the author and his subject.

However, if a writer notes defects in his personality, he may want to refurbish his personality before pushing his pen any farther. One way to accomplish this is to prayerfully develop interpersonal relationships. Some of the most effective Christian authors are the most genuine and sincere in their one-to-one relationships. Mature personalities develop from these empathetic interactions. Knowing and helping people on an individual basis gives writers insight and inspiration. A systematic physical fitness program will help develop a stimulating personality.

Not many evangelical writers can meet readers' needs by staying in the seclusion of their studies, imagining what real people and crises are like. Direct contact with the primary resources (people) will strengthen a writer's personality and provide significant subjects.

A new writer will certainly benefit from analyzing the style of an accomplished author. But mimicking slavishly will only result in frustration and disappointment intensified by rejection slips.

Overuse of a dictionary of synonyms can produce a stilted style. Naturalness in style comes from using words derived mostly from the author's functional vocabulary. A synonym reference such as Roget's *International Thesaurus* or Webster's *Dictionary of Synonyms* can help achieve variety of diction so that the same key word is not repeated ad nauseam.

Some of the common characteristics of an effective style include clarity, brevity (word length, sentences, and paragraphs), sincerity, creativity (the author's personality coming through), and direction.

Conclusion

A Christian writer should not let all the procedural and technical details turn down the brightness control on the vision of how dedicated writing can be used of God to win people to Himself.

In 1964, James Engel was a young associate professor of marketing at Ohio State University. He had obtained his Ph.D. and was becoming known nationally for his writing on consumer behavior.

He had never come into contact with evangelical Christianity in his entire life. But during the 1964–65 school year, a friend began giving him copies of *Faith at Work* magazine. Its personality sketches illustrating the Christian life amazed him. In his thirty years of living, Engel had never met any people like the ones described in those articles. Later he went to a conference where some of the *Faith at Work* staff showed him how he too could become a follower of Christ and have new motivations and a new pattern of life. He made his decision for Christ, became a witness for Him on the Ohio State campus, and now serves his Lord as chairman of the Billy Graham Program in Communications at Wheaton Graduate School.

Praise God that He continues to use the print medium to show people of all ages how He can transform their lives.

BIGFOOT
XING
NEXT
5 MILES

3
The First-Person Narrative

A narrative is basically an interesting or exciting true story that is generally told in chronological order. Often a dramatic incident is pulled out of the natural time order and used as the introduction. After the reader is drawn into the story, a flashback transports the reader to the beginning of the narrative.

Benton Patterson, *Guideposts* editor, believes each writer has had one experience worth publishing. He suggests that authors get that experience out of their systems by writing it as soon as possible. Patterson feels that free-lancers will then be able to move on to more significant and interesting subjects that require substantial research.

This advice can be modified if a writer is leading a creative life and is meeting new people and having exciting or meaningful experiences that would interest at least a specialized readership.

The first step in planning this type of writing is listing—writing in chronological order each of the details in the narrative, no matter how insignificant. The second step is selection—determining which of the many details will fit in the article and which ones are the most relevant to the main point (thesis) of the narrative. Although all points in a narrative may be of equal relevancy to the thesis, they are not all of equal importance. Therefore, a writer should not feel obligated to give equal space to each detail in the narrative.

Whenever possible the first-person singular pronoun (I) perspective should be used. The first person plural, or the "editorial we," often confuses the reader. If antecedents (words to which pronouns refer) aren't planted nearby, the reader constantly wonders how many people are contained in those two letters, "w" and "e."

One variation of the first-person narrative is the "as-told-to" article. In this subtype, another person tells his story to a writer, who then writes it from the first person (I) perspective. In this case, the names of both the subject and the author should appear under the title, with "as-told-to" preceding the author's name.

This type of article usually requires interviewing the main subject. The chronological sequence serves as a natural structure. Description, dialogue, and anecdotes are woven together to form the fabric of the story.

The monotony of the pronoun "I" in the first-person narrative can sometimes be lessened by using descriptive and explanatory passages stated in the third person (he, she, it, they) or a proper noun.

Minimal research is necessary with this article type because the author is the world's leading authority on the topic. Even so, care should be taken to have a good structure and to select significant details. Interviewing others who were involved in the experience can sometimes provide additional insights and information.

The integration of description in a narrative splashes color on the story being told. Description, along with anecdotes and direct quotations, allows the writer to show the story rather than merely tell it.

Multi-sense descriptions of narrative settings provide the reader with wide-screen shots of the story's environment. Spatial description (what is seen) should be included as the author functions like a TV camera, panning the setting for the reader. However, if the scene includes sounds, aromas, touch sensations, and even emotional stimuli, these should be shown to achieve higher degrees of realism.

Whenever possible in narrative writing, the leading personality should be shown in relationship to the physical setting. Concrete details such as objects on a desk, book titles within a bookcase, and quotations on a bulletin board may reveal much about the main subject. The point of view in descriptive writing, as well as in narrative writing, can change with the passage of time, with variations in the location of the observing point, and with fluctuations and attitudes towards the subject.

Some books on feature writing list another type of narrative: the third-person. The main difference between this type and the first-person narrative is the perspective. The third-person narrative is an experience told by someone other than the one who had the experience. As the title for this type of narrative indicates, the author uses the third-person pronoun (he, she, it, they) as the main perspective.

In recent years evangelical editors have not been publishing third-person articles as much as the first-person variety. The first-person narrative generally possesses more of an intimate, authentic tone.

The adventure article based on an exciting personal experience is a subtype of the narrative. The following six components have been suggested as the main outline for the adventure story: the lead, flashback, suspense and buildup, conflict element, climax (success or failure in the adventure), and projection into the future. The amount of space devoted to each of these components depends on the facts themselves. All points do not have to be given equal word length.

If the story being recounted is interesting or even exciting and has significance for the reader, the author can have a stimulating experience recreating the account in the rich tradition of Mark Twain and other masters of the narrative.

"Lord, I Believe You Want Me to Live"

Marilyn Henderson

Everything seemed sunny that Saturday afternoon, and there was the most beautiful, cloudless blue sky. It was a perfect place for a weekend retreat—a Colorado dude ranch. First we rode horses, and later we were scheduled to have a barbeque down by the river.

But then the weather changed. The clouds began to look ominous, and the air was very still and eerie.

So, instead of the barbeque, we ate at small tables in a room close to the river. Then we moved to a building called the People's Barn and started sharing stories about the women's summers and what the Lord had done. We met from 7:30 to about 9:30. I remember praying that our lives would be different as a result of the week, but I was, of course, thinking of our upcoming training with the rest of the field staff at Colorado State University.

Then we heard over a loudspeaker that a flash flood was coming and that we needed to evacuate immediately. We rushed to our cars, leaving everything behind.

When we had arrived at the ranch earlier that day, we had driven downhill to get there, so now we followed the police toward the highway, which we considered higher ground. We stopped by some railing, then heard an explosion and, when lightning flashed, could see the water coming through the trees in the distance.

But we felt very safe, and at that point, it was all exciting to me—like watching "Emergency" on TV. I never thought that anyone would be hurt.

As we drove on, a policeman stopped us. Over the muddle of calls coming on the radio in his car, he told us, "Go east toward Loveland. NOW." I thought the reason he was so emphatic was that he smelled the propane gas from the exploding storage tanks.

Then it started to thunder and lightning hard. My secretary, Carol Rhoad, who was driving, was very afraid of thunder. That's when I told her, "Carol, stop the car and I'll drive. We're going to be okay." So I crawled out from the back seat where I had been with June Fujiwara and Precy Manongdo, to drive the '75 red Granada, with Carol sitting on the hump beside me and Melanie Ahlquist in the other bucket seat.

As we drove, it began to rain. We approached a bridge, and I could see cars' taillights that had gone just before us. The bridge was about 50 feet in front of us when we started to drive through a low spot in the road where a stream of water crossed the road and hit our car. Much to our amazement, the engine stalled.

Later we found out that the water was rising a foot every 15 seconds, and the water on the road was actually the river moving over its boundaries. Because of the rapid rise of water, cars made it safely across the river just in front of us, and 15 seconds later no one would have dared to try to cross. But our car and the one behind us (which I didn't realize was even there at the time) were there at just the right second to be caught up on the river as it moved over its normal boundaries.

We couldn't believe it was happening. Where did the water come from? What was going on? There was nowhere to go. The water was very, very swift, and it moved us broadside. The first thing we knew our car was jetting into the river; it was like being in a boat without a motor. We were heading right toward a huge house trailer that was floating down the river.

We were kind of excited, but there was a real peace. I can remember we were praying aloud, almost reassuring God: "Lord, we love You, and we aren't doubting that You love us. We're okay." We told each other that we loved one another and that we were going to see Jesus. Carol said, "Mar, I would rather see Jesus with you than anybody in the world except my mom and dad."

As I look back, I wonder why that was the initial reaction and not, "We have got to get out of here." I really believe that was dying grace for Carol, June and Precy. When Carol said she was going to see Jesus with me, I thought, "Yeah, that's true," but in my mind I knew I was supposed to get out of there.

So I rolled down the window and sat on the door's windowsill, and Melanie did the same. I pulled Carol out, and she was sitting next to me. We still were heading toward this trailer; I could almost touch it now. Then I got knocked off the door by the force of the water rising and fell in a two-yard space between the trailer, which was almost submerged by then, and the car. The water was so strong, it was like being hit by a truck.

I went down and I thought, "Lord Jesus, I'm coming to be with You." I was taking in a lot of water and knew I was drowning. "Am I with You now?" I asked, not sure if I were alive or dead.

But then I came to the top. I still didn't really know if I was with the Lord or what because I couldn't see anything—it was totally dark. I grabbed a tiny board, but it wasn't big enough to hold my weight.

I went down again, and I thought, "Well, now I'm with the Lord." Then I was up again, and I opened my arms and ran into a clump of sticks. It was as if the Lord had put them right there in the water for me to grab.

Now I could float and my head was above water. "I've *never* skied this fast," I thought. Later I heard that a policeman had driven down the highway at 80 miles an hour and the water was moving ahead of him.

At that moment I thought, "Lord, I believe You want me to live." Later in the hospital I remembered one of the messages I was going to give at Staff Training to the women. It was about assuming rightful responsibility for their lives, not looking for someone else to take care of them. God had given them their lives as gifts.

In my message I was going to talk about how God gave the children of Israel the land, but He made them fight for it. It was as if God were giving me my life now, but I had to fight for it.

At that point I came to a shallower, calmer part in the river, and I was washed up to this huge, huge tree root. I pulled myself up on it. Then I made my way from the root to the tree itself. I hugged that tree and even said aloud, "I love you, tree!"

I ended up standing on one foot on a small twig four inches long. I leaned all my weight on my foot and then waited for over an hour. I felt safe from the water.

My mind was razor sharp at this point. I could watch cars going by on the highway, and I thought, "There are people there, and they're living, but no one knows I'm here except the Lord. I've never been so alone before."

A "beaver dam" of debris was being built up between the bank, about 30 feet away, and me, and I thought, "Lord, if you made a path for the children of Israel through the Red Sea, you can build a road to the bank for me." I thought I was going to have to wait there until morning and then cross over the dam to the bank. Lightning began flashing again at about 11 p.m., and then I could see better as the dam built up—trees and brush came to add to it.

Then I slipped from my little branch and my body started shaking violently. I think my muscles had had it. I knew then that I couldn't make it until morning.

"Have You brought me this far, Lord, and now am I going to die?" I asked. "Lord Jesus, please either take me home now or send somebody to help me. I know that You are my Savior, but if You save me now, again, I will tell the world that You are the Savior."

It couldn't have been five seconds later that I saw car lights coming. It looked like the car was being driven right down the river bank, but there was a little road that I hadn't seen before. The headlights shone on me, and I called out, "Here I am!" just knowing that God had sent them and that they were looking for me.

The two men from the car started for me and kept saying, "Stay right there, stay right there." I was so excited I kept shouting, "Here I am!" They got two long poles and stabilized themselves over the debris, walking over to me.

One of the men, a rancher named Clifford Moore, picked me up in his arms; nothing ever felt so good. I couldn't say it, but I thought, "I felt this way before—when I became a Christian."

They took me to a house nearby and wrapped me in blankets and then drove me to the hospital. Mr. Moore stayed at the river, and he's the one who found Melanie and Carol's body.

Later Mr. Moore told me, "Ma'am, I don't know what made me turn off the road. I was driving and thought I just had to turn off. Then I thought of an older lady who lived in a cabin down by the river and wondered if she had gotten out okay, but that was almost an afterthought."

After I got to the hospital, I refused to go to sleep until the next afternoon because I knew Melanie had arrived, and I kept waiting for them to bring Carol in. I didn't know another car was involved, but I was pretty sure June and Precy couldn't get out of our car.

Melanie and I were the only people to be rescued that night. A man was brought in early in the morning; as far as I know, we were the only three people who were in the water and lived.

On Monday my roommate, Ney Bailey, told me about the other women. I cried. I had had no idea *seven* of our women had died.

After the flood and being so close to death, at first nothing else seemed real to me. I remember coming home from the hospital and seeing some kids playing in a yard and riding bikes, and I thought, "Why are they doing that?" It was almost like culture shock to see people living normally.

I have never been a particularly heavenly minded Christian, but the flood gave me a clearer perspective of heaven. I knew the women were experiencing such joy that I almost felt left out when I couldn't join them.

Questions plagued me. Why did I roll down the window? Why did I get out of the car? Why did I pull Carol out? Did I fight and she didn't? I remembered thinking as we sat on the windowsill of the car, "She's so limp beside me." In contrast, I was super-strengthened and alert and calm and ready for something. Did I love the Lord enough? Or is it just natural to fight for life? Did Carol fight? Or June? Or Precy?

Then one morning I was reading the newspaper and there was the ad that was put in the papers across the country, explaining how the women were still alive in heaven. I cried, "Lord, how come I'm not there? I love You enough! . . . I think I do . . . maybe I don't."

That day I read in Hebrews 5 in the Living Bible: "Yet while Christ was here on earth He pleaded with God, praying with tears and agony of soul to the only one who would save Him from (premature) death." And in the footnote it explains that there is a strong case that Satan tried to rob Him—to take His life prematurely—so that He couldn't finish the course He came to run. I saw that Jesus fought for His life, too, because it was the wrong time. And then I realized that the issue wasn't my love for God, but rather was that the right time for me to die.

I saw, too, as a result of the flood, the hideousness of death and what Jesus Christ conquered when He died at the right time. Because now I've seen what death is—the fruit of sin—and that death apart from God is the worst thing.

And I'm seeing that not only did Jesus have victory over death, but He also has the gift of life—now and forever. Those realizations caused my desire to share the gospel to be heightened. Now I'm praying for myself, "Restore unto me the joy of my salvation. Teach me what I was saved from. What it means for You to be my Savior. What people are going to face apart from You. What it means for people to be lost."

I've come to realize that I don't want to spend the next year telling *my* story. I want to share the gospel because the Lord's story is the only one worthy of being told. If He can use the flood as an example, that's great. But I know that He doesn't want me to live July 31, 1976, for the rest of my life. More than ever, now that I've gone through the flood, I just want it to make a difference that I've been here on earth and shared the gospel these few years I'm alive before I take the next natural step—this time really into heaven.

CRITIQUE OF "Lord, I Believe You Want Me to Live"

Forrest Boyd, President of International Media Service of Washington, D.C., judged Marilyn Henderson's article as the first-place winner in the First-Person Narrative category of the 1978 EPA Awards Contest. Four main criteria have been established for this type of article: dramatic quality, sincerity and believability, relevance and reader identification, and writing style.

The subject of this article has universal appeal. Most people, when they have time or when jolted by a crisis, wonder what it is like to face death and how they would react. Both secular and Christian media reported the 1976 flash flood in Colorado. Therefore, a first-person narrative by a flood survivor would interest thousands of readers, both Christian and non-Christian. This account was of special interest to readers of *Worldwide Challenge,* because seven Campus Crusade staff members died in that flood.

The dramatic quality throbs within the experience itself, and Marilyn Henderson recounts it well. She narrates clearly by using basic Anglo-Saxon prose that communicates well to a general readership. This narrative contains not a hint of insincerity, which would undercut any article's impact.

Henderson uses a descriptive lead that establishes the setting for the account; its tranquility contrasts sharply with the rapid sequence of events that follows.

Techniques of fiction writing can often be used by the nonfiction author to reveal the subject rather than merely telling about it—a special danger in narrative writing.

Foreboding, a fiction device, is used in paragraphs two and three. The reader soon gets the feeling that something dire is about to occur (paragraph two). Flashback provides perspective in paragraphs four and twenty. From paragraph thirty-five to the end, Henderson provides the reader with an aftermath explaining her reactions and struggles following the flood. She employs dialogue sparingly to move her narrative along. The re-creating of her thoughts as she went through the disaster helps the reader to identify.

More dialogue and more multi-sense description would have helped paint a sharper word picture. The recounting of her body shaking violently (paragraph twenty-five) is the type of description that adds depth to a narrative. All five senses were involved in this terrifying experience.

In general, concrete details such as at "thirty feet" and "11 P.M." (paragraph twenty-four) establish vividness. The conclusion (paragraphs thirty-six through forty-two) is a bit long for an article of this length; five percent is the recommended ratio. However, even though the ending contains lessons from the author's experiences, they do not sound like deadly sermons. I think most of the article's readers stayed with it through its completion.

Above all, this first-person article contains the ultimate criterion for a successful narrative: It makes the reader feel that he has lived through the experience and the subsequent reflections.

—The Editor

The Ones Who Are Left

Elisabeth Elliot

"It's gone." I could see the yellow-spoked wheel of the spare tire, perched on the back of a 1934 Plymouth, disappear over the hilltop. The car in which I might have got a ride home from elementary school on this rainy day had gone and I was left.

"It's gone." The trainman stood at the only lighted gate in Penn Station. The train had gone, leaving me behind to figure out how on earth I was to make a speaking engagement on Long Island in an hour and a half.

We've all experienced the desolation of being left in one way or another. And sooner or later many of us experience the greatest desolation of all: he's gone. The one who made life what it was for us, who was, in fact, our life.

And we were not ready. Not really prepared at all. We felt, when the fact stared us in the face, "No. Not yet." For however bravely we may have looked at the possibilities (if we had any warning at all), however calmly we may have talked about them with the one who was about to die (and I had a chance to talk about the high risks with my first husband, and about the human hopelessness of his situation with my second), we are caught short. If we had another week, perhaps, to brace ourselves. A few more days to say what we wanted to say, to do or undo some things, wouldn't it have been better, easier?

But silent, swift, and implacable the Scythe has swept by, and he is gone, and we are left. We stand bewildered on the sidewalk, on the station platform. Yet, most strangely, that stunning snatching away has changed nothing very much. There is the sunlight lying in patches on the familiar carpet just as it did yesterday. The same dishes stand in the rack to be put away as usual, his razor and comb are on the shelf, his shoes in the closet (O the shoes! molded in the always recognizable shape of his feet). The mail comes, the phone rings, Wednesday gives way to Thursday and this week to next week, and you have to keep getting up in the morning ("Life must go on, I forget just why," wrote Edna St. Vincent Millay) and combing your hair (for whom, now?) eating breakfast (remember to get out only one egg now, not three), making the bed (who cares?). You have to meet people who most fervently wish they could pass by on the other side so as not to have to think of something to say. You have to be understanding with *their* attempts to be understanding, and when they nervously try to steer you away from the one topic you want so desperately to talk about you have to allow yourself to be steered away—for their sakes. You resist the temptation, when they say he's "passed away," to say "No, he's *dead*, you know."

After a few months you've learned those initial lessons. You begin to say "I" instead of "we" and people have sent their cards and flowers and said the things they ought to say and their lives are going on and so, astonishingly, is yours and you've "adjusted" to some of the differences—as if that little mechanical word, a mere tinkering with your routines and emotions, covers the ascent from the pit.

I speak of the "ascent." I am convinced that every death, of whatever kind, through which we are called to go, must lead to a resurrection. This is the core of Christian faith. Death is the end of every life and leads to resurrection, the beginning of every new one. It is a progression, a proper progression, the way things were meant to be, the necessary means of ongoing life. It is supremely important that every bereaved person be helped to see this. The death of the beloved was the beloved's own death, "a very private and personal matter," Gert Behanna says, "and nobody should ever dare to try to get in on the act." But the death of the beloved is also the lover's death, for it means, in a different but perhaps equally fearsome way, a going through the Valley of the Shadow.

I can think of six simple things that have helped me through this valley and that help me now.

First, I try to be still and know that He is God. That advice comes from Psalm 46, which begins by describing the sort of trouble from which God is our refuge—the earth's changing, or "giving way" as the Jerusalem Bible puts it, the mountains shaking, the waters roaring and foaming, nations raging, kingdoms tottering, the earth melting. None of these cataclysms seems an exaggeration of what happens when somebody dies. The things that seemed most dependable have given way altogether. The whole world has a different look and you find it hard to get your bearings. Shadows can be very confusing. But in both psalms we are reminded of one rock-solid fact that nothing can change: Thou art with me. The Lord of Hosts is with us, the God of Jacob is our refuge. We feel that we are alone, yet we are not alone. Not for one moment has He left us alone. He is the one who has "wrought desolations," to be sure. He makes wars cease, breaks bows, shatters spears, burns chariots (breaks hearts, shatters lives?), but in the midst of all this hullabaloo we are commanded, "*Be still*." Be still and know.

Stillness is something the bereaved may feel they have entirely too much of. But if they will use that stillness to take a long look at Christ, to listen attentively to His voice, they will get their bearings.

There are several ways of looking and listening that help us avoid being dangerously at the mercy of our (heaven forfend!) "gut-level" feelings. Bible reading and prayer are the obvious ones. Taking yourself by the scruff of the neck and setting aside a definite time in a definite place for deliberately looking at what God has said and listening to what He may have to say to you today is a good exercise. And if such exercises are seen as an obligation, they have the same power other obligations—cooking a meal, cleaning a bathroom, vacuuming a rug—have to save us from ourselves.

Another means of grace is repeating the creed. Here is a list of objective facts that have not been in the smallest detail altered by what has happened to us. Far from it. Not only have they not been altered; they do actually alter what has happened—alter our whole understanding of human life and death, lift it to another plane. We can go through the list and contemplate our situation in the light of each tremendous truth. It is simply amazing how different my situation can appear as a result of this discipline.

The second thing I try to do is to give thanks. I cannot thank God for the murder of one or the excruciating disintegration of another, but I can thank God for the promise of His presence. I can thank Him that He is still in charge, in the face of life's worst terrors, and that "this slight momentary affliction is preparing for us [not 'us for'] an eternal weight of glory beyond all comparison, because we look not to the things that are seen but to the things that are unseen." I'm back to the creed again and the things unseen that are listed there, standing solidly (yes, solidly, incredible as it seems) against things seen (the fact of death, my own loneliness, this empty room). And I am lifted up by the promise of that "weight" of glory, so far greater than the weight of sorrow that at times seems to grind me like a millstone. This promise enables me to give thanks.

Then I try to refuse self-pity. I know of nothing more paralyzing, more deadly, than self-pity. It is a death that has no resurrection, a sink-hole from which no rescuing hand can drag you because you have chosen to sink. But it must be refused. In order to refuse it, of course, I must recognize it for what it is. Amy Carmichael, in her sword-thrust of a book

If, wrote, "If I make much of anything appointed, magnify it secretly to myself or insidiously to others, then I know nothing of Calvary love." That's a good definition of self-pity—making much of the "appointed," magnifying it, dwelling on one's own losses, looking with envy on those who appear to be more fortunate than oneself, asking "why me, Lord?" (remembering the "weight of glory" ought to be a sufficient answer to that question). It is one thing to call a spade a spade, to acknowledge that this thing is indeed suffering. It's no use telling yourself it's nothing. When Paul called it a "slight" affliction he meant it only by comparison with the glory. But it's another thing to regard one's own suffering as uncommon, or disproportionate, or undeserved. What have "deserts" got to do with anything? We are all under the Mercy, and Christ knows the precise weight and proportion of our sufferings—*He bore them.* He carried our sorrows. He suffered, wrote George Macdonald, not that we might not suffer, but that our sufferings might be like His. To hell, then, with self-pity.

The next thing to do is to accept my loneliness. When God takes a loved person from my life it is in order to call me, in a new way, to Himself. It is therefore a vocation. It is in this sphere, for now, anyway, that I am to learn of Him. Every stage on the pilgrimage is a chance to know Him, to be brought to Him. Loneliness is a stage (and, thank God, only a stage) when we are terribly aware of our own helplessness. It "opens the gates of my soul," wrote Katherine Mansfield, "and lets the wild beasts stream howling through." We may accept this, thankful that it brings us to the Very Present Help.

The acceptance of loneliness can be followed immediately by the offering of it up to God. Something mysterious and miraculous transpires as soon as something is held up in our hands as a gift. He takes it from us, as Jesus took the little lunch when five thousand people were hungry. He gives thanks for it and then, breaking it, transforms it for the good of others. Loneliness looks pretty paltry as a gift to offer to God—but then when you come to think of it so does anything else we might offer. It needs transforming. Others looking at it would say exactly what the disciples said, "What's the good of that with such a crowd?" But it was none of their business what use the Son of God would make of it. And it is none of ours. It is ours only to give it.

The last of the helps I have found is to do something for somebody else. There is nothing like definite, overt action to overcome the inertia of grief. The appearance of Joseph of Arimathea to take away the body of Jesus must have greatly heartened the other disciples, so prostrate with their own grief that they had probably not thought of doing anything at all. Nicodemus, too, thought of something he could do—he brought a mixture of myrrh and aloes—and the women who had come with Jesus from Galilee went off to prepare spices and ointments. This clear-cut action lifted them out of themselves. That is what we need in a time of crisis. An old piece of wisdom is "Doe the next thynge." Most of us have someone who needs us. If we haven't, we can find someone. Instead of praying only for the strength we ourselves need to survive, this day or this hour, how about praying for some to give away? How about trusting God to fulfill His own promise, "My strength is made perfect in weakness?" Where else is His strength more perfectly manifested than in a human being who, well knowing his own weakness, lays hold by faith on the Strong Son of God, Immortal Love?

It is here that a great spiritual principle goes into operation. Isaiah 58:10–12 says, "If you pour yourself out for the hungry and satisfy the desire of the afflicted, then shall your light rise in the darkness and your gloom be as the noonday. And the Lord will guide you continually and satisfy your desire with good things, and make your bones strong; and you shall be like a watered garden, like a spring of water, whose waters fail not, and . . . you shall be called a repairer of the breach, the restorer of streets to dwell in [or, in another translation, 'paths leading home']."

The condition on which all these wonderful gifts (light, guidance, satisfaction, strength, refreshment to others) rests is an unexpected one—unexpected, that is, if we are accustomed to think in material instead of in spiritual terms. The condition is not that one solve his own problems first. He need not "get it together." The condition is simply "if you pour yourself out."

Countless others have found this to work. St. Francis of Assisi put the principle into other words in his great prayer, "Lord, make me an instrument of thy peace. Where there is darkness, let me sow light, where there is sadness, joy. . . . Grant that I may not so much seek to be consoled as to console. . . . For it is in giving that we receive; it is in pardoning that we are pardoned; it is in dying that we are born to eternal life." The words of this prayer were like a light to me in the nights of my husband's last illness, and I wondered then at the marvel of a man's prayer being answered (was I the millionth to be blessed by it?) some seven hundred years after he had prayed it. St. Francis was most certainly during those nights in 1973 an instrument of God's peace.

Perhaps it is peace, of all God's earthly gifts, that in our extremity we long for most. A priest told me of a terminally ill woman who asked him each time he came to visit only to pray, "The peace of God which passeth all understanding keep your hearts and minds through Christ Jesus."

I have often prayed, in thinking of the many bereaved, the words of the beautiful hymn "Sun of my Soul":

> Be every mourner's sleep tonight
> Like infant slumbers, pure and bright.

There they are—six things that, if done in faith, can be the way to resurrection: be still and know, give thanks, refuse self-pity, accept the loneliness, offer it to God, turn your energies toward the satisfaction not of your own needs but of others'. And there will be no calculating the extent to which

> From the ground there blossoms red Life that shall endless be.

CRITIQUE OF "The Ones Who Are Left"

Elisabeth Elliot is an established literary figure in the Christian world. This tightly written article, "The Ones Who Are Left," which appeared in the February 27, 1976 issue of *Christianity Today,* forms a model of a "First-Person Narrative." One can readily understand why this contribution was evaluated as a first-place winner in the 1977 Evangelical Press Association's Higher Goals Contest.

Judges in the contest were provided with four criteria for selecting winners: dramatic quality, sincerity and believability, relevance and reader identification, and writing style.

1. *Dramatic quality.* The hidden drama of the author's painful experience of losing her first husband to murderous jungle tribesmen and her second to the slow attrition of cancer is recounted in quick, bold strokes. The starkness of her situation is heightened by her disciplined writing. She never stoops to overdramatize the situation nor wallow in her grief. But the sharpness of the pain comes through.

In her lead paragraph she cites two common experiences—missing a car ride home from school on a rainy day and watching a train depart in Penn Station. The reader quickly identifies with the feeling of being left. The unobtrusive craftmanship of "hooking" the reader by commonly experienced events gets one into the story immediately.

After setting the picture of her own deep loneliness, the author quickly moves into describing the means of grace that enabled her to deal with her grief. Thus there is a practical, helpful justification for writing the article.

2. *Sincerity and believability.* You sense these qualities when the author describes the ongoing sameness of life—the patches of sunlight on the carpet, the dishes stacked on the sink, the razor and comb on the bathroom shelf. She gets out one egg, not three, in preparing breakfast. These pictures register immediately. There is no circumlocution or vagueness to destroy the mood of sincerity and believability.

3. *Relevance and reader identification.* Not all of us have lost a spouse, but by the illustrations of the missed ride, the departing train, or the homely details of everyday life, the author sets herself alongside us in our human situation. She is describing emotions that affect us all. This *mood* works for believability.

4. *Writing style.* No one better illustrates the effectiveness of straightforward declaration. She employs Bible and literary quotations to give strong substance to her thesis. The quotations are apt, not dragged in.

One senses the presence of God and His grace. Here is no false piety, but direct, relevant consolation that emerges from the Word of God without being preachy.

—Russell T. Hitt, judge
Editor Emeritus
Eternity magazine

RESEARCH

1. Begin a collection of first-person narratives that you can use as models for your own manuscripts. Select three or four from *Reader's Digest* and note the outstanding characteristics and techniques of each article by underlining, highlighting with a color marker, or by writing notes in the margin. Look for effective use of chronological structure,

flashbacks, dialogue, description, narrator's perspective, and anecdotes.

2. Start a parallel collection of first-person narratives from Christian magazines. Look for examples in the interdenominational periodicals, such as *Christian Herald* or *Moody Monthly*. This article type is often found in Sunday school take-home papers such as *Power for Living, Freeway,* and *Connect* by Scripture Press, and *Sunday Digest. Looking Ahead,* and *Christian Living* by David C. Cook Publishing Company. Scripture Press has a "Tips To The Writer" packet that contains sample take-home papers and lists of editorial needs (P.O. Box 513, Glen Ellyn, IL 60137). David C. Cook editors have prepared a booklet of editorial requirements for *Sunday Digest*. They also have single information sheets for *Looking Ahead* (for junior-highers) and *Christian Living* (for senior-highers). These may be obtained by writing to the David C. Cook Publishing Company at 820 N. Grove, Elgin, IL 60120.

Mark up the outstanding parts of these first-person narratives from evangelical publications as was suggested in Research item 1.

3. Visit your college or public library and make a survey of how frequently the first-person narrative is being used in some of the leading secular magazines. List the magazines that print this article type. Then look through the last six issues of one periodical that regularly uses the first-person narrative and make a list of these articles by issue giving author, title, and page numbers.

4. If you are attending a Christian college or have access to a Christian college's library or a church library, make a frequency survey of evangelical publications in the same way as suggested in Research item 3.

5. Use one article selected for Research items 2–4 and study the use of anecdotes. What is the approximate time span in each anecdote?

PRACTICE

1. Make a list of your personal experiences that you feel are significant enough to be of interest to an editor and his readers.

2. Construct an article overview of the personal experience you believe has the best chance of being published. An overview is a one-page list that contains the following items: subject of the article; article's purpose (e.g., "to show the reader the challenges and rewards of serving Christ in the inner city"); sources (people, publications, and places that need to be researched in preparation for writing the article); intended readership; slant

or focus (some particular emphasis or aspect of the subject that will heighten the interest for the intended readership); three potential publications (ones that your survey of the evangelical market has shown might be interested in your proposed article).

3. (a) Using the subject you selected for Practice item 2, make a list in chronological order of all the details that you can recall of that personal experience. (b) From this list of details, select the ones that you feel are the most important and could be handled effectively within the framework of a 1,000–1,500-word article. (c) Write three different leads for an article based on the subject selected for Practice items 2 and 3.

4. Using the details selected for Practice item 3(b), write a thesis (one-sentence statement of the main point of the narrative) and construct a topic outline.

5. Write your personal narrative article based on your thesis and topic outline. As you continue to think about this article, you should feel free to revise or reorganize your outline. However, after you have determined your thesis, don't change it. The thesis will serve as your ultimate standard as to the relevancy of every fact, point, description, quotation, and anecdote. If these do not support, amplify, clarify, or illustrate your thesis, they should not appear in your article.

Show your rough or second draft to a friend or classmate. Study the evaluations you receive before typing the final draft. Submit the article with a cover letter to your first choice of potential publications (point six on your overview).

DISCUSSION

1. Which characteristics of a good title are observable in Elisabeth Elliot's article?

2. Compare the introductions of the two first-person narratives in this chapter. Identify the type of each one and its purpose in relation to the rest of the article.

3. How many examples of multi-sense description can you find in "Lord, I Believe You Want Me to Live"?

4. How does each author employ the flashback technique?

5. Compare the conclusions used in these narratives. What labels can you give them? What is the purpose of each conclusion? Where does the conclusion start in Marilyn Henderson's article?

4
The How-to-do-it Article

This type of article is extremely popular because of the almost universal desire among people to improve themselves. This article form shows readers how to do or make something. In some journalism textbooks this type of feature is called the process or utility article.

Two main approaches are possible: "how-to-do-it" and "how-it-was-done." The first approach shows the reader how he can do this process himself in the future and the second type is a variation of the third-person narrative, explaining how someone else went through a process such as building an outdoor nativity scene or learning how to witness for Christ more effectively. This second type generally has more of an authoritative tone, giving it a slight advantage over the first.

Anecdotes must be used in this type of article so that the reader can see and experience the step-by-step process. Each step should be preceded or followed by a vivid anecdote that illustrates that part of the process being described.

Some of the anecdotes in a "how-to" article can be humorous, showing how the author made mistakes. This technique helps the reader by subtly warning of chuckholes to avoid in the process. These brief narratives also help the reader realize that the author is human and struggles before succeeding.

Early in this type of article the readers should be shown why this subject is significant or important to them personally. If the writer fails to do this on the first page, the readers probably will not finish the article.

One of the built-in hazards of this kind of article is the preachy tone, since the second-person pronoun perspective is often used. The humorous anecdote can help turn down the preachy tone.

Ed Eulenburg, long-time feature reporter for the late *Chicago Daily News*, says the supreme challenge in this type of writing is to get someone excited and involved in the process who has had no previous interest in the subject.

The structure of this kind of article should answer at least three of the reportorial questions: what (resources needed in the process), why (significance of the procedure to the reader), and how (illustrated steps in the process).

The writer should be excited about the subject in order to get enthusiastic reaction from readers.

How to Produce a Children's Film Without Actually Crying

Glenn F. Arnold

The lights in the sanctuary dimmed, the rumble of the timpani began to build to a crescendo through the public-address system, and members of the children's church staff tensed. Then there it was in pulsating hues on the seventy-by-seventy-inch screen in the chancel—our Children's Day production in super-eight color, "The Good Samaritan"!

This moment—so exhilarating for both children and adults—climaxed nine months of dreaming, planning and producing by the children's church of the First Baptist Church of Park Ridge, Illinois.

"Why, if I had known what this film was going to be like," enthused one mother, "I would have brought my neighbors. Why didn't you tell me?"

To such a question there was only one answer. "Not even those of us who had been working on the project for months really knew what the final product would be," commented Dorothy Crane, junior church director. "This was a first-time experience for adults as well as children."

The idea had first gripped both the youngsters and their elders when Dennis Shippy, a communications major at Moody Bible Institute, showed a film he had directed and produced in his home church when he was in high school. Using an eight-millimeter camera he had purchased from a dime store for $10, he and the young people of his church had created an impressive film on Christ's nativity.

A showing of Dennis's film to the children's church staff and to the board of Christian education pushed everyone involved across the bridge of uncertainty. They had been hooked on a 400-foot line of celluloid!

The first step was to ask the children if they would be interested in a film project. Their enthusiastic affirmative left no doubt as to their feeling.

The staff, concerned that the children participate from the beginning, next asked them what Bible story they wanted to present.

"Jesus walking on the water!"

"Noah and the ark!"

After explaining as diplomatically as possible that these first suggestions might involve technical difficulties, Curt Pinnell, primary church director, suggested that the children research in Bible-story books so they could see for themselves some of the physical problems involved in recreating their favorites. This research, done in small groups using Bibles and books from the church library, led to the children's choice of the parable of the Good Samaritan.

Further study followed. First the account in Luke was read in a number of translations and versions. Pictures of the dress and houses in first-century Palestine were carefully observed. Drawings were made of costumes, designs for the inn and murals of outdoor scenes. Donna Wadsworth, a dramatically oriented high schooler, assisted in writing a script.

Solomon's wisdom was needed for the next step. Which children should take the leading roles? In general, the children agreed to the suggestion that the oldest be given such leading parts as the victim, the good Samaritan, the Levite and the innkeeper. Eventually each child had at least one part although from a standpoint of numbers the way to Jericho looked more like a modern interstate highway than a lonely road.

Pleas went out through the church paper, by phone and through the children themselves for help in collecting the needed properties and costumes. A flood of bathrobes, scarfs, sandals and towels poured into the Christian education office with many parents wondering what kind of rummage sale the staff was running now.

Rehearsals began indoors during the winter as part of the weekly program with the children practicing according to the scenes. At the same time, boys and girls on the art staff began drawing murals of what they thought the outdoor and inn settings should look like.

One adult leader suggested that the road scenes be shot outdoors instead of against a mural, and a tour of a nearby forest preserve quickly revealed an ideal setting complete with a huge boulder—a perfect hiding place for the attackers.

Early in the spring after one or two fresh-air rehearsals, the outdoor scenes were filmed. These were completed in three weeks. The attack incident was filmed from a number of angles and was acted out so enthusiastically that leaders were relieved to see the victim get up by himself. The emerging foliage and the progressive deepening of the green hues as the weeks passed gave the producers some uneasy moments, but these problems were largely unnoticed in the final film.

The stage in the church's Fellowship Hall made a good location for filming the inn scenes. All went smoothly here with the exception of the appearance of a very modern light switch at the inn's entrance and an over-zealous innkeeper and his wife who nearly suffocated the attack victim under a mound of blankets.

Editing was the most traumatic step for the adult staff. For several weeks, the Christian education office was decorated with dozens of strips of super-eight film along the walls, each identified as to scene. Previously, not one of the adult leaders had done any film editing beyond work on home movies.

After initial help from the Bible school student, staff members found themselves on their own in their attempt to get the right section of film, at the appropriate time, in the correct place.

Background music was transferred to a master tape and by means of the "add-a-track" feature on the church's tape recorder, the narration and taped background of children's voices were added. Making the tape took several evenings.

As each roll of film came back from the camera shop, it was shown to the children the following Sunday. Interest was high. Finally on the Sunday before Children's Day the film in nearly complete form was presented at the children's church service. The children's enthusiastic response forecast a sanctuary overflowing with parents and friends one week later.

The Children's Day program became a double feature because each major step had been filmed and several cassette recordings had been made as the children worked on their project. These activities provided footage for feature one, "The Making of a Movie," a twenty-minute documentary of the previous nine months' activity in children's church. Then, following announcements and offering, "The Good Samaritan" was shown for fifteen minutes to an appreciative and enthusiastic congregation.

Some had been concerned about showing the films in the sanctuary. In fact adult leaders had found themselves praying for a cloudy day so that the pictures would have a brighter image on the screen. These prayers were answered in the form of a cloudburst shortly before service time. Though advance preparation had been made to darken the sanctuary by masking some of the windows, the heavenly help made it possible for everyone to see clearly.

What does it cost to produce a mini-spectacular? By borrowing cameras, lights and projectors from adult members, expenses were held to $150 of the $200 set aside in the budget. Most of that amount went to pay for film and processing.

Does this seem expensive? When the benefits and values of the project were considered, most of those involved agree that it was a small and very worthwhile investment. The teaching value of the project was recognized by all. The children who made the film and the parents who saw it received new insights into the parable. Each child was asked what the story meant to him.

In addition the children were given many opportunities for self-expression through writing, drawing, painting, planning and acting, all with focus on the Bible's teaching. The participants also learned team-work. Finally, the church now has its own uniquely effective film of the Good Samaritan parable for use in Sunday school, children's church and vacation Bible school.

While there were times when tears might have been used instead of splicing tape or glue to splice the film, almost everyone—children, adults and youth—agree that the total effort was one of the richest Christian education experiences the church has ever offered.

CRITIQUE OF "How to Produce a Children's Film Without Actually Crying"

The key to all "how-to-do-it" articles is to choose a subject that has significance in terms of innovation and need. Many "how-to" articles deal with similar subjects, such as how to teach, how to hold a Bible study, how to witness when it's ten below zero, etc. Most of these, if not all, are overdone and reader interest is not very high.

The author here chose something fresh, something not so old, something actually original, and something that could be of tremendous encouragement to people who are frantic to find ideas on how to get their children involved in biblical material they will remember. Any Christian education director, Sunday school teacher, youth pastor, or parent who is keenly desirous of having children come to some meaningful involvement in biblical areas would find this article of immense interest.

But the "how-to," in order to get off the ground, given the subject, given the title (which here was a bit confusing), depends very heavily on the lead. Here it is anecdotal, and without such an opening, the how-to article seldom gets off the ground. This lead set the proper tone and captured the reader's interest by carrying him directly into the situation. One key line in the opening is the hooker, "and the members of the children's church staff tensed." No reader is going to let go until he finds out why. This is the essential part of all article writing, but the "how-to" needs it even more because it does not carry natural elements of thunder and lightning in the first place.

Secondly, the successful "how-to" must tell what the idea is, expand it properly, and provide enough clarity into the procedures to not give the reader a feeling of being overwhelmed by complexity. This "how-to" is about something that had already occurred. Now the author must piece it together from those who experienced it in such a way that others could do the same thing with equal success. If there is any weakness at all in this "how-to" article, it is that sometimes there is a feeling of a lot of work going into a project that already appears a bit complicated.

However, as one moves through the exposition step by step, there is an emerging consciousness that something *exciting* is happening. Something is actually being produced. And in light of that, whatever feelings of excessive labor that might have hung over it soon fade away in the prospect of kids creating a biblical story on film in their own way.

The various steps are well-illustrated throughout the exposition, and any author who can take a "how-to" experience and get it all across in this way has done his homework well. Fuzziness about procedures and superficial examples of how something is done can destroy the interest value of material. But this one is carefully laid out, so that anyone who wanted to get into this project could do so by the steps presented.

The paragraph near the end which opens with "Some had been concerned about showing the films in the sanctuary . . ." is not necessary. It's nice to know how God cooperated by providing a thunder storm, but it might have been better to say: "On the day of the film showing, it was cloudy and the auditorium was properly darkened in order for everyone to see. But those who do these projects should consider when and where the film will be shown."

The important area that this "how-to" brought in at the end was the cost. There are projects that sound great until the bill is faced. Here the author shows exactly what it cost, and that it was really cheap considering the result. The final summation of the project's value to the church was also very important, because readers often ask, "Is it worth it in the end?" It proved to be profitable in every sense.

The final proof of a good "how-to" article is that the reader feels he or she wants to get up and do what is suggested. In this case, there is no question that the project came across as exciting, practical, and inexpensive. Undoubtedly, many will be guiding children in producing their own films "without crying."

—James L. Johnson
Coordinator of Journalism/Print Program
Wheaton Graduate School

The Mature Person Takes Inventory

Jeanette Lockerbie

January Sales. They are as much a part of American economics as the Christmas shopping binge that produces them.

Why, we might ask, do business firms make such a production of their yearly inventory? To be sure, it is not to give the shopper a once-a-year chance to paw through the high-piled merchandise on sales counters. Business has a dual purpose in these extravaganzas: one, to scrap the no-longer-profitable merchandise; two, to restock with proven profit-makers and to make room for new items.

And people of all ages can learn from this practice.

In particular, what are some items the mature person can profitably discard?

Regrets: Nothing produces more misery than does dwelling on past mistakes and shortcomings. With what insight the poet Whittier wrote:

"For of all sad words of tongue or pen, the saddest are these: 'It might have been.' "

It is sheer futility to expend emotional energy on something that is beyond hope of recall or change. Yet, so many persons, in their later years, let themselves be snared into this trap.

When regret is mingled with remorse over sin—whether sin of omission or commission—there is one sure way of scrapping it. If a person has repented and has confessed the sin to God, then God has forgotten it. His Word tells us so (Isaiah 43:25). Why then spend years in needless regretting that drains the emotional energy needed for each day?

We need to forgive ourselves, when we have sought and received the Lord's forgiveness. Yet I find, as I speak to various groups (and write on the subject) that forgiving oneself seems to be something many people have never considered. When they do, and when they act upon it, they begin to experience a totally new release (as many have written and told me).

Another expendable as we start a new year is intolerance.

If we would enjoy good relations with the people around us, we need to be flexible. In order to do this we may have to temper our feelings and monitor our words to a degree. Especially is this so when we make comparisons of how different some things are from what they once were.

If there is one thing more than another that tends to infuriate younger people, it is the smug attitude of some older folk, that theirs was a "better day"; that people were more virtuous, courageous, ingenious, thrifty and appreciative than young people are today. Whatever the evidence, the subject is explosive, and filibustering on it merely creates resentment.

So this kind of intolerance can profitably be gotten rid of. (There is, however, a commendable intolerance of sin in all of its forms. God requires of us this kind of intolerance.)

One of the true marks of maturity, as Dr. Clyde Narramore repeatedly states, is the ability to face up to reality and not live in a world of unrealistic hopes. Chief among these for many persons is the hope that things will go on as they always have. Especially is this so when one of the marriage partners goes on to be with the Lord. The home may have to be broken up or an equally traumatic change made. And all too often, for the one left, life becomes filled with unrealistic hope that somehow things can be as they have been. But this can never be. We're not living in a world of "As it was in the beginning is now and ever shall be"; we're living in a world of swift change which all too often invades our everyday life.

Frequently, unrealistic hope leads to selfish demanding that others rearrange their lives to accommodate the one who so hopes. Such attitudes may make the person feel loved and wanted, for he's living in his own unreal world.

There is nothing unrealistic, however, in putting one's hope in God. "Hope to the end . . ." the Apostle Peter exhorts us (1 Peter 1:13). This is healthy hope.

In our own stocktaking, then, we need to take a good hard look at these areas we have mentioned. We may find, too, some other traits, habits, attitudes that need to be scrapped for our own well-being as well as for their effect on others around us, both emotionally and spiritually.

And, may I suggest, do not neglect the physical. As never before, experts are telling us how important it is that we maintain our bodies through proper diet and sufficient exercise. If you will pardon a personal illustration, my son is the one who encourages me to jog. Not only so, but a few Christmases ago, he gave me a regular suit. Now he diligently inquires both by mail and on the phone, "Mother, are you jogging; are you getting proper exercise?" There's something uniquely motivating about "doing what is good for you," when it comes from someone who loves you and you know it.

Now for the restocking of the shelves of our life. This too must be planned and carried out with care. The whole "line" is there in Galatians 5:22,23; love, joy, peace, long-suffering, gentleness, goodness, faith, meekness, temperance.

What a stock to have on hand with which to face this new year!

CRITIQUE OF "The Mature Person Takes Inventory"

Jeanette Lockerbie proves with this piece that an article need not be long to be effective. She has written a short and subtle "how-to-do-it" article, thereby not offending readers with a heavy hammer approach or giving them time to get bored.

The introduction is a model that can be studied to good advantage by beginning writers. The reader's attention is snared by the impact of a two-word sentence fragment, "January Sales." This is a beautiful example of starting where the reader is. I can easily visualize the January issue of *Psychology For Living* arriving in a reader's home simultaneously with the after-Christmas sale announcements and advertisements from Sears, Penneys, Montgomery Ward, and the discount houses. Most readers would immediately identify with this subject.

In the second paragraph, Lockerbie expertly helps her readers see the subject from the businessman's perspective. This introduces the subject of inventory, which is speedily applied to the reader's personal life. At the end of paragraph two, the reader is given the outline of the article in embryonic form: scrapping and restocking. Paragraph three is the thesis. This article reminds authors that an effective piece can have as few as two main points.

Without being preachy, Lockerbie shows what items within the reader's inventory need to be discarded: regrets, intolerance, and unrealistic expectations.

Support for these three subpoints comes from literature (paragraphs five and six), the Bible (paragraphs eight and sixteen), and experts in the field (paragraph fourteen).

The title of this article shows that it's not necessary to have the phrase "how to" in the title of this type of writing. The word *mature* in the title has a strong self-improvement hook; many readers would stop to read an article bearing this word in the heading in order to learn how to become more mature. Also, a sincere compliment is paid to the reader through the adjective *mature*.

The placement of the jogging recommendation was somewhat confusing. It comes at the end of the section about aspects of life to discard (paragraph 18), but before the concluding step of restocking (paragraph 19). This might have been presented as a new or restockable item dependent on the reader's previous involvement in physical fitness.

Above all, Lockerbie has given her readers some practical and positive steps for taking a self-inventory that could help them have a much happier and fulfilling new year.

—The Editor

RESEARCH

1. Start your collection of how-to articles. While surveying secular and Christian publications, look for examples of both "how-to-do-it" and "how-it-was-done" types.

2. Which of the two types seems to be the most popular in secular magazines? Which one in evangelical periodicals?

3. Using one of the articles obtained while completing Research item 1, analyze the reader that the author of the article had in mind (e.g., age, sex, marital status, interests, personality traits, and attitudes).

4. Locate and summarize in your own words at least two articles in *Writer* or *Writer's Digest* on writing the "how-to" article.

5. Select three "how-to" articles from the last six issues of *Reader's Digest*. Study the relationship of the anecdotes to the steps in the process. Which comes first most often—the steps or the anecdotes illustrating the steps? Which sequence do you think is the most effective? Why?

PRACTICE

1. Make a list of six subjects from your church or family activities, hobbies, or job that might be good possibilities for a "how-to" article.
2. Select three subjects from the six compiled for Practice item 1, and use them to write three overviews (subject, purpose, sources, readership, slant or focus, and three potential publications).
3. Using one of the overviews completed for Practice item 2, construct a topic outline that includes a working title, the thesis, the lead, the steps in the process, and the conclusion.
4. Construct three possible display window units (title, subtitle, and lead) for the outline completed for Practice item 3.
5. Write a "recommendation for action" conclusion for the article outlined in Practice item 3. This is the type of conclusion that encourages the reader to try the process himself.

DISCUSSION

1. In what ways has the author of "How to Produce a Children's Film" attempted to warn the reader of potential hazards in this type of project?
2. In what instances was humor used to explain the process? Did this seem natural or forced?
3. Was the passive voice overused in Glenn Arnold's article? If so, how would you reconstruct some of these sentences?
4. Why did Jeanette Lockerbie write this article for the January issue of *Psychology For Living?* What are some examples of effective noun and verb selection that were especially relevant to the article's subject?
5. What were the two main points in "The Mature Person"? Why didn't Lockerbie develop the second major idea of the article: restocking life's shelves?

5
The News Article

Evangelical editors have trouble publishing "hard news" in their magazines. When a periodical is issued quarterly, monthly, biweekly, or even weekly, any information that was news at deadline time is slightly stale by the time the magazine gets to the reader's mailbox.

The news editor of a Christian magazine is then forced to publish a series of items listing the most important religious news of continuing interest to his readership. Or he can write up announcements of coming events. He can also write in-depth featurized news reports on one or two of the major stories as space and time permit. This latter approach includes a heavy emphasis on the "why" of the story that may not have been covered in the secular or other religious media. Sometimes the news section in a Christian periodical will be a collection of short items (one or two paragraphs per story) and one or two featurized stories. *Christianity Today, Moody Monthly, Eternity,* and *Christian Life* can be studied for methods of covering evangelical news.

No matter what the length or the approach of the news article, an attempt should be made to answer the six traditional reportorial questions: who, what, when, where, why, and how. Rudyard Kipling called these his "six serving men."

The structure for a news story has often been pictured in an inverted pyramid or triangle:

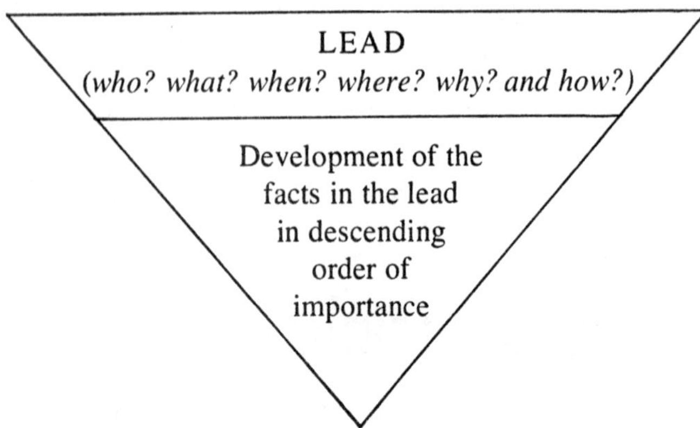

The lead in a news story is generally the first one or two sentences (usually the first paragraph). The rest of the paragraphs put flesh on the six interrogatives in descending order of importance. This permits an editor to cut a news article toward the bottom if there is a space problem.

However, the longer featurized news story that may include interpretation of the event usually is constructed differently. It starts with a more creative lead and then builds to an important concluding paragraph. This type of news article can not be clipped by an editor as brutally and easily as the straight news story.

The news story should be characterized by accuracy and thoroughness of the facts. It's something like the old *Dragnet* program; the news editor also wants "the facts, ma'am, just the facts." If complete objectivity is not a possibility, fairness should certainly be a primary goal for the writer of religious news.

The World of WIM[1]

Jerry Ballard

In an address in Kingston, Jamaica, in October, Cuban President Fidel Castro declared that the Cuban people have religious freedom but warned church leaders not to try to block "the triumph of the socialist revolution." His word came while meeting with a cross section of Jamaican church leadership. He added that church leaders should not stand in the way of "the inevitable process of history, the triumph of the socialist revolution."

This fragile balance between freedom and restraint was evidenced during WIM General Director J. Allen Thompson's September visit to Cuba. The Cuban-born leader, returning to his birthplace after a 17-year absence, was impressed with the freedom granted him to visit churches and preach without restrictions. And everywhere he went the churches were filled with believers. Not only the old-timers who wanted a touch with the past, but also scores of young people who are finding a dynamic faith amidst the "socialist revolution."

Such is the ministry climate today in WIM's field of mission birth. And a half century of God's blessing is seen throughout the island as decisively as anywhere in the world of WIM. "We are somewhat smaller in number than when I left Cuba in 1960," Thompson reported, "but the spiritual qualities I saw in the lives of our Cuban brothers and sisters in Christ are as real and deep as anywhere. We praise the Lord for this continuing demonstration of His love and power in individual lives. We're learning how to live in a Marxist society in Cuba, and I found the church more awake, alive and coping than here in North America."

Thompson underscored that church life in a socialist society like Cuba is not without its difficulties. "But we are proving that the gospel is valid in any context, that individuals in their personal relationship with the living God are finding a simpler life-style conducive to spiritual growth."

In general, Thompson found believers in Cuba more spiritually oriented than in many other areas of the world. "They are examining their value system in light of the Word of God, rather than swallowing a secularized value system as we tend to do in North America. I saw little hunger for material possessions. Instead, I saw Christians diligently searching the Scriptures for truly Biblical values."

The seminary at Los Piños Nuevos continues to prepare men and

[1]West Indies Mission.

women for ministry. Thirty-five students are enrolled this year with churches giving sacrificially to meet the school's budget. "I was impressed with our young pastors," Thompson shared. "They have the same quality of life and strength in the Word as those trained in earlier years. Momentum in the work is being maintained. They might lack the theological breadth we would like to see, but they are learning the Word for living, not just for knowing."

How is an uncompromising Christian world view sustained in a competitive ideological environment? What are Biblical imperatives from which there can be no retreat? What in adopted Christian life-style is nonessential and can be discarded? Here is the area of struggle for Cuban believers. And we here at home would do well to come back to the Scriptures on this one, too.

CRITIQUE OF "The World of WIM"

(The article, "The World of WIM," from *Harvest Today* magazine, was judged a first-place winner in the Evangelical Press Association's 1978 contest. It was evaluated "outstanding" in objectivity, timeliness, significance for intended audience, and clarity and economy of expression; it received a "good" in thoroughness.—The Editor)

The article dealt specifically with the community of Christians in Castro's Cuba, and more generally, with a question of profound significance for all Christians—in the words of the author, "the fragile balance between freedom and restraint. . . . How is an uncompromising Christian world view sustained in a competitive ideological environment?"

The author, Jerry Ballard, avoided the temptation of dealing with a saccharine or easy Christian topic. The author took up an issue—communism—that has often been treated very emotionally and one-sidedly in the Christian press in the years since World War II. Ballard found unexpected hope for Christians in the Marxist society of Cuba as well as relevance for Christians in America.

The article was balanced, probing, courageous, fair, and most important, it sought truth. Technically, it was well-constructed, weaving the secular background, the present situations, and the spiritual implications. It could, and probably should, have been expanded into a much longer article. This would have permitted the use of specific illustrations, which were lacking.

The author began by quoting Castro's statement that the church must not interfere with the socialist revolution. Despite these ominous words, the author said that WIM General Director J. Allen Thompson discovered freedom to preach as he wished and churches were filled with Christian believers. In fact, Thompson found believers in Cuba more spiritually oriented than in many other areas. But the author did not conclude on a Pollyannish note.

"How is an uncompromising Christian world view sustained in a competitive ideological environment?" the author asked. "Here is the area of struggle for Cuban believers. And we here at home would do well to come back to the Scriptures on this one, too."

This was a superb article. It dealt with a burning crisis for many Christians elsewhere in the world. My only criticism—tell me more!

—Wesley G. Pippert, judge
White House Correspondent
United Press International
Washington, D.C.

A Minister Is Missing

Edward E. Plowman

For ten weeks bands of parishioners gathered nightly at First Baptist Church of Maine, New York, to pray for the safe return of their pastor, Donald LaRose. The 34-year-old minister disappeared on Tuesday, November 4, under mysterious circumstances involving suggestions of foul play by Satan worshipers. As of late last month he was still missing. The prayer meetings, however, ended abruptly at mid-month when the official board of the 150-member church announced it had terminated the pastoral relationship.

Head deacon William Brigham, a printer, said an extensive investigation indicated that LaRose had planned his own disappearance. Yet authorities and private investigators were unable to establish any motive. LaRose was in good health, family members and close friends told *Christianity Today* that they had noted no changes in his personality, there were no major hassles at church, and his wife Eunice said there were no family tensions (the couple have two daughters, ages 10 and 13). He had little life insurance, he was abreast of debts and taxes, he had told his family and friends he was happy in the ministry, and no amorous connections were uncovered. Neighbors described him as "the happiest man on the street."

"We're at our wit's end," said Adam LaRose, the minister's father, a business executive in Reading, Pennsylvania.

In a statement issued to the news media, Eunice LaRose appealed for her husband to return home. Despite the problems caused by his sudden disappearance, she said, "we can work things out."

LaRose grew up in the Lancaster, Pennsylvania, area, where he attended the large Calvary Independent Church with his parents and sister. After graduating from Moody Bible Institute, where he met Eunice, he returned to Lancaster to work with the Youth for Christ organization. Next he entered the Christian radio field and worked at stations in Indiana, Wisconsin, and Maryland. He then moved to Syracuse, New York, where he became an executive with WMHR-FM, a station he helped to organize. After nearly five years, he left as a result of a dispute over business strategy. In October, 1973, he accepted a call to First Baptist in Maine, a village northwest of Binghamton. The church is loosely affiliated with the General Association of Regular Baptists.

Last October LaRose's name appeared in local news stories in connection with a series of messages on the person and work of Satan. The talks were given at the mid-week services on Wednesday nights, and they were advertised in a widely distributed newsletter that the church publishes.

As the series progressed, LaRose reported to state police that he had received threatening letters and telephone calls. The letters, postmarked from Maine, were pasteups of words cut from printed sources. Investigators later determined that the cutouts came mainly from issues of *Broadcasting,* a secular trade magazine published in Washington, D.C., and the church's newsletter. (LaRose was one of *Broadcasting's* few subscribers in the Binghamton area.)

Said one letter: "Rev. LaRose: For blasphemy against Satan I condemn you to the wrath of Lucifer, son of the morning, ruler of this world, and victor over all opposing forces."

Another announced that "for continual public blasphemy against Satan, the most high Lucifer requires your blood as a sacrifice so your rip-off can be stopped."

At least one of the threatening telephone calls was answered by ten-year-old Joyce LaRose.

Pastors of two neighboring Baptist churches reported they too were getting similar notes and telephone calls. The calls, said Pastor Harvey Sumner of First Baptist Church in Vestal, sounded like tape recordings played into the telephone. In all, there were ten calls, most of them taken by his wife. The voice came through in low, gutteral tones, saying that Satan was upset by Sumner's preaching. During an interview, Sumner, 37, was asked if the voice tones resembled what happens when a tape recorder is played on weak batteries or deliberately slowed down. "Exactly," he replied.

After LaRose disappeared the letters stopped coming to the other two ministers. The last letter received by Pastor Derwin G. Hauser of Bethel Baptist Church in Vestal arrived the day after LaRose disappeared. It had been postmarked at 10:30 A.M. on November 4.

November 4 was election day. LaRose accompanied his wife that morning to a polling place. Something odd was happening, he commented to her. He said he had received a phone call informing him that one of his church members would be operated upon in an Endicott hospital. When he went to the hospital earlier that morning, he said, he found that no operation was scheduled for the parishioner.

After voting, Mrs. LaRose proceeded to her part-time job at a school cafeteria, and the minister said he was going to get a haircut.

At 12:20 P.M. church secretary Beida Lawton looked out the office window and saw LaRose on the church parking lot. It was the last time anyone remembered seeing him that day.

When he had not returned home by 7:00 P.M., Mrs. LaRose and church members began checking area hospitals and country roads. The next day police found his 1970 station wagon abandoned in an urban renewal area of Binghamton, near the bus station. Because of the sensational Satanism angle, the story of LaRose's disappearance got national news coverage.

Hauser told reporters that there were indeed Satanist activities in the Binghamton area and that he knew of a witch's coven there. He declined to specify where "because of the risk." (Police said they knew of no such group.) Sumner meanwhile purchased a revolver.

State police officials early in the case cautioned the public against jumping to conclusions. They said there was no solid proof that the minister had been abducted. Some press stories left the door open to the possibility of a hoax.

The church posted a $10,000 reward for information leading to the pastor's safe return or $5,000 for the whereabouts of his body. It also spent thousands of dollars on private detectives. Private investigator Charles Reagan of the Michigan-based Finkler Detective Agency turned up some of the key evidence that led to the church's decision to fire LaRose (and to withdraw the reward offers).

It was discovered that LaRose had purchased carry-on flight luggage at a Sears store last July. In September he got $675 in cash advances from a bank through the use of credit cards. He also cashed in $3,500 worth of stock in the Syracuse radio station. Mrs. LaRose knew nothing of these transactions. The day before he disappeared he gave her $60 of his $235 weekly paycheck for household use, as was his custom. It was also his custom to deposit the remainder in the bank, but the deposit was not made. Thus at the time he disappeared he could have been carrying at least $4,350, all legally his.

In an interview, Reagan said there were other "minor" shreds of evidence suggesting that LaRose had arranged his own disappearance, but both he and Deacon Brigham declined to divulge them.

At month's end the authorities (including Federal Bureau of Investigation agents working quietly in the background), LaRose's family and his friends were still pondering the two main questions: Where is Pastor Don LaRose and why is he missing?

LaRose is nearly six feet fall, weighs 190 pounds, is a bit paunchy, may wear glasses, and he has blue-gray eyes and light brown hair, a prominent dimple on his chin, and a freckle or mole near his left eye.

A tragic sidelight in the case involved fundamentalist leader Carl McIntire and an anti-Satan rally he and his followers held in front of the Maine church on January 3. Mrs. LaRose and First Baptist's leaders tried to discourage McIntire from coming, and they said they would not participate if he came. But McIntire said the rally was a demonstration against Satan on behalf of all Christians, and that it would kick off his group's Revival '76 program.

En route to the rally, one of McIntire's five busses overturned near Binghamton, injuring twenty persons. Ten were hospitalized with fractures and cuts; three suffered spinal fractures. Among the latter was Franklin Faucette, 75, dean of McIntire's Faith Seminary in Philadelphia.

CRITIQUE OF
"A Minister Is Missing"

Edward E. Plowman of *Christianity Today* was on top of a breaking story of national interest—the mysterious disappearance of Donald LaRose. Plowman brought all the skills of a top-flight investigative reporter to bear on this intriguing, fascinating chronicle.

The story is fair and balanced. It received the "outstanding" mark (5) for objectivity. Plowman doesn't accuse the minister of masterminding a hoax, yet neither does he use the article to slash at Satanist groups, jumping to the conclusion that the devil's disciples made LaRose do it.

"A Minister Is Missing" also received the highest score for thoroughness. Note attention to detail: the 150-member church, the two daughters' ages, the church secretary's name, for example. The reader is told that Beida Lawton "looked out of the office window and saw LaRose on the church parking lot. It was the last time anyone remembered seeing him that day." This is much more graphic than merely: "The church secretary was the last person known to have seen him that day."

Plowman's article also scored "outstanding" for timeliness. Though *Christianity Today's* news deadline is about two weeks ahead of the issue date, the unfolding drama was still hot when the magazines hit subscribers' mailboxes. Note how Plowman gives exact times and dates when he can: "disappeared on Tuesday, Nov. 4" (Election Day); "postmarked 10:30 A.M. Nov. 4"; "At 12:20 P.M. church secretary Beida Lawton looked out. . . ."

But he protects himself and the magazine when the time factor might be crucial: "As of late last month, he was still missing." (If LaRose had turned up the day after the magazine came off the presses, the article would still be correct.) And earlier, Plowman says the nightly prayer meetings ended "abruptly at mid-month," probably because he or his sources weren't sure of the exact date.

I rated this article "4" (good) on its significance for the intended audience. The running story was of interest to practically everyone (we all like a mystery) and was carried by national media. Because LaRose's church was Baptist ("loosely affiliated with the General Association of Regular Baptists"), it would be of special interest to evangelical *Christianity Today* readers. The story's significance, of course, is less than one of news affecting nearly all churches or Christians.

The story reads smoothly and the suspense builds. Plowman uses to good effect a fiction-writing technique: He doesn't let us in on the flight luggage and cash until more than three-quarters into the story.

Clarity and economy of expression were rated "5" (outstanding). A minor point: I had to go back and reread who "Hauser" was when I came upon only that last name on the second page, five paragraphs after he is first identified. More clear, for a second reference here, might be: "Hauser, *one of the neighboring Baptist pastors,* told reporters. . . ."

The ending is nineteen lines about the "tragic sidelight"—the bus accident. This detracts somewhat from the impact of the main story, in my opinion. Better to have made the bus sidelight a sidebar—a short separate story set adjacent to, or at the end of, the main story, with its own smaller headline.

After this surgery, would the end of the major story be further improved by transposing the remaining final two paragraphs?

The previous paragraph would end: ". . . Deacon Brigham declined to divulge them."

Next: "LaRose is nearly six feet tall . . . (etc.)

Finally: "At month's end . . . still pondering the two main questions: Where is Pastor Don LaRose and why is he missing?"

Incidentally, these questions were answered in a subsequent *Christianity Today* article. It told how and where the missing minister was found—because someone in Minnesota read Plowman's first account, recognized LaRose and . . . .

But that's another story.

—Russell Chandler, judge
Religion Writer
Los Angeles Times
Los Angeles, California

RESEARCH

1. Look in your daily newspaper for six news stories. Clip an example of one that emphasizes the "who" of the story, and five others, one each that highlights one of the five other interrogatives (what, when, where, why, and how).

2. Compare the structure and style of the news stories in your local newspaper with those in your denominational magazine or some other favorite Christian periodical.

3. Study the differences and similarities of the news stories in the news sections of *Time* and *Newsweek* with your denominational magazine or some other favorite Christian magazine.

4. Study the news section of an evangelical magazine and on the basis of the article's content, attempt to determine the news deadline for the issue you are examining.

5. Locate and study three articles in Christian periodicals that emphasize the "why" of the news story.

PRACTICE

1. Using the examples of the six interrogative leads in news articles, rewrite each of these so that one of the other five interrogatives is highlighted. Do not repeat types of interrogatives in your rewrites.

2. Listen to or view a local newscast and then rewrite some of the stories by emphasizing one of the other five interrogatives.

3. Using the inverted pyramid structure illustrated at the beginning of this chapter, write a news story announcing a coming event, activity, or ministry of your church. Make certain all six interrogatives (who, what, when, where, why, and how) are answered (when appropriate to your subject). Submit it to the editor of your weekly newspaper through your pastor, the church's publicity committee, or directly to the paper—if your church approves.

4. Look for a news story in your local newspaper that has significance for evangelicals in other parts of the country. Send the clipping to the news editor of *Christianity Today, Eternity,* or *Moody Monthly*. The news department at *Christianity Today* has compiled "Guidelines for *Christianity Today* News Correspondents," which they send to people who are interested in submitting news clippings, memos, or articles for the news section.

5. Write a news article about an unusual religious happening or ministry in your church or community that would interest the readers of your denominational publication or a nondenominational periodical. You can test your "nose for the news" by observing how many of your news articles are accepted by newspaper and magazine editors.

DISCUSSION

1. Why was the Cuban subject of the "World of WIM" significant to the intended readers, the supporters of the West Indies Mission? Why was the subject especially significant in the light of current events in 1977?

2. In what major way does this article depart from the standard news story?

3. Where should the illustrations be added that Wesley Pippert mentions were missing? What type of illustration would be the most appropriate in each case?

4. How many news interrogatives are answered in the lead of "A Minister Is Missing"? Has this article met the news story goal of fairness? If so, explain.

5. If you had been the *Christianity Today* news editor when this story broke, how would you have researched it? Did an evangelical news editor have any advantages over secular newspeople in covering this story? If so, what were they?

6
The Interview Article

As the name indicates, this type of article is based on statements obtained from someone during an in-depth interview, conference, or press conference.

As Joyce Booze suggests in her outline at the end of this introduction, the homework done prior to the interview will determine to a large extent the success of the interview. This homework includes reading everything that can be found in print about the person in reference works like *Who's Who In America,* and in newspapers, magazines, journals, and books. Material written by the interviewee should be read as time permits.

Fresh and relevant questions should flow from this type of research. These can be listed in the order they come to mind. Then they need to be reorganized into topical subdivisions or on the basis of difficulty or sensitivity. Of course, if an editor has assigned the interview, the free-lancer needs to be certain he knows what information the editor wants from the interviewee.

John McCandlish Phillips, a feature reporter for twenty-one years on the *New York Times,* found that rapt attention was the most important technique for interviewing. He warns writers against trying to become stars of the interview session. If the interviewer is to be successful, the interviewee must be permitted to do almost all the talking. Later, at the manuscript stage, the author also needs to step back and let the subject speak directly to the reader.

Phillips recommends a ninety-minute interview session: forty-five minutes of formal questioning following the prepared questions and forty-five minutes of informal conversation that often yields some of the most interesting information.

Courtesy requires notifying the potential interviewee of the free-lancer's desire for a conference. According to the time available, a one-page letter requesting an interview or a phone call can be the means of the initial contact. The letter can state the purpose for the interview, some of the basic questions that will be asked, the intended publication, and a statement about when a telephone call will be made to learn if the person will grant an interview.

If the interview is to be conducted by phone, a letter sent in advance will give the interviewee time to think about the questions posed in the letter and will provide the subject with a general idea of when to expect the call.

Among several variations of the interview article, the question-and-answer (Q-and-A) is the type most commonly used. Even though the Q-and-A is the least creative, it is still requested frequently by editors. Even with this relatively unimaginative format, selection and arrangement of the questions and responses need to be carefully planned.

Helen Patterson, in her book *Writing and Selling Feature Articles*, suggests the following four ways of structuring the interview article:

> The interview article may (1) consist almost entirely of direct quotation, with a limited amount of explanatory material concerning the person interviewed; or it may (2) be made up partly of direct and partly of indirect quotation, combined with necessary explanation; for greater variety it is advisable (3) to alternate direct with indirect quotation; and (4) a description of the person and his surroundings, generally by way of introduction, gives the reader a distinct impression of the individual under characteristic conditions.[1]

Whenever possible, the subject of the interview article should be a person who interests the author and who has the potential of saying something significant that will grab the attention of an editor and subsequently his readers.

At the 1976 EPA convention in Springfield, Missouri, Joyce Booze, editor of *Good News Crusades*, presented the following excellent outline in her workshop session on interviewing.

[1] *Writing and Selling Feature Articles*, 3rd edition (Englewood Cliffs, N.J.: Prentice-Hall, Inc., 1956), p. 72.

Outline for "Show Me" Session on Interviewing

I. Techniques of Interviewing
   A. Prepare for the Interview
      1. Do your homework
      2. Outline questions
      3. Prepare your attitude
      4. Dress appropriately
   B. Create a Good Interview Situation
      1. Choose a private setting when possible
      2. Make interviewee comfortable
      3. If taping, have machines ready
      4. Establish good rapport
      5. Explain who you are and give interviewee a copy of the publication you represent
   C. Do the Interview
      1. Start with easy questions
      2. Keep control, listen carefully but don't edit
      3. Use standard English
      4. Avoid questions that can be answered "yes" or "no"
      5. Don't waste time but don't rush
      6. Conclude on an optimistic note
      7. Don't promise to publish interview
   D. Get Photos
      1. Interviewee may have photo he wants to use
      2. Have photographer on hand

II. Editing the Interview
   A. Secure an Accurate Transcript
   B. Decide How You Can Best Use Material
      1. Consider slant needed for your publication
      2. Arrange material in order and form desired
      3. Consolidate information on one subject and delete repetitions
      4. Put in transitions
      5. If you keep interview form, don't be afraid to rearrange questions
   C. If Advisable, Send Copy to Interviewee for Approval

The interviewer basically serves as an ambassador for his readers. He needs to ask questions that he feels many of his readers would raise if they had the opportunity to meet the interviewee personally.

A writer who continues to develop interviewing skills will find these techniques helpful in researching for personality, third-person narratives, how-to-do-it articles, and other types of articles. Interviewing can become one of the most thrilling steps in research as the free-lancer has the opportunity to meet stimulating people who can provide important information, insights, and additional sources that can be investigated.

Serving a Hungry World

A *HIS* Interview with Samuel Kamaleson

Samuel Kamaleson, loved by students who have heard him sing and preach, was a pastor in his own country of India. Then God gave him a worldwide ministry as vice-president-at-large of World Vision International.

He has degrees from the University of Madras and Asbury Theological Seminary, and a doctorate from Emory University. At Urbana 76 he spoke on "Declare His Glory in a Suffering World."

HIS: First we'd like to know something about your personal background and your early life.

SK: I was born and grew up in southern India, in the state that is now known as Tamil Nadu. I came from a family of about six generations of Christians, but I did not know the Lord as my Savior until I went to the University of Madras, where I was enrolled in the school of veterinary medicine.

HIS: How did you meet the Lord?

SK: Through my roommate Shankar, who came from a Hindu background. He met a street-preaching team and heard the gospel through their presentation. The message captivated him and he said he wanted to try Jesus Christ as an experimental option.

So the Lord took him, accepted his challenge and changed his life. And it was his life, because he put his body where his words were, that profoundly impressed me. It was his life that ended my argumentations against personal faith in Christ. It corroded my resistance, and finally I came to the point where I was willing to say, "There is truth in what this fellow is claiming."

Then when we were working as student veterinarians on a government farm one summer, I had some pressing needs which I had to meet somehow. I was willing to use God or anyone else to satisfy them. So I went to this fellow and said, "Will you not pray for me?" He said, "Yes, I'll pray. But before we claim God's promises, don't you think we should satisfy God's conditions?"

I said, "What are God's conditions?" He said, "Sam, are you a Christian?"

That shook me, because I thought he had no right to question me that way. But I had to have him pray for me. So, controlling my anger, I said, "What do you mean, am I a Christian?"

He said, "Sam, are you born again?"

I told him my genealogy, my church membership and everything else, including my name being Samuel. He said, "All of them are good, but not any one of them will qualify you to be a Christian." So then I challenged him, saying, "Where does the Bible say that I must be born again?" He had a little New Testament, and he pulled it out and took me to the third chapter of John's Gospel.

For the first time I saw Christ the ultimate authority, saying that you must be born again. And the person he addressed was a man called Nicodemus, a ruler of the Jews and a morally good man. So in the long run, the statement included me also. Finally I came to the end of searching. I was ready to find.

I turned to my friend and I said, "What do I do to be born again?" He said, "Sam, you can do nothing. God has done everything for you. If you know you are a sinner in need of a Savior, Jesus Christ is here, available, ready to give himself to you." So we knelt down on a dusty farmyard road and that's where I received Christ.

My approach to him was, "Lord, I can see that you have done things for this fellow. It's real. I don't know if you're interested in me; just because you're interested in him doesn't mean that you're interested in me. But if you are, you must give me victory in defeats," and I named some of my problem areas.

And from that night onwards to this day I have had no occasion to turn back to those habits again. God gave me victory. He vindicated the fact that his interest in me and his care for me were real. And since that day I've walked with him.

HIS: What are some of the experiences that led you to devote your life to feeding the hungry?

SK: No man can be absolutely callous to the needs of his own people. They are too obviously present all around you. And so my awareness of the suffering of people in India, and the need for interpreting the message of the redeeming love of Jesus Christ in terms of participating in their suffering, came very early after I became a Christian.

In fact, four or five of us in the university who came to know the Lord at about the same time prayed together and formed an agricultural fellowship where we lived with people, taught them new methods of cultivation, and so on.

That was in 1961, and it's still growing today. Through that fellowship we are now taking care of 480 destitute children. Some of them have gone on to college and have become very respectable citizens in India.

HIS: So you had direct contact with poor people?

SK: Yes. Many things have impressed me about the humanity of those who do not have some advantages that others seem to have.

Way back in the fifth- and sixth-century poetry of the Tamil people, there are statements in which the poets observe that the most sickening thing that happens to a poor person is that others regard him as if he was a carrier of some contagion—if you go close to him, he'll give it to you. So people avoid the poor.

The complaint of the poor is, "What has happened to me? I'm still human—the only change is that the wealth I once had is gone. Why do you treat me as if I'm not human?"

That is the number one thing that appeared to me. Unconsciously I was also caught in that trap. I was afraid of poverty becoming a contagion in my life. I had been taught to maintain my middle-class respectability and every ounce of education that had been poured into me was a safeguard against my degeneration into the subhuman level called poverty.

HIS: How did you change?

SK: When I met the poor people, they had such a beautiful humanity in them. I remember one Sunday evening on the way home from church: I was carrying my three-year-old boy. I went to a little shop across the street to buy a box of matches for my wife.

A poor man was going by whose shirt was torn, and sweat was caked all over him. He had his child by the hand. He was buying for that little child one small strip of candy. Before the shopkeeper could give it to the child, my little boy, whom I was not watching, grabbed the chocolate.

So I pulled his hand back, slapped it and said "No!" I took the candy and gave it to the child. Do you know what that man said? "Don't do that, sir. He's a little boy, he doesn't know better."

And then he turned to his little child and said, "Honey, don't you want to share your candy with your brother?" And he broke a little piece and gave it to my son. And his child said yes to that. And I noticed the sweetness with which that child did not even object to his daddy. I couldn't refuse it. At first I thought I shouldn't take it. But then something higher than my own self told me, "Don't be a fool, let them do it. This is love they are expressing. Just take it." And I've never forgotten that.

Another incident took place with a rickshaw man some years ago in India. We had human beings pulling rickshaws. I wanted to give him extra money for the work he did, and so I paid him double what he had asked for.

He took it and pulled the rickshaw a few paces away, stood underneath a street lamp, and counted his money as I walked away. He came chasing after me. He said, "Sir, by mistake you have given me double the money." I said, "It was no mistake, it was my joy to give it to you."

You see, this is the poor. And it seems to me that we, by isolating ourselves from them, prove that we are still in bondage to fear. Then we deprive ourselves of what we could be taught by them. We need to learn a great deal from them.

What we consider as being a "developed" status may not be developed at all. It could be over-developed. And we may be doing the wrong thing in running through the world's resources much more quickly than God intended. So I feel that they have much to teach us.

HIS: How did you come to work with World Vision?

SK: My involvement with World Vision was a total surprise to me. I had never thought about it and I never considered myself a candidate for it. I was one of the speakers in Lausanne. Dr. Stanley Mooneyham was there, and clear out of the blue sky he asked me if I would not come in and take the place of Dr. Paul Rees, who was retiring. I still don't consider myself as a successor, but I fit into his job description.

HIS: Tell us more about your own university years and about the equivalent of Inter-Varsity there, the Union of Evangelical Students of India (UESI).

SK: After I came to know the Lord, I looked around for a place where I would have spiritual nourishment. It was then that I met Tom Turley, a fellow student in the school of veterinary medicine. He told me about a group that met for prayer, and asked me to come.

So I went. Just two, three, or four fellows would meet, but there was a lot of love. They were genuinely interested in me. They seemed to be so happy that I had become a Christian. They would talk about everyday affairs and relate them to the Word of God. They spoke about the Word of God as if it were the centrality of life, and one could receive guidance from it for one's total life.

There was a man by the name of Professor Enoch, who taught biology and zoology in the university. We used to meet in his home. We were a small group then, and nobody knew we existed. But that's what I needed at that time.

And then Dr. Norton Sterrett came from the United States, sent by IFES to help the Evangelical Union of students in Madras University. And Norton became one who very patiently worked with me. Our relationship was a warm, tender one. It became a natural thing. He taught me how to sing.

Then I became secretary for the chapter. And later, president of the chapter (the EU) in Madras.

HIS: Besides your zeal for the poor and hungry, you are also a gifted preacher. How did you first receive your call to preach?

SK: The call to preach came as a result of street preaching. Once I found the relevance of the gospel in my life, I felt a compulsion to share it with people. Sometimes I'd be going to buy groceries and the compulsion would come on me. I'd stand on the street corner, put the grocery bag between my feet and start singing. And you know, you don't have to be a good singer to stop a crowd! All you need is a pretty strong voice.

Then when people would stop, I would quickly tell them who Jesus is, what he can do, what he's done for me. (All this you've got to do in five, six, or seven minutes; otherwise they are gone.) And after I told them that, I'd pick up my bag and walk away apologetically.

But you know, one day a fellow followed me, tapped me on the shoulder and said, "I want what you've got." And I led that first fellow to the Lord.

That whetted my appetite. Then I organized a street preaching team. We went out two or three times every week to preach on street corners. Little by little the Lord affirmed in me the sense of a call to proclaim his message. I stayed to finish my veterinarian's work, graduated, and then went to the theological program.

Until the World Vision invitation came, I turned all other invitations down because I felt that the congregational ministry was the most vital, meaningful, biblical ministry—the people of God as a community expressing their knowledge of the love of God in creative action which included proclamation. It was in the context of preaching that I did this action, so that my action got into my preaching and my preaching got into my action. I couldn't have preached meaningfully if I did not get involved meaningfully. This is what I like about World Vision.

HIS: What are some of the ways that the average American student can put his faith into action for the poor and hungry?

SK: I think an American student can do a great deal. He can (1) minimize wastage, which is possible for anybody to do. I avoid large statements about stopping a multi-national corporation from making profits and all that, because I think many people give up at that point. I want to talk to the freshman who is a Christian and who says, "What can I do?" To him I would say, "Don't waste."

Avoid wastage even if it is pushed on you—wastage in terms of overeating, wastage in terms of too large a helping. We sometimes get angry if they don't give us more than we can eat. We think they have insulted us. That need not be true for a Christian.

(2) One must not make his spiritual hunger a reason for physical indulgence. I feel that a great many of us are manipulated by the advertising media at this point. "Are you feeling lonely? Why don't you go buy a new suit?" Or, "The latest fall fashions are out and if you wear this you will be like Johnny Carson." It's really a spiritual hunger that they are playing on and we are being fooled all the while. I think I would tell my freshman friend to watch out for that.

Kneel down and talk to God. Take your spiritual needs to him. If you are lonely, talk to him. If you have problems that give you anxiety, let him give you his support. And then you will find that the urge to buy—and externalize your spiritual need—decreases.

Then (3) take to the Lord whatever money you have saved by following the first two steps and ask, "Lord, how should I invest it?" And keep on doing this. It will help you look deeper and deeper, and larger involvements will be possible.

When my daughter was a freshman in high school, she had her own fasting program. She went without food for a weekend on behalf of those who suffer, and her classmates who knew her pledged a certain amount of money for every hour of every day that she would be without food. At the end of the weekend she had $50 she could send to feed people who are hungry. Something like that can be done even by people who are not very influential. I think it can be done.

HIS: Sometimes it seems that anything we could do is too small to matter.

You would say we should do it anyway, even if it's just on a personal level?

SK: Yes. If my conversion was the result of one boy living the life faithfully, then I will never minimize the effort of one person anymore, all my life. Shankar was faithful in those weeks and months. The result? I came to know Christ and I've been preaching the Word around the world so many times now. One can never minimize the effect of one person relating himself to one other person and saying to him, "Look, this is Jesus."

HIS: Shankar was just simply obedient and you happened to be watching; he probably didn't think that would count for anything.

SK: This is right. You don't obey Christ in order to influence another person. You obey him and as the observer watches it, the Holy Spirit witnesses and says, "Hey listen, the life this guy is living is true. It's authentic." I think it's scriptural. We witness and the Holy Spirit also witnesses. But without the succeeding witness of the Holy Spirit our intent can be perverted.

HIS: What should be our motive for giving money or food to the hungry?

SK: One caution: never respond to the hungry out of a feeling of personal guilt. It is not biblical. It is not the task of the Christian. The Bible says very plainly, "Now there is no condemnation for those who are in Christ Jesus." If the Holy Spirit reminds me that I am eating too much, then I need to obey him and not keep on eating and feel guilty about it. If the Holy Spirit reminds me that I ought to get involved in an area where my action is needed, I ought to get in and get involved. Guilt and a personal whipping such as the flagellants do is no substitute for the wholesomeness of the joy of obedience.

In Corinthians Paul says, "They first gave themselves to the Lord and then of their means they gave to you." This is always the progression of the Christian's concern for the needy. He gives himself to his Lord, and because this God is a self-giving God, he then gives. The Christian is not giving this as if it's part of his karma to win his salvation. That's already done and paid for.

Now I act because he has set me free, because he is this kind of God. And so my plea would be, do not ever get under the harness of guilt. Be free, act free, love free, give free. Don't quench the need for your enjoyment. But there is a difference between needed enjoyment and indulgence. Let the Holy Spirit guide us.

HIS: Do you become bitter or angry when you come to the United States and see so much food on cafeteria trays going into the garbage?

SK: I find that among students who are activists there is an uncontrolled anger against those who seem to live in callous indifference. This is understandable. Commitment involves emotion and where there is no emotion, there may be superficiality of commitment.

But if this resentment and anger drain a major portion of a Christian's emotional energy, they become dangerous. We then become negative activists. We don't have the energy to do the positive things. In fact, I would almost make it mandatory that a person who would be called by the Lord to be involved in this task will also ask the Lord for grace to overcome this hatred.

If a brother has a lot of money and is enjoying it in extreme self-indulgence, I would ask the Lord to give me grace not to be negative toward him, but to know that myself minus Jesus Christ plus all the wealth that this brother has will be the same kind. The only difference is the input of Jesus Christ.

So negativism can be a killer. Mahatma Gandhi, when he worked against the British government in India, avoided negativism like poison because he said you cannot make truth a force for you if you become negative, bitter or intolerant. These things will then oppose the truth force and nullify it. Mahatma Gandhi got his insight from Jesus Christ. We ought to be able to do it better.

HIS: What is going on with the church in India at present?

SK: The church in India is very active. Extremely active. And it's got a lot of promising leadership emerging. There's a lot of hope on the horizon. The Indian church refuses to be merely the receiving church. She's now purposely giving. When they had drought in England, the church in India sent a thousand pounds as relief. This thing is happening everywhere. A brother in PACLA (Pan-African Christian Leadership Assembly) in Nairobi said that Christians in Zaire are supporting retired missionaries in Europe by sending money to them. Missionaries from Belgium and France who have come and returned now. We never hear about these things.

HIS: They support the missionaries in retirement back home?

SK: Yes.

HIS: So it's not "sending countries" and "receiving countries" anymore?

SK: No. This is a glorious day. I am part of a missionary fellowship in

India. They've sent about eighty people into north India, into the unreached areas. One of the persons who gives regularly is a grass cutter. She cuts grass to sell as fodder. At the end of the day all her labor will bring about 75¢ U.S. She tithes it immediately. Every day she pays her tithes at the mission office saying, "This is for my missionary."

HIS: 75¢ would buy what? Barely her food and clothes?

SK: Yes, it's minimal. She probably lives in a mudwall hut and drinks rice gruel, with an occasional piece of meat. And yet she does it joyfully. You can't tell her, "Don't give," because she's not giving it to you—she's giving it to her blessed Lord.

HIS: Is it possible to get into India now as a missionary?

SK: It is hard now to get in. But if traditional mission board avenues are closed in countries like India, I think the student who has the call of the Lord should look into other ingenious ways of entering.

One way would be to join the Peace Corps. Then you have access to India. You can be the kind of person that the earliest missionaries were.

Second, there are scholarships offered by Indian universities to American youth in reciprocal relationship to the scholarships offered to Indian students by American universities. A believer can make this a wonderful opportunity to enter the country and serve the church while studying.

HIS: How does one find out where to write for that kind of information?

SK: The Indian high commissioner in Washington, D.C. or San Francisco can give a full list of their universities that offer scholarships.

The third thing: Oil companies, rubber companies, Xerox, and other multi-national corporations have wonderful opportunities for a person to go to foreign countries. They give you a salary and sometimes an extra bonus for volunteering to go out of the United States. You can't find anything better than that.

I knew a fellow who was with a U.S. oil company in Bombay who became the leader for the Youth for Christ work there. And I knew two men in Madras who were with Mansfield Tires. They became powerful witnesses in my church as long as they were there.

Then doctors. If there are six young men in med school who want to be doctors in India and the door is closed, they can then divide their ministry in India. Each can offer two months every year, so that among the six of them they can cover one spot in India around the year. They can make up the money that they will lose in that two months during the other ten months in the USA.

HIS: How do they get into India like that? On a tourist basis?

SK: Yes, tourist. Tourists are welcome.

There are beautiful ways in which you can do it. It may not be the same settled pattern that our forefathers knew. But then mankind has changed also. And so maybe this kind of methodology will be sufficient and right at this time in history.

CRITIQUE OF "Serving a Hungry World"

Although I am not particularly visually pleased with a four-column format, part of the success of "Serving A Hungry World" was nevertheless its highly readable layout. Short paragraphs, the boxing of significant quotes, and the introductory page grab the reader's attention.

This article placed first in a section of the EPA awards called "Personality Articles." It is not clever writing, turning a neat phrase, flashback technique, or the unusual life story of the personality that make this article a winner. It is the personality himself. The technique (the interview format) lets the person speak for himself in contrast to the hundreds of other "personality" articles which suffer from lack of balance and the tendency to build a myth about a person.

The strength of this article is found in the following:

1. The reader meets more than the facts about the person; he meets the person and interacts with his ideas. The interviewer lets Samuel Kamaleson tell his own background with an initial long quote. But it is well told and sets the pace and the response to the rest of his ideas. Here is a Third World person who *knows*, talking about a critical, timely issue.

2. The issue or subject behind the personality *is* critical and timely. The reader becomes involved in ideas about poverty, but the force of the ideas is in the personality telling the story. It is neither an article on Dr. Kamaleson nor an article on world hunger. Hence, points one and two focus on the two major reasons for the quality of this article.

3. The personality emerges as a *real* person who is working through the issues of world hunger which consume his life. He is afraid; he is open to new lessons about what it means to be human. (See the fourth question in the interview.) World hunger is handled with realism, yet without gimmicks, tearjerker tales, or hysteria. The entire interview has a sane balance for the audience to whom it is written and is highly credible.

4. The reader's benefit from reading this article goes beyond "What an interesting man!" or "Isn't world hunger awful!" The article has spiritual benefit beyond the issue of world hunger and beyond the personality speaking. The reader is involved in practical areas of personal responsibility not by direct challenge, but by the personal sharing of the personality who speaks in the first person. (See the twelfth question.)

The strength or weakness of the interview format is the *personality* being interviewed. In this case Dr. Kamaleson is both highly articulate and highly motivated to communicate his concerns. The interview questions (which are not particularly profound) provide a kickoff for Dr. Kamaleson to share himself. Other persons equally interesting and doing equally significant work may require much more involvement from the interviewer, particularly if the person is not verbally skilled or a natural communicator.

—Gladys M. Hunt, judge
Author, lecturer, journalism major
Michigan State University

You Can Pray If You Want To

An Interview with Jesse Jackson, by Glenn F. Arnold

Jesse Louis Jackson is the founder and national president of PUSH (People United to Save Humanity). From 1967 to 1971 he served as a national director of Operation Breadbasket within the Southern Christian Leadership Conference. He attended Chicago Theological Seminary after graduating from North Carolina Agricultural and Technical State University and is an associate minister of Fellowship Baptist Church in Chicago. He leads national PUSH campaigns for excellence in city schools and conducts crusades against sex and violence in the media. Glenn Arnold, associate professor of journalism at Wheaton Graduate School, conducted this interview.

Question. Do you recall spiritual experiences from your childhood?

Answer. Well, of course, I remember that the environment was "join the church," but I was never pressured to do it. But when I made that decision—I was in the third grade—I could sense the delight in my parents. I remember crying as if some burden had lifted.

Q. What do you recall about your early church experience?

A. Sunday school, church attendance, and Baptist Training Union on Sunday afternoons were all part of our life-style then, to be sure. The first stage I ever spoke on was a pulpit during some Christmas or Easter pageant. The church for us was a social, cultural, spiritual matrix around which a lot of our life revolved, a place where we could express our talents, whether playing a piano or organ or singing, and gain acceptance, as it were, in the broader community.

Q. Is it true that you were a delegate to a Sunday-school convention at age nine?

A. Yes. That became a great source of growing up. When you went to these conventions, your mother was waiting to get a report back from the counselor. She would ask, "How was his conduct away from home?"

Q. Do you remember any particular pastor especially well?

A. The Reverend James S. Hall. He was the pastor who first introduced me to social action—Jesus and social change and Mahatma Gandhi. He was a young pastor, twenty-six or twenty-seven, and I was fourteen or fifteen at the time. Jackie Robinson was coming through Greenville. He couldn't get off the plane to use the rest room or eat at the local airport. So Pastor Hall led a march, over much resistance from the community, because they just couldn't understand why a preacher would do such things. He began to interpret the Gospel in its broader application.

Q. Would you describe your conversion experience?

A. Well, you know, I'm very sensitive about trying to interpret that, because I think that many people have been driven from the church by seeking some classical form that their conversion took. You know, "I remember the day! I remember the hour! I felt the power!" "I fell off a horse and woke up on a certain street." I think people have been locked into a certain cataclysmic event, and people who may not have felt that way after trying often have felt that they haven't been called or that they haven't been converted. I really think that one can have high moments, but one in my judgment should never associate a convulsion with a conversion.

Q. What happened after you felt called to the ministry?

A. There was some equivocation in my mind about coming to seminary here in Chicago. I was first accepted at law school at Duke. I finally decided to come on a trial basis, because it was within the context of the civil-rights movement, and we would be downtown marching. When I first came here to Chicago, I drove all the way with my wife and baby. I sat down on the side of the bed; it was a fairly dreary day, and I cried. I was leaving one period and going into another. There are two significant periods in a person's life—that's to know when you were born and then to know why. It was clear to me why I was born and what my mission was.

Q. Did you feel that this was more like a confirmation of your call?

A. Yes, a real inner confirmation. And then of course during the years since that time, I've had other expressions of confirmation. Sometimes I've been at particular places at particular times that could not have been planned or predicted, circumstances that only God could have arranged. I was with Dr. King in Memphis when he was killed. That experience—the tragedy and the trauma of it, as well as the opportunity to interpret it—was unique. Other kinds of events also indicate to me that it is possible for man's feet to be planted by God.

Q. Do you still enjoy preaching?

A. Oh, very much. It is the supreme joy of my life. I'm always humbled by the size of the crowds. I'm acutely aware that people don't have to come to hear me preach. They don't come to hear other people preach. I think when I was a little younger, I may have preached for reputation; but the older I get, I preach for edification. And when I see the crowds come in, I don't feel so much good as I feel obligated. They come from so many walks of life, and they expect so much. A lot of them don't even come to church ordinarily; and so to have prepared myself as best as possible as a vessel through which the Word of Truth might come is a very obligative state of existence.

Q. What kind of sermons do you preach?

A. Well, first of all, I speak to situations. But I tend to put my situations in biblical contexts. I've never experienced a situation where there was not a text that could adequately fit the situation, a biblical text.

When Mayor Daley died, for example, people were searching for profound things to say and searching for ways to interpret it. I remembered the last verse in the last chapter of Judges when there was no king in Israel, "And each man did what was right in his own eyes." And that's exactly what happened; all that breaking up into little groups and coalitions—the Jews, the Irish, and the blacks, and the Croatians—"there was no king and each man did what he thought was right in his own eyes." You can just go on and on, searching for ways to marry the situations.

I think just talking about Ezekiel and describing the circumference of Babylon—describing the geography of Babylon and using some literal interpretation of bones and talking about physiological anatomy without any serious application to the valley in which you now stand—is a misuse of people's time. That is not good preaching.

Q. Do you consider yourself an evangelical?

A. I consider myself an evangelical, but white evangelicals don't. They shy away from me because of my social activism.

Q. Do you believe in the virgin birth of Jesus Christ?

A. Yes. It can't be disproved. God is capable of all things.

Q. What do you believe about the doctrine of original sin?

A. Well, one has to know that Adam and Eve is a myth; I separate myth from a fairy tale. A fairy tale is a story that has no original truth. It was designed to be false. A myth is a way of conveying a message wherein there is a kernel of truth even though certain peripheral elements may not be literal.

Q. Do you believe in the bodily resurrection of Christ?

A. Well, you know, I do. If that tomb was guarded by military soldiers and they were not able to report that they were overthrown by some element and left, something happened. The disciples would not have lied to the point of each of them being destroyed through some violent death. They not only came back to protect themselves; they came back with enough convictions themselves to be crucified.

Q. Do you believe that Jesus Christ is the Son of God?

A. Oh yes, I do. I don't believe Jesus is the only Son of God. I think God's world is too big for that.

Q. Would you explain that?

A. I think that God has many sons. There are people all over the world—some who never heard of Christian faith—who will be saved because they're God's children. I don't think 900 million Chinese today who never heard the word "Jesus" are lost eternally because some white Christian missionary didn't make it to China. I don't believe that.

Q. Do you believe that they would have some awareness of God through nature or other means?

A. Through nature and through other people. God is not limited to his use of people and events through which to speak. Sometimes when he tries to speak through a given vehicle that is insufficient, then God will raise up others. But, you know, Jesus went on to define how you get to the Father. And even though we always say that you go through Jesus to get to God, Jesus did not always put on that restriction.

Q. What do you do with Acts 4:12, "There is no other name under heaven that has been given among men, by which we must be saved"?

A. I just take that as the evangelism of *that* day. It's a good sermon. One might say that there is "no other way under heaven whereby man may be saved except through love."

Q. Are there major differences between white and black evangelicals?

A. I told somebody one time that the classical difference between Dr. King and Billy Graham—both were evangelicals—was that Billy Graham would have preached to the slaves in Egypt and converted their souls and told them to go back to the fields; then he'd have gone and played golf with Pharaoh. Dr. King would have preached to change their souls and then taken them to Canaan.

See, it's not enough to change people's appetites and desire for freedom and then send them back to slavery, while you go play golf with Pharaoh. God wants the mind, body, and soul of his people. God is more likely to manifest himself when you change from the tendency of the oppressor to him as the liberator.

I think evangelicals by and large have been too insensitive to the environment in which God has sent us to evangelize. A part of the mission is the creation of a just world.

Q. What is the relation between your Christian faith and politics?

A. My religion compels me to be concerned about economics and international affairs. I would be violating the tenets of the faith if I were not involved in helping in housing, urban development, HEW, war and peace. How can you be a messenger for the Creator without a concern for the creation, for all the creatures?

Q. When did you first see Christianity functioning in a social context?

A. My mother was a real social servant of sorts. She had graduated from high school, and in our neighborhood in Greenville, South Carolina, she was one of the few people who could read. A lot of old people, when they would try to apply for Social Security, would come by the house, and Mama would fill out the papers for them. If they were sick, she would go to their house and try to make certain they got what was coming to them. A lot of them couldn't even count well enough to take their money to the store. I appreciate the impression that made upon my own mind.

One experience stands out in my memory. Mr. Dave Robinson used to come by the house all the time. He couldn't read or write. He got real sick, and Mother used to go down to his house every day and help him with his medicine and his liniment.

Anyhow, this Christmas, Daddy lost his job, and Mama had been ill, and we didn't have any money. They were debating not going to church because we didn't have any gifts to share. I remember Mama saying, "We don't have any gifts to give, but we are members of the choir." She was a lead singer in the choir. "We aren't taking any gifts and we don't expect to have any gifts. It's okay; we can still participate." So then we walked to church, three or four miles across town.

Later we came back home and walked up the flight of seventeen stairs. I shall never forget it. There were about six bags of groceries on the porch. They didn't have any name written on them, and we assumed it was an accident. We saw some meat and we figured we'd at least put the meat in the refrigerator until someone claimed it. We wouldn't dare touch it.

The next day Mr. Dave came by and said, "I don't understand. You got the groceries in the living room. Somebody should have put them up."

But Mama said, "No, nobody can put it up, because they belong to someone else; they were left here by accident."

He said, "Oh no, it was not an accident. My Social Security check came, and I bought that for you and Charlie and the children for Christmas."

That was a very spiritual experience and made an imprint on my mind. The reason there was no writing on the groceries was that Mr. Dave couldn't write. That was really "bread cast on the water," returning toasted, with butter on it.

Q. Why don't white evangelicals have a Jesse Jackson on the front lines of social issues?

A. Racism. I think that one great flaw in the American character is that of race, and the quicker that that cataract of race is pulled off the eye of the evangelicals and the Golden Rule is applied to all of God's children and a compassion for those that have less is communicated, then the power of the evangelical will expand; his power will be unlimited.

Q. What should be the relationship between Christianity and the government in the United States?

A. One of the great dangers of Christianity in this country is that Christianity is determined by color and limited by culture. And too often we end up with a state religion where the flag flies higher than the cross. We end up respecting the cross but worshiping the flag. If God is the ultimate concern, that is what we will live and die for ultimately. There aren't many Christians who will die about the cross.

Q. What lies behind your PUSH for excellence in inner-city public schools?

A. Our basic notion is that the death of ethics is the sabotage of excellence. There must be ethical standards. We've said in PUSH that the triangle is our symbol. We have economic generation, spiritual regeneration, and discipline. You need all three; because if you're spiritually regenerated and disciplined, you can get economic generation.

Q. Do you think prayer and Bible reading should be reinstated in the public schools?

A. Well, you know, actually they were never taken away. I think that in a pluralistic society that is heterogeneous, you cannot impose your religion on people of other religions. If a child is trained in Islam, you cannot have him standing up and saying the Lord's Prayer. The court didn't say that *you* couldn't pray; the court said that you couldn't make *me* pray. That's all the law has said. I've been to many schools around this country where they still have prayer. And it's not unconstitutional either.

Q. In your very busy worldwide schedule, what priority do you give to your own family members and their needs?

A. I try to share with them a qualitative use of my time, but quantity, too. In summertime, periodically I'll take my daughter on weekend trips with me so she can say things she'd never say if she wasn't away from Mama and the boys. Then the next weekend I might take three of my boys with me. We begin to communicate. I have a basketball goal in my back yard, and we play ball together. And I sign my children's report cards.

Obviously their mother sends them off to school more than I do, but they finally got to come back this way before that report card goes back.

Q. If you could get one message across to the readers of *Christianity Today* or white evangelicals in general, what would it be?

A. When you say "Our Father," draw the "O" big enough to include all God's children.

CRITIQUE OF
"You Can Pray If You Want To"

The key to a good interview story is the selection *and* order of the questions to be asked. Since the Reverend Jesse Jackson is a well-known clergyman whose Christian beliefs (evangelical) sometimes come under a cloud of suspicion, the questions had to burrow in on that area. The author of this article did that in light of the readers he was communicating with—middle-of-the-road evangelicals who are educated, who cleave to biblical truth, and yet who are open to a broader spectrum of applying truth in social dimensions.

One sensitive area the author dared to enter was that of Jackson's spiritual beliefs. In questions ten through fifteen, the questions that form the very nub of concern with Jackson are spelled out and Jackson did not welsh on them. These areas of his life have perplexed evangelicals for some time, and without being clarified by Jackson, we still would not know where he stands concerning the "critical" dimensions of biblical Christianity.

In other words, the value of an interview with any personality depends on how well the cloudy points in that person's life — or if not "cloudy" certainly rather gray—are illuminated. In this case, the answers to the key questions were adequate, not dragged out nor heavily theological. The author undoubtedly had to cut material and keep the very grist of answers in order not to slow down the "Q-and-A" pacing.

An excellent question, which revealed the personality of Jackson, came in number eighteen where the author asked: "Are there major differences between white and black evangelicals?"

Jackson's answer is classic, probably the gem of the entire interview; he illuminated the distinctions in a telling way. Whether he was right or wrong is not the issue; what matters is that a good question received a frank answer. The man himself is revealed concerning the subject in a way no other query and response could have done.

Question nineteen on politics is an excellent and necessary one because Jackson is known for considerable commentary in this area. The key, of course, is how an evangelical or any Christian can relate to politics with a militant position such as Jackson's. This might have been expanded some to learn the various dimensions of what he considers "politics."

One thing this interview did was bring the man Jesse Jackson to the fore, out of the aura of PUSH and into the elements of his humanity. The author did this by digging out both his personal history as well as his contemporary concerns. Many interviewers make the mistake of spending too much time on history or too much time on the total context of a person's life and work.

There is an expanded answer to the question of when Jackson first saw Christianity functioning in a social context. This answer shows a side of the man few people in evangelical circles today know. It is a poignant insight because it shows Jackson's roots, especially in terms of his social activism today.

Possibly a better approach at the beginning would have been to save the questions about his childhood spiritual experiences and jump immediately into his philosophy and theology in the context of PUSH. Asking about a man's early spiritual life at the opening tends to force the reader to learn about something at a time when he doesn't want to; later on the question would have been more timely.

But this interview story is an excellent example because it brings out the man and not simply the crusader for justice in the black community. After reading this interview, Jesse Jackson means much more to me. That is the task of a good interviewer, and this author has accomplished it.

—James L. Johnson
Coordinator of Journalism/Print Program
Wheaton Graduate School

RESEARCH

1. Find and read carefully three interview articles from three separate secular magazines. Attempt to find the pattern or rationale that the author used for the order of the questions.

2. Locate and read carefully three interview articles in three different Christian magazines. Look for one that is the straight question and answer, one that mixes direct and indirect quotations, and one that contains narration or description of the interviewee. Use these six articles collected for Research items 1 and 2 as the beginning of your file of interview article models.

3. Ask a published free-lance writer or local newspaper reporter which interview techniques have proved the most productive.

4. Read two articles on interview techniques in the last year's issues of *Writer* or *Writer's Digest*. Construct a topic outline of the most important content in each article.

5. Go to your college or public library and read the most relevant chapters from a book on interviewing for the media (newspaper, magazine, radio, or television). Take notes of the techniques and principles that you may want to use in your interviewing in the future.

PRACTICE

1. Make two lists of people in your town or nearby who would make good subjects for an interview article. One list should be for possible articles for your community or county weekly newspaper. The second list should contain names of people who would be of interest to the readers of a Christian periodical.

2. From the list of possible subjects for local newspapers, select the person whose occupation, hobby, church activities, or community service has the highest reader interest. Write an overview using this person as the subject (e.g., subject, purpose, intended readership, slant or focus, and three newspapers that might be interested in an article on this person). Contact an editor of one of your local papers to see if he or she is interested in your proposed article.

3. If an editor approves your subject, then you should construct questions you want to ask your interviewee. These questions should be revised and reorganized as you continue to think about the interview. Make arrangements to interview your subject. Research this person through print and people resources. Use a cassette recorder, if the interviewee approves, so that you can verify and complete your notes and later replay the tape to listen for ways you can improve your interviewing techniques.

4. Decide whether you want to cast the article in the question-answer format or the combination direct and indirect quotation structure. Then construct a thesis and topic outline. Next write the article following your outline and using the statements you obtained in the interview. Revise your article at least twice before submitting it to the newspaper editor.

5. Using the same sequence as suggested in Practice items 1-4, plan and write an interview article for your denominational magazine or one of the EPA publications listed in the market guide at the end of this book.

DISCUSSION

1. Read the entry on HIS magazine in the market guide at the end of this book and then explain why the HIS editors interviewed Samuel Kamaleson for their readership.

2. What other evangelical publications might be interested in publishing an interview with Kamaleson?

3. What other article type is integrated into the HIS interview?

4. Explain the rationale behind the sequence of questions in the Jesse Jackson interview. Why did the interviewer ask the last question?

5. The ninety-minute interview with Jackson produced thirty pages of typed manuscript. What were some of the questions that the interviewer probably asked that didn't appear in the article?

7
The Personality Article

The personality and interview articles are first cousins. Both focus on one individual. They differ in that the interview emphasizes what the subject says while the personality article highlights the person's accomplishments.

The most effective personality articles focus on a narrow but highly productive or important segment of the subject's life. No effort should be made in this type of article to cover the subject's entire life story. The biographical article tackles that tornado.

The challenge of the personality article recalls the old western motto, "Bring 'em back alive." Through anecdotes that show the subject in action, combined with comments from the subject, associates, family, friends, and even rivals, the subject of the personality article comes alive for the reader. Description can also help establish the personality in his environment.

Usually, interviews with the subject are necessary to obtain the required documentation. Whenever possible, interview other people who know the subject to get a well-rounded picture.

Researching for personality and interview articles can provide the author with rich learning experiences and blessings that would not have been possible otherwise.

Many evangelical editors have increased the people emphasis in their publications in the last several years. This has been true of Sunday school take-home papers as well as magazines.

Whenever possible, an editor should be queried about a personality profile or an interview article before contacting the subject. More interviews will probably be granted if the free-lancer can say that *Christian Life, Eternity, Moody Monthly, Sunday Digest,* a denominational magazine, or some other well-recognized publication is interested in publishing an article about that person.

The potential purposes of the personality piece can range from inspiration, teaching, challenge, and guidance to entertainment.

Closely related to the personality sketch, the biographical article is usually written about a deceased person and attempts to give an overview of the subject's entire life. Biographical writing about well-known people or people with universal experiences has always been popular because readers like to read about interesting people. Much of the research for this type of article has to be done through printed sources and in some cases with friends and relatives of the subject.

Biographical articles can also be written about older living subjects who have achieved outstanding accomplishments. This type should begin with an interesting anecdote from youth or adult life and then flash back to birth and childhood. The significance of the person should be stressed as often as possible, and the latter part of the article should emphasize development to the present, adult accomplishments, and future plans. Each section should be liberally illustrated with quotations, description, and anecdotes.

In both the personality sketch and the biographical article, the reader should see the subject's struggles, philosophy and perspective of life, and significance to other people.

Don't Tell Mama

Marinus M. Swets

My Pa never defied my Ma to her face. He respected and admired her too much to do that. For one thing, she was better educated than he was; she had finished eighth grade, Pa had never gotten beyond sixth. Ma also had more resources for being an authority on many subjects. She had a large collection of old wives' tales and proverbs to back her up. She also could point to biblical references which might be interpreted to pertain to the problem at hand. She also had a supply of unique epigrammatical utterances drawn into the strict Dutch church mythology, utterances from published sermons of old Dutch ministers who were feared almost as much as the Lord was feared. She having this lore of wisdom, Pa viewed Ma as having a much better understanding of what Ma called "the realities of life" than did others.

But Pa still maintained a tension in the family. He was sly. Ma called him a sneak. "Stiekemert!" Ma would shout at him when she caught him in a sneaky act. Pa really didn't mind that, it seemed. His sneaky manner might have stemmed from the days in Holland when he would, on the sly, follow his older brothers courting their girl friends in the shadows of the big dike that held back the waters of the Lek River which flowed by his home.

Let me tell you what Pa was sneaky about. Should there be in the icebox on Saturday some lunch meat purchased for next week's lunches, half of it would disappear over Sunday. To nibble at any of it was strictly forbidden, yet half disappeared even under Ma's dark, watchful eyes. Of course, everyone knew that Pa had sneaked it, but no one ever confronted him directly, mainly because he often made others a part of his conspiracies. Thus, as I caught him once with his hand in the meat tray, he calmly took out two slices, shoved one in his mouth, and, with a wink, gave the other to me. You can see that his deceits, which were nearly all of the meat-snitching variety, weren't like those of others who might chase women on the sly or drink too much and pretend they don't, two things Pa never did.

Ma, of course, got annoyed by his small tricks, and her awareness, when it was let out, created tension in the family. It was not an unhealthy tension; there was no danger that the family would break up or anything like that, but the tension gave us three boys an edge of awareness of the dynamics of the family we were a part of.

We were aware, for example, that Ma was far more serious about her religious life than was Pa. She urged us to church three times each Sunday with the strength of her will, and at year's end we were in church almost more than out of it: three times on Sunday, twice on Christmas, again three times on Sunday, New Year's Eve, and again once on New Year's Day.

Pa was permitted to sleep Sunday afternoons. We had to go to all services. We didn't want to. Sermons were in Dutch, services lasted all of an hour and forty-five minutes, and there was generally an atmosphere of gloom, it seemed, for people wore dark clothes, dark stockings, drove dark cars, and had somber corners of their mouths turned down.

Whenever Ma was sick, and that was rare, Pa would take us boys to church without her. Church was a two-mile walk (we did not get a car until the forties). Between home and church were two hazards: one, a lovely park with a pond in it teeming with goldfish; two, another church with English services that lasted only an hour and fifteen minutes at most, Coldbrook Church.

I cannot remember the exact first time Pa did it—not take us all the way to church—but he did once, then twice, then every time Ma was sick. We would go to the Coldbrook Church services where they sang hymns, not gloomy Dutch chorales, and where people smiled and where instead of getting the collection from you in black velvet bags at the end of long poles, they passed shiny brass plates in which coins went "clink."

After church we had time for a romp in the park, careful not to get grass stains on our knickers, and as we approached our house, blowsy and sweaty, Pa would wipe our faces with his big handkerchief and wink and tell us, "Don't tell Mama."

It wasn't only "Don't tell Mama." It was also "Don't tell the boys" to her, or "Don't tell Adie" to me, or "Don't tell Marinus" to Ade, my brother. An instance: We would walk to church on winter nights, my brother and I each with a hand in Pa's. Jack, the youngest, would ride with a neighbor. As we passed through dark shadows between streetlights, I would feel Pa's hand leave mine to fumble in his great coat pocket. It would emerge with a piece of Hershey's chocolate. He would thrust it into my hand and mutter to me, "Don't tell Adie." I didn't know then, but I know now that he was treating Ade the same.

Pa had to have a confidant with whom he could share his jokes. Sometimes they weren't jokes. Once, when I was about sixteen, Pa called me into the kitchen late at night. He was, maybe, fifty-two or fifty-three at the time. He unbuttoned his trousers, pulled up his shirt, and said to me,

"Feel, here." I was ashamed and squeamish, but he said, "It's okay. Here." And he took my hand and placed my fingers against his lower abdomen. "Hernia. Rupture," he said.

"How bad is it, Pa?" I asked.

"Terrible," he said, "sometimes it hurts so bad when it all sags down. Then I have to sit down—on the curb, even, sometimes—and push it all back in."

"Pa, you have to get that fixed. You can't go on that way," I started to say. But he cut me short.

"Ya, well, no. I can't afford to get laid up." He was right. He couldn't afford that. He was sole support of the family, had no benefits like hospitalization, no savings, no unemployment compensation. He knew what it took to keep things running.

We had some small talk, and before I returned to my bedroom to sleep, he grabbed my arm and said, "Don't tell Mama."

Only after he and Ma were gone did I realize that his deceptions ran to more than sneaking lunch meat and skipping church. It was not in his character to allow himself to get caught at being less than able. He stole lunch meat to put a small joke over on Ma. That was a game. But it was no game when he concealed his ruptures. It was no game when once he got a two-dollar cut in pay from sixteen dollars a week to fourteen dollars a week. He found an early-morning, part-time office-cleaning job and spared Ma the knowledge of his extra work, merely stating that his hours were extended.

There was another side still to his "not telling." He wouldn't let on sometimes that he knew something. For example, one summer I discovered that Pa had a cigar box of loose change on the top shelf of the hall closet. When no one was around, I hooked a quarter for a soda. I was about eleven or twelve at that time. I felt terribly guilty about it, resolving to earn a quarter and replace the stolen money. A few days later the taste of a soda grew stronger than my guilty feelings, and I did it again. A few days later my compunctions were weaker still, and I slipped over to the closet while Pa and Ma were out on the porch. Well, Pa came in for a drink and caught me in the act.

He could have caught me, I should say, for even though he saw me and saw what I was up to, he stared out, over, and beyond me without uttering a word, went into the kitchen and got his drink, and returned to the porch. I knew. He knew that I knew. More unease and distress I couldn't have suffered had he thrashed me.

Pa had a non-condemnatory attitude toward his entire family. He was a most accepting person. As it was in the coin-sneaking episode, even when he might have good cause to really blow his top at us, he didn't. Should we come in too late, should we not clean our rooms, should we take up smoking, should there be a telltale smell of beer on our juvenile breath, he let us know that he knew, but never let on overtly. In these situations when he justifiably could have lambasted us physically or verbally, he kept quiet. Maybe he could do that because we were inculcated by Ma's continuous admonishments to be good boys. It might have been Ma's overt behavior that made Pa's silence effective in circumstances wherein we were misbehaving, apprehended by Pa, and never upbraided, only left alone, yet aware of his awareness and necessary feelings, and, maybe, of his silent sufferings about us.

Ma, of course, was more forthright, and made more fuss about our behavior than did Pa. She was the disciplinarian in the family, meting praise and punishment in proper intervals. Whenever she despaired because of us, Pa would say to her, "Don't worry. It will all turn out all right." You can see, that was a variation of "Don't tell Mama." She didn't learn as early in life as Pa did that there are just some things you can't remedy. Therefore, his unimportant deceits gave Ma moments of irritation. But the larger ones that he withheld from her gave her rest that she wouldn't have gotten had he let it all go. His sometime physical pain, mental distress, and awareness of other things if revealed, would probably have created more turmoil than mere tension. His sense made our home a sensible place to live, and not one that we left eagerly.

I have too much of my mother in me. I can't shut up when I ought to, look the other way when it would be wiser. I have Pa's sense of snooping but not his sense of keeping quiet about what I discover when I snoop. I can be sneaky about my own misbehavior, but let me have the slightest bit of evidence of my teen-agers' misbehavior, real or imagined, and I am out with it. Confrontation. Dark looks. Unnecessary accusations and resulting recriminations, and a cold, hurt feeling in the house for weeks.

I can't condone his teaching us bad habits. For in a way he was doing that when he made us co-conspirators against others. He was telling us that it was okay to be a bit sneaky. To tell the truth, part of that did rub off on me. But not the good part. I have to learn to look the other way, see over and beyond, keep quiet, ostensibly ignore human foibles in my teen-agers, misbehavior that I can't do anything about anyway. I have to adopt his fine philosophy, "It will all turn out okay." After all, our family now isn't that much different from the one we had at home. And my kids are better, if anything, than I was then.

CRITIQUE OF "Don't Tell Mama"

I felt that in the relatively restrictive confinement of a short personality article, Mr. Swets executed well the most difficult of assignments for a writer: developing characters. It is a rare ability and has been the mark of some of our better short story writers (O. Henry, John Cheever, and others). Even though the story followed familiar lines—a son's fond recollections of the influence of his parents—I found it to be told in such an appealing manner that it was irresistible.

The mark of good writing is not "style" but the ability to hold a reader, and in this Mr. Swets was flawless. He demonstrated an excellent command of the language—often the key to getting a reader into the next paragraph. He used punctuation in such a skillful manner that fairly complex sentences appeared simple. He used conversation well and carefully avoided the pitfalls of the overuse of vernacular.

A good story well told is often exemplified by memorable scenes and episodes, times when the writer relies less on words and more on examples and anecdotes. Mr. Swets depends not on heavy rhetoric but on "dark clothes" and "dark stockings" to capture the gloominess of some church services. More importantly, he catches up the reader in the characterization of Pa through harmless "deceits" (lunchmeat theft, etc.) and thus makes him much more believable when it comes time to present more serious matters and the consistency of his (Pa's) silent suffering.

I think, however, that it was Mr. Swets' ability to define the less sympathetic figure of the mother that won me. He was able to make me appreciate the mother's role in effecting the necessary balance that makes a family work and to empathize with his own development along those lines.

—John Underwood, judge
Senior Writer
Sports Illustrated
New York, N.Y.

Solzhenitsyn—Whose Face in the Mirror?

Cheryl Forbes

For years he wrote in secret. Neither his colleagues nor his students suspected that the man then teaching physics would in a few years become a Nobel Prize-winning novelist, a world-renowned prophetic figure, and an exile from the land he loved. In an autobiographical sketch he says, "During all the years until 1961 not only was I *convinced* that I should never see a single line of mine in print in my lifetime but also I scarcely dared allow any of my close acquaintances to read anything I had written because I feared that this would become known. Finally . . . I decided to emerge and to offer *One Day in the Life of Ivan Denisovich*."

That small novel (it has no chapter divisions and reads more like an extended short story) catapulted Alexander I. Solzhenitsyn to worldwide literary fame. Soviet reviewers were nearly unanimous in praising book and author: "The story . . . is written with the sure hand of a mature, unique master. A powerful talent has come into our literature." "As befits a real artist he has told us a truth that cannot be forgotten, that is staring us in the face." "The effect of this novel, which is so unusual for its honesty and harrowing truth, is to unburden our minds. . . . It . . . strengthens and ennobles us."

One Day was published in November, 1962. In December, 1963, the Union of Writers of the U.S.S.R. nominated it for a Lenin Prize. Four months later it was removed from the list of nominees and taken off library shelves. *One Day* was the only one of Solzhenitsyn's novels to be officially published in the Soviet Union; the others circulate in *samizdat,* a word meaning "self-publishing," used for typescripts of books forbidden publication.

By 1967 members of the Writers Union not only refused to help Solzhenitsyn get *Cancer Ward* published but denied that he was an artist of unusual standing. They criticized the work for unevenness and said it was mere sloganeering. But one member urged its publication. He recalled the immense impression created by *One Day* and asked why it had not been forgotten as had other stories about prison life during the Stalin era. The answer to that question lies with Solzhenitsyn himself—with his view of the artist's role in society and his view of the nature of literature, both of which stem from his Christian faith. One of his enemies recognized this in part: "The works of Solzhenitsyn are more dangerous to us than those of

Pasternak: Pasternak was a man divorced from life, while Solzhenitsyn, with his animated, militant, ideological temperament, is a man of principle."

Solzhenitsyn is, in a sense, a *Soviet* writer; he was born in 1918, a year after the Bolshevik revolution (and six months after his father was killed in a shooting accident), and he grew up as a committed Communist. Although he wanted to write, the only school to which he could go did not have a literature major. He studied physics and mathematics instead and graduated in 1941 with a double major. That same year he finished a correspondence course in literature.

After graduation he went into the army, was decorated for bravery twice, and was promoted to captain. In 1945 he was arrested for criticism of Stalin (unnamed) in private letters to a friend. His scientific training probably saved his life; because of it he was sent to a special camp for scientists instead of the usual prison camp. His experiences there were the basis for his first novel, *The First Circle* (the title and image are taken from Dante's *Divine Comedy*). He served his eight-year sentence and was then sent into a "perpetual exile." Shortly after that, near death, he entered a cancer hospital. He survived that, too. He was released from exile in 1956 during a general political thaw. A year later the Soviet supreme court issued a statement saying he had been rehabilitated.

All but one of Solzhenitsyn's books reflect his own experiences. *One Day* and *The First Circle* deal with prison life, and *Cancer Ward* is about the treatment of dying patients. Solzhenitsyn characterizes *The Gulag Archipelago I–II* (volume two, containing "The Destructive-Labor Camps" and "The Soul and Barbed Wire," was published in English late in 1975) as "an experiment in literary investigation," a history of the development of the vast underground prison world existing in the Soviet Union. *August 1914,* the first fascicle of a longer work that probably will include *October 1916, March 1917,* and *R 1917,* concerns the first two weeks of World War I. The heart of the novel, the defeat of General Samsonov's Second Army, was conceived in 1936 when Solzhenitsyn wrote an essay on that disaster.

Solzhenitsyn's major concern is with the soul of man, and with the effect evil and good, truth and falsehood have on the soul. He believes that the duty and purpose of an artist is to serve his readers by writing the truth. Without that moral purpose there is no artist, and there is no literature, he believes.

To use an unpopular word, we could say that Solzhenitsyn writes with a *didactic* motivation. He is trying to teach his readers. As he writes, the images of thousands of confused, hungry, searching people never leave his mental sight. He wants to present them with the truth that evil lies not within the system but within each of us. Yes, he reveals the evils of the prison system, but he does so by baring the sins of individuals. Each of us, the author included, is culpable. In a sense his writing is an outgrowth of his repentance for participating in the Soviet system, for his former faith in it. And Solzhenitsyn wants to do more than inform: he wants to move his readers to repent along with him.

His Nobel Prize lecture is the fullest, most systematic explanation of his view of literature and the moral responsibility of the artist to his audience, a theme present in each of his books. The great writer is "the teacher of the people . . . a second government." To compromise that goal is to forsake literature for mere words: "Of course, they couldn't write much of the truth. But they consoled themselves with the thought that someday things would change, and then they would return to these times and these events, and record them truthfully revising and reprinting their old books. Right now they must concentrate on that quarter, eighth, sixteenth—oh, all right, that thirty-second—part of the truth that was possible" (*The First Circle,* Harper & Row, 1968, p. 360). And what do you have left? asks Solzhenitsyn. Not a real book. Not real literature. Not any part of the truth. Just lies. Lies that will work against consolation that *someday* . . . : someday will never come unless someone now begins to lead the people to repentance. Satirizing shallow discussions of the business of literature in *Cancer Ward,* Solzhenitsyn shows his attitude toward a false view of truth. One girl wants it to be "uplifting, optimistic." First we need to repent, says Solzhenitsyn. And how can we repent unless we face our sins?

Our secular culture has subverted and twisted our conscience, he says. We compromise, we excuse, we cannot feel the truth. But prison changed that for Solzhenitsyn. It forced him to face himself as he was. Few of us have that opportunity; he offers it to us in his realistic retelling of prison life. "Sometimes he was not at all sorry to have spent five years in prison," he writes in *First Circle*. "Those years had come to mean something in themselves. Where could one learn about people better than here? And what better place to reflect about oneself? How many youthful hesitations, how many wrong starts, had he been saved from by the iron path of prison?" (p. 253).

He elaborates on this in part four of *Gulag,* "The Soul and Barbed Wire." The epigraph for this section is First Corinthians 15:51: "Behold, I show you a mystery; we shall not all sleep, but we shall all be changed." Prison presents us with a paradox, a mystery. The reason for a prison term is to punish a person and cause him to repent and reform. But many people were sent to prison guilty of nothing criminal. How can one repent if one is not guilty? Or is each prisoner tainted?

Solzhenitsyn seems to say yes to the latter question. True, he was innocent of that for which he was sentenced, but he was still guilty of personal sins:

"In the seventh year of my imprisonment I had gone over and re-examined my life quite enough and had come to understand why everything had happened to me: both prison and, as an additional piece of ballast, my malignant tumor. And I would not have murmured even if all that punishment had been considered inadequate.

"Punishment? But . . . whose?

"Well, just think about that—whose?" (*The Gulag Archipelago II*, Harper & Row, 1975, p. 614).

The reader must stop to consider that subtle but pungent question. Prison changed Solzhenitsyn. He learned from whom his life came and for what purpose he, an artist, had been born. The following poem, composed in prison and published in *Gulag II*, explains more fully than anything else he has written what happened to him during those eight years:

When was it that I completely
Scattered the good seeds, one and all?
For after all I spent my boyhood
In the bright singing of Thy temples.

Bookish subtleties sparked brightly,
Piercing my arrogant brain,
The secrets of the world were . . . in my grasp,
Life's destiny . . . as pliable as wax.

Blood seethed—and every swirl
Gleamed iridescently before me,
Without a rumble the building of my faith
Quietly crumbled within my heart.

But passing here between being and nothingness,
Stumbling and clutching at the edge,
I look behind me with a grateful tremor
Upon the life that I have lived.

Not with good judgment nor with desire
Are its twists and turns illumined.
But with the even glow of the Higher Meaning
Which became apparent to me only later on.

And now with measuring cup returned to me,
Scooping up the living water,
God of the Universe! I believe again!
Though I renounced You, You were with me!

And thus he blesses prison life.

Even without this poetic statement about the living water we would know of his rebirth through his views on art, his insistence on the truth, the resurrection movement of his stories, the hope on the lips of his characters. We have also his essays and some of his letters. *Solzhenitsyn: A Documentary Record,* edited by Leopold Labedz, includes among other things the Postscript to *August 1914* not printed with the English translation of the novel, several letters and interviews, and his Nobel Prize lecture. In this lecture Solzhenitsyn pulls together ideas scattered throughout his books. An artist should be an educator and, one could almost say, a prophet-priest. As he works he is responsible to both God and men. Since that is so, he bears the burden "to be more keenly aware than others of the harmony of the world, of the beauty and ugliness of the human contribution to it, and to communicate this acutely to his fellowmen." His purpose: salvation.

The steps to achieving this goal also become clear. First, recognize your own sin, confess your own culpability. Repent. "Repentance," he says, "is the only starting point for spiritual growth." Change. "Repentance loses all sense . . . if we have a good cry and then go on as before." Submit your will to God's. And dedicate yourself to *telling the truth* for God's sake and the world's. The latter is perhaps the hardest for each of us to do. Who can easily face the truth about himself? For Solzhenitsyn the task is further complicated by the shroud of lies covering society.

Solzhenitsyn is not a political figure. Many Western journalists forget that he is an artist, a poet-priest who follows in the steps of the great Russian and Western writers like Dostoevsky and Milton. The recent BBC interview with Solzhenitsyn is a case in point. The questions were political; Solzhenitsyn's responses about the state of the West were moral. As Malcolm Muggeridge pointed out on "Firing Line" when the interview was broadcast there, Solzhenitsyn was talking about good and evil. The concessions he feels the West has made have been to misunderstand, and therefore to encourage, evil. Much of what he said in that interview is more concisely stated in the essay "On Repentance and Self-Limitation."

Solzhenitsyn has become a political figure because he has written the truth of what he knows about the U.S.S.R. That brings us back to the original question: Why have his stories, unlike other horror tales of prison life and corrupt governments, grown rather than diminished in importance? It is because he is not a journalist merely recording events, like *Post* reporters Woodward and Bernstein; he is an artist who has transcended the bare facts to tell us the truth not just about the Soviet system or prison life but about ourselves.

CRITIQUE OF "Solzhenitsyn—Whose Face in the Mirror?"

Bill Willoughby, Religion Editor for the *Washington Star*, served as judge for the Personality Article category in the 1977 EPA Awards Contest. He selected Cheryl Forbes's article on Solzhenitsyn as the first-place winner. He wrote:

> Far and away, both by content, structure, and style, I list Cheryl Forbes's article on Solzhenitsyn in *Christianity Today*. I believe it showed what can be done in the way of religion writing that would be of interest not only to the religion-oriented individual but the diffident person as well—a criterion I believe should be high on the list.

When Forbes wrote this article, she was an assistant editor at *Christianity Today*. This personality profile is an excellent example of an article written by an editorial staff member. In some Christian magazines over the past few years, there seems to be a slight trend toward using more staff-written pieces that come out of editorial conferences.

This piece definitely meets the main criterion for a personality article in that it concentrates on an important slice of the subject's adult life and does not attempt to be a biography. Solzhenitsyn's early adulthood is summed up nicely in two paragraphs (five and six).

This article also proves that a quality personality article can be produced when a personal interview with the subject is not possible or practical. Forbes let Solzhenitsyn speak to her readers directly through paraphrases, allusions, and direct quotations of his writings. The subject's major concerns and purposes in life come through clearly in paragraphs eight, nine, and eighteen, as well as his internal struggles produced by imprisonment (paragraph eleven). The article's organization takes the form of a chronological tour through Solzhenitsyn's writings.

Forbes's style is appropriate for her subject and readership. The paragraphs are much longer than the journalistic average, but the more thorough development correlates with the subject's international stature and *Christianity Today's* readership. The literary allusions (e.g., paragraph twenty) would be especially meaningful to *Christianity Today's* readers.

Showing the subject's struggles is one of the marks of a good personality article. Forbes has shown this mainly at the point of Solzhenitsyn's imprisonment.

Forbes has done a masterful job of indicating the significance of her subject for her reader. This can be seen in the concluding paragraph and the little "how-to" insert in paragraph eighteen ("The steps to achieving . . .").

—The Editor

RESEARCH

1. Look up and take notes on at least three articles on the subject of personality or biographical articles that have appeared in *Writer* and *Writer's Digest* over the past three years.

2. Find three personality articles in Christian magazines and three more in secular periodicals. Study these to see if the authors "brought their subjects back alive" for their readers. What techniques did the authors use to accomplish this goal? Use these articles to begin your collection of personality articles.

3. Can you reconstruct the thesis and outline in each of the personality articles located for Research item 2?

4. Examine three consecutive issues of *Reader's Digest* to see how many personality articles are used. Do the same with the *New York Times Magazine*.

5. Among the articles located for Research item 2, determine which ones have the best "display windows" (title, subtitle, and lead package).

PRACTICE

1. Locate a person in your community whose accomplishments or experiences may be of interest and help to the reader of a *Sunday Digest, Power for Living,* or a similar Sunday school publication distributed by your denomination.

2. Write an overview on the person selected in Pratice item 1. List your subject, purpose, sources, slant or focus, readership, and publication.

3. Obtain permissions for the interviews needed (the subject and related people) and conduct the interviews.

4. Type the interviews, write a thesis, and then construct a topic outline for the article.

5. Write the article, revise it at least twice, and then submit it to your selected "take-home" paper.

DISCUSSION

1. Explain how the author of "Don't Tell Mama" used anecdotes to show his father to his readers.

2. Why did the editors of *The Banner*, a denominational publication, decide to publish "Don't Tell Mama," a personality article that focuses on the family? What other evangelical magazines might be interested in a reprint of this article?

3. "Solzhenitsyn—Whose Face in the Mirror?" differs from most personality profiles because the subject is viewed through his writings. How many different types of Solzhenitsyn's writing did Cheryl Forbes allude to or quote in this article?

4. In the EPA Awards Contest, why did the Solzhenitsyn article receive high ratings on the following criteria: *significance* (Is the person featured of adequate stature to command attention or does the experience show God at work in some unusual way?), *timeliness,* and *credibility* (Is the person presented as a whole person with real struggles?)?

5. Readers often turn to personality or biographical articles to obtain a moral or a lesson for living. Is this element present in the articles by Swets and Forbes?

8
The General Expository Article

The general article is usually expository. Therefore, its main purpose is to explain a subject to the reader.

The expository article usually has a lead, a transition, a body (three to five main points), and a conclusion.

Wayne Christianson, senior editor of *Moody Monthly*, recommends the following structure for the basic general article. He says the lead (not more than ten percent of the article) should introduce the subject in an interesting way and present the thesis. Mr. Christianson says the transition points up the significance of the article to the reader and prepares him for what is to come.

The body should be organized into three to five major points that will assist the reader in grasping and retaining the material. Christianson envisions the main points in a general article as shopping bags into which the total subject is subdivided into logical subcategories for reader convenience. A shopper expects a supermarket to supply bags and a clerk to sack all the items in basic groups instead of trying to catch all the canned goods, eggs, vegetables, milk, and meat as they come tumbling off the checker's conveyor belt. An alert reader, another type of consumer, will also be expecting the author to group the contents of the article. These primary divisions are generally the major components of the subject being explained.

The body provides the main opportunity to let the reader see the subject through anecdotes, illustrations, statistics, description, and direct quotations.

The introduction of a feature should not exceed ten percent of the total manuscript and the conclusion should consist of no more than five percent.

If the general article deals with the exposition of a problem, an early section of the article can briefly review its history. This background information then can be followed by a section that shows the reader the present state and outworkings of the problem. The conclusion can suggest possible solutions to the problem.

The following outline prepared by Judy Downs Douglas, editor of *Worldwide Challenge,* gives some valuable tips for researching and writing the in-depth version of the general article.

THE STORY BEHIND THE STORY—THE KEY TO GOOD FEATURE WRITING

Good feature writing involves finding the story behind the story and presenting it effectively.

I. What is the story behind the story
  A. The story the reader doesn't suspect is there
  B. The unique under the obvious
  C. The extraordinary in the ordinary
  D. The fresh, interesting twist
II. How to find the story behind the story
  A. Look for the human element
  B. Concentrate on ordinary people
III. Be committed to the story behind the story (don't settle for the superficial)
  A. Develop curiosity and enthusiasm
  B. Wonder about people
    1. What makes them tick?
    2. Why do they do what they do?
    3. How do they see the world?
    4. What is it that makes them unique?
  C. Practice with people you know
IV. Presenting the story behind the story
  A. Research the story
  B. Determine your focus
  C. Use two types of focus
    2. On one person
    2. On one aspect of a person's life (usually a personality feature)
  D. Organize your story—use an outline.
  E. Look for an unusual fact or twist for your lead to catch the reader's attention.
  F. Maintain the pace set in the story in the ending.

The Price of Praise

Virginia Stem Owens

I have a friend, an artist, who says the first thing she notices about a person is the colored splotch on the inner part of the eye socket where it curves upward to become a part of the nose, whether it is blue or purple or maybe slightly green. When she told me this, it startled me, and I was glad I was wearing glasses that hid my own little spot of color until I could go home and check it out for myself. If she had said that the first thing she noticed was the firmness of a person's handshake or the warmth of his smile or any of a dozen other characteristics by which we are admonished to judge people, I would not have felt self-conscious. But the inside of one's eye socket? That suddenly seemed a naked, vulnerable spot.

Charles Williams, in *Descent of the Dove,* (Oxford, 1939, pp. 57–62), says people have sought God in two seemingly contradictory ways: through the senses (that is, by apprehending his creation) and through the suppression of the senses, what is called the *via negativa*. "The Way of Affirmation was to develop great art and romantic love and marriage and philosophy and social justice," he says; "the Way of Rejection was to break out continually in the profound mystical documents of the soul, the records of the great psychological masters of Christendom."

But the way of rejection is one that few have followed. Williams cites an ancient canon, dating from the second or third century, to illustrate the church's official attitude toward the material world: "If any bishop or priest or deacon, or any cleric whatsoever, shall refrain from marriage and from meat and from wine, *not for the sake of discipline but with contempt,* and, forgetful that all things are very good and that God made man male and female, blasphemously inveighs against the creation, let him either be corrected or deposed and turned out of the Church. And so with a layman." (Italics mine.)

Now in no way would I want to undermine the validity of the *via negativa*. It has had little enough honor, especially in the Protestant tradition, where deprivation of the senses is usually "for your own good" rather than for God's good. Indeed, how *any* good could derive from fasting, retreat, silence, or celibacy (despite our Lord's practice of them all) has often escaped our notice as we clucked our tongues over the Roman monastic tradition. At least part of the success of the recent rapprochement between Protestants and Catholics can be attributed to the changes by which nuns dress like "normal people" and priests insist on matrimonial rights.

However, our defense of the former way, access to God through the full use of our senses, has of late been truncated and confused. The reasons are numerous and tiresome. For a start, most of the population is surrounded not by primary creation—the things that only God can make, such as trees—but by secondary or even tertiary creation—the things that God's creatures can make or the things that God's creatures' creations, i.e., machines, can make. And those secondary and tertiary products are often shoddy enough to merit only the cursory attention they get.

So that when my friend speaks of the subtle colors on human faces, it strikes us as extraordinary, a little odd, even faintly amusing, but not of the earth-shaking importance it truly is. For how are we to give thanks for something we've never noticed? How shall we praise God for the world we've not paid proper attention to? Our practice of pigeonholing our praise into broad categories—family, friends, country, health, and the like—reminds me of the all-purpose five-second prayer I devised as a child for use on cold nights: "God bless everybody in the world. Amen." When we pray in terms of everybody-in-the-world, we imagine ourselves to be dealing with a divine, omniscient bureaucracy. But God doesn't love everybody-in-the-world. He loves each of us singly, knowing the hairs of our heads and the shadows of our eye sockets.

One of the chief champions of this way of the senses in the Protestant tradition is, surprisingly, Jonathan Edwards, whose reputation as a dour example of asceticism is due to his overly anthologized and journalistically interpreted sermon, "Sinners in the Hands of an Angry God." On the contrary, Edwards' early attention was absorbed by the natural sciences, the careful observation of spiders being his specialty. But natural science was not a mere sideline to his theological thought. His scrutiny of creation provided the full heart out of which he wrote his doctrine of creation, with which physics is only now catching up. "God not only created all things, and gave them being at first, but continually upholds them in being," he says. "It will certainly follow from these things, that God's *preserving* created things in being is perfectly equivalent to a *continued creation,* or to his creating those things out of nothing at each moment of their existence" (*Works,* II, 487ff.).

Think of it. With each breath we take, God is again pumping into our lungs his exhalation of the breath of life, just as he did for Adam. If he withdrew his breath from the bubble of our world, it would instantly collapse. We are not a clock, once wound, running down. Developing this sense of continuous creation pulls the mask from our eyes, enables us to see creation hanging on God's breath, dependent, contingent. And the precariousness makes it all the more precious.

The world's existence hangs on God's continuing to pay attention to it, and to be properly thankful we in turn must pay rapt attention to his crafting. But there are dangers. In *Pilgrim at Tinker Creek,* Annie Dillard tells of her meticulous search of her surroundings in rural Virginia, from the single-cell algae in her pond to the view of Alpha Centauri from her backyard. Sometimes the evidence is devastating: nature is wasteful, extravagant, cruel, predatory. Never does the evidence point to chance, mere random agitation of atoms; and sometimes it points to the universe as the creation of a madman, a sadist. Yet it is beauty itself that is ultimately the answer to her questions, the fact that we desire and seek out beauty, that we separate the beautiful from the broken in creation. "No, I've gone through this a million times, beauty is not a hoax," she testifies. "Beauty is real. I would never deny it. The appalling thing is that I forget it" (Bantam, 1974, p. 273). It takes attention, rapt attention, to keep that reality before us. But our attention span is limited. Is this not perhaps the meaning of sleep, that dark bed of mystery in which our consciousness must rest in order to be restored to its task of thanksgiving?

When Jesus instructed us to "consider" the lilies of the field and the fowls of the air, he wasn't making some moralistic point, as in the dreadful fable of the ant and the grasshopper that was used to goad earlier generations into productive activity. The point of considering lilies is just the opposite: they are lazy lilies, occupying space amid the common field grasses for no reason other than that it pleases God. Can we appreciate God's creative prodigality? The idea of trillions of stars and cells offends our sense of proportion, especially as they keep exploding and dying. How can we praise such a wastrel, we who now are sweating out every barrel of oil and ton of coal? It's all very well for *him* to frivol about with wildflowers, but what about us—what shall we eat, what shall we drink, where shall we find fuel for the morrow?

Yet our business is not to be anxious about these matters but to praise God, to exult in him. And the most accessible way for most of us is through God's creation. What we call nature—flowers and trees and birds and bees, scorpions and hail and sharks—this is primary creation and reveals the "nature" of its Creator, the way he is. We know what steadfastness is because we see eons of predictability in the physical world. We know what surprise is because of sudden storms.

Andrew Wyeth once told an interviewer, "I love to study the many things that grow below the corn stalks and bring them back into the studio to study the color. If one could only catch that true color of nature—the very thought of it drives me mad." *That* is considering the lilies of the field. And it effectively drives out utilitarian anxiety.

Or take for an example Rachel Peden, a woman of uncommon considering power, who in her book *Speak to the Earth* describes the exploration of a hound's-tongue seed: "The dime-sized seed pod is enclosed by five sepals and marked off into four parts with a single spike rising at the center. I pinched open one yellow-green, burry section of this fruitlet and saw the watery unripe seed inside. The brown stalk gave out an uninviting smell, sometimes compared to mouse smell. . . . I like it because it is pretty and interesting and we were having a good time fishing when I first saw hound's-tongue" (Knopf, 1974, p. 82). On God's scale of knowledge, which weighs heavier: knowing the market value of Nielsen ratings or knowing that a broken stalk of hound's-tongue smells mouselike?

Unfortunately, there is unrelenting pressure not to pay very close attention to creation but instead to consume oneself with anxiety about survival. A bizarre example of such pressure comes from a recent book called *Language and Woman's Place:* the author cautions women not to make fine color distinctions—not to speak of mauve and lavender, for instance, because powerful people in our society lump them all together as purple. (While Andrew Wyeth meticulously studies the various shades of snow.)

The demonic line of reasoning runs like this: If human senses, often employed to subvert the spirit, can also be a primary access to God in this world, then humanity must be harassed into not using them. "You see one mountain, you've seen them all," a friend, since demitted from the ministry, said to me. I felt the cold wind of blasphemy on my face. Really seeing a mountain would take a lifetime, I protested silently. Or longer than that if we are to believe Dante, who pictured purgatory as mountain-shaped.

When Thornton Wilder wrote *Our Town,* his notion of purgatory was attention paid too late, misplaced in an afterlife of awareness devoid of action. When Emily dies in childbirth and joins the dead in the hillside cemetery, she wants to go back and observe just one day of her short life. "Choose the least important day in your life," the dead advise her. "It will be important enough." Emily's final soliloquies echo the lament of the psalmist who dreads to go down into the pit where there is no longer the possibility of praise. "I love you all—everything," she cries out to the world that can no longer hear her. "I can't look at everything hard enough. . . . Wait! One more look. Good-by, Good-by, Grover's Corners . . . Mama and Papa. Good-by to clock's ticking . . . and Mama's sunflowers. And food and coffee. And new-ironed dresses and hot baths . . . and sleeping and waking up. Oh, earth, you're too wonderful for anybody to realize you. Do any human beings ever realize life while they live it?—every, every minute?" (*Treasury of the Theatre*, ed. John Gasser, Simon and Schuster, 1960, p. 948).

And the Stage Manager replies: "No. The saints and poets, maybe—they do some."

My friend the artist, the observer of eye sockets, consented to give me drawing lessons. "It's simple eye-hand coordination," she insists impatiently. Although I learned to excel in only two areas, long-haired sleeping dogs and aspen bark, I learned concomitantly to give thanks for a great many aspects of creation I had never known existed before. The great gaping holes in my universe were suddenly filled with such intricate detail that my eyes began to grow bulgy from looking. They felt too small to admit all the things there suddenly were to see: where the whiskers grow on a cat's nose and how exceptionally long they are, the receding ridges within a sandstone cave, the rounding slope of my daughter's upper lip.

"Divinity is not playful," Annie Dillard warns us. "The universe was not made in jest but in solemn incomprehensible earnest. By a power that is unfathomably secret, and holy, and fleet. There is nothing to be done about it, but ignore it or see" (p. 278). Sometimes when I have been focusing overlong on the miniscule world of leafhoppers hatched in mold still damp from snowmelt, or when I feel physically assaulted by the bombardment of stimuli from a supposedly dead, silent winter day at my back door, I think it costs too much. The whole human race is not enough to search out each cunning device of its untiring creator. But attention is the price we must pay for awareness—without which there is no thanksgiving.

CRITIQUE OF "The Price of Praise"

In "The Price of Praise" Virginia Stem Owens has accomplished something that is rarely done. She has combined universality of topic with uniqueness of approach. Her article appeared in the November 18, 1977, issue of *Christianity Today* at the same time most other Christian periodicals ran one or more articles on Thanksgiving. Ms. Owens's piece was different—she never once suggested that food is to be a major object of our thanksgiving.

Throughout the article the reader is struck by the economy and the artistry of her phrases, the effective use of imagery and emotive stimuli: "Our practice of pigeonholing our praise," "creation hanging on God's breath," "God's creative prodigality," "utilitarian anxiety," "the cold wind of blasphemy," "eyes . . . bulgy from looking," and "each cunning device of its untiring creator."

One area of improvement might be to delete or change the focus of paragraphs two, three, and four at the beginning of the article since they seem almost parenthetical to the thrust of the rest of the piece. The quotation from the ancient canon that focuses on affirmation (paragraph three) could have been included in some other way to follow the line of thought she develops.

The sources used to illustrate Owens's argument of the importance of paying attention to God's crafting are a fascinating combination. Picture a discussion of the topic among Jonathan Edwards, Annie Dillard, Jesus, Andrew Wyeth, Rachel Peden, Thornton Wilder, and Dante. Such use of diverse sources enlarges the dimension of the article and its ability to communicate.

Owens helps us, her readers, to focus our imagination on the smaller details of nature, to see what is special. We are challenged to reflect, "On God's scale of knowledge, which weighs heavier: knowing the market value of Nielsen ratings or knowing that a broken stalk of hound's-tongue smells mouselike?" Owens's use of imagery is free of hackneyed phrases which slip so easily into an article on the topic of praise or thanksgiving. While her major emphasis is on seeing, she includes the sense of smell. Though the article is already rich in stimuli, its impact could have been increased by illustrations of touch, taste, and hearing.

The Dante reference may cloud the point of the paragraph in which it appears. Although Dante's purgatory follows the idea of the "demonic line" referred to in the beginning of paragraph fourteen, it seems contradictory to the heavenly emotion Owens expresses in, "Really seeing a mountain would take a lifetime."

The author's second reference to her artist friend with whom she captured our attention in the first paragraph, and her reference to her own vastly increased awareness, give Owens's writing the power of personal testimony while rounding out the effective development of the central idea.

Fifty-four other articles were judged in the same category. Of this group, less than six could be considered at all competitive in writing style with "The Price of Praise." Owens's choice of idea was both timely and timeless, simple and profound, pertinent to every Christian's daily life.

—Marilyn Kunz, judge
Associate Director
Neighborhood Bible Studies, Inc.
Dobbs Ferry, N.Y.

The Small Tribe Living Down By the Old Orchard

Monte C. Unger

There is a small, relatively unknown "tribe" of 1,500 people living on the edge of the city of Grand Rapids, Michigan. You probably haven't heard much about them either in the newspapers or on TV. But they are there, nevertheless.

Because of man's "territorial imperative," each family has its own "living space," though the boundaries separating most of the living units directly adjoin the next one.

Tribe members reside in 667 living units in less than one square mile of what used to be an open field. Perhaps there had once been an orchard nearby. Though each family has its own cooking and bathing areas, there is a communal swimming hole where the tribe can relax in the hot summer months. And there is a sort of tribal "longhouse" set aside for communal gatherings of various kinds. These gatherings are generally accompanied by the noise, laughter and eating common to such festivities.

Once off the larger arterial highways and roads, tribespeople use the same pathways for reaching their individual living areas.

None of the tribe's families, strangely enough, are blood relatives, though this is generally one of the reasons for this type of community closeness. Instead, they live together simply because accommodations were available: someone had built all these living units in this one area, and the rent is reasonable.

The typical problems of such tribal living are prevalent: sexual freedom, for example, as 27% are divorced. There is much drinking, though no more perhaps than in any other comparable group, and fortunately, there is little traffic in drugs.

Basically, according to one observer, there is a lack of direction and purpose in the lives of the tribespeople. It appears that most of them do want, however, to have a faith in a religion in order to gain the security and the resource-of-strength which faith in a Higher Being will bring.

One young couple living in this tightly packed little society had been trained by The Navigators. This couple has dedicated their lives for the past few years, and will do so for the foreseeable future, to bring Christianity to the fellow-members of their community.

This missionary couple resides in exactly the same kind of living unit which all the others live in. They eat basically the same type food and have the same general life-style. The father has a job as a tool-and-die maker. The mother is a typical housewife, and their small son plays with the other children, sharing the common playground.

Recognize the tribe yet?

This is simply *suburbia*.

The living units are not grass huts or sod houses, but a contemporary apartment complex called Old Orchard. The "tribe" members are middle-class Americans, who make average monthly rental payments for their one- and two-bedroom apartments.

In fact, this "mission field" is not unlike tens of thousands of such mission fields nestled in the suburban areas of the major cities of the industrial world.

One doesn't have to go to the forests and jungles of Ecuador or Zaire or New Guinea, for not all Christian workers are called by God to go to those exotic places. The mission field is often thought of as jungle huts, natives vacillating between their clay gods or the spirits of the forest and a simplistic belief in Christianity as taught by white people from rich countries far beyond the mountains. This is the "foreign" mission field. But what about the "domestic" mission field?

What about the Christians who do live out their lives in suburbia, in apartment complexes, in high rises and in new housing developments? That place of residence is their "mission field." It starts there, right where they live . . . it starts in your neighborhood, right where you live.

The ultimate goal of The Navigators international disciplemaking ministry is to help Christendom accomplish the Great Commission, which Christ gave in Matthew 28:19: "Go therefore and make disciples of all nations. . ." The Navigators are in 30 countries, but each missionary out there first learned right on his home "mission field," just like Dean and Lyn Berkompas, the Navigator-trained workers at Old Orchard apartments in Grand Rapids.

After Dean and Lyn were trained in the basics of Christ-centered living, they caught the Navigator vision of passing this on to others. This is called spiritual multiplication. The scriptural principle for this is found in II Timothy 2:2, which says, ". . . and what you have heard from me . . . entrust to faithful men who will be able to teach others also." Paul taught Timothy who was to teach others and those others would in turn pass the training on to yet others. Spiritual reproduction.

Dean has a discipleship training program and a community outreach program built into a schedule which married businessmen and professional men can readily adapt to. This is a couples' ministry.

The key intake of the Word, which builds the individual and equips him to reach others, occurs at a Monday-night Bible study in Dean's apartment. Up to 30 attend this.

Thursday nights provide further individualized training and the Old Orchard evangelistic outreach. This night is reserved for what Dean calls a "Timothy training program," the "Timothy" coming from the verse quoted above.

Dean started this a year ago with a butcher and a dentist and their wives. These three couples were trained Navigator disciples. They each recruited another young couple to help begin the evangelism in the community.

When they go to the other apartments to share the claims of Christ, each new couple first observes Dean and Lyn or one of the other more experienced couples. The next time the new couple will try some of the steps of personal evangelism on their own. This practical experience is gained gradually, in a series of well-coached steps.

After the visits, they all return to Dean's apartment to discuss results, questions and problems.

Some of the people now doing this at Old Orchard are an electrician, a school teacher, a clerk, a carpet salesman and an accountant.

A segment of the working community of Grand Rapids is hearing about the life-changing power of Jesus Christ because a tool-and-die maker is starting with his own "tribe."

CRITIQUE OF
"The Small Tribe Living Down By the Old Orchard"

Monte Unger's story caught my attention, I suppose, because I happen to know that in a certain area of Chicago's Northside lives the largest concentration of American Indians outside a reservation.

And I suppose Unger's startling opening sentence would catch the attention of other evangelical Christians (even though they might not know about the Indians in Chicago), because all of us are so schooled in concern for missionary work among foreign tribes.

By the time I got to the fourth paragraph I realized I had been tricked. Unger is not talking about a tribe of "foreigners" at all, but a typical residential apartment complex in American suburbia. But the simile is so appropriate and he has managed it so well that, instead of being angry that he misled me, I applaud his ingenuity. He has me in the palm of his hand. He is not being clever or cute. He is imaginative and creative.

The facade is maintained throughout much of the article. Not until you are nearly half finished with the piece do you find confirmation of what by now you may be expecting: It's an apartment complex complete with swimming pool, community center, and bicycle paths that is being described as a mission field. And all the logic of the missionary approach to a community and its culture overseas are now set forth as the approach of the Navigator "disciplemaking ministry."

This is effective writing supported by equally effective layouts and graphics [in the original].

How would you have written the story? Suppose you had begun, "Dean and Lyn Berkompas view the Old Orchard apartment complex, where they live just outside Grand Rapids, Michigan, as a mission field just as truly as if they were serving in Ecuador or Zaire or New Guinea." That's the story, but with none of the burst of insight Monte Unger provides with his imagery.

I gave him a "4" (good) in every category on the "attitude scale," only because I reserve "5" for near perfect writing, which I seldom see. The only addition I can think that might have been made to this article is a coupon the reader could sign to inquire about getting into a ministry of this sort. But even that is not needed. Anyone God is calling through such an article will take the time and trouble to respond. And all the rest of us will see American suburbanites from a slightly different perspective henceforth. Monte Unger has raised our consciousness and given us a new way of seeing.

—Walden Howard, judge
Editor, *Faith at Work* magazine

RESEARCH

1. Look up definitions for the word *expository* in three dictionaries and see which ones apply best to the general expository article.

2. Find three general expository articles in recent Christian magazines and three from secular magazines. Remember, these are articles whose main purpose is to explain. Use these as the beginning of your collection of general expository articles.

3. Make a list of issues, concepts, principles, and conflicts that need explaining by means of a general article in an evangelical publication or in your campus or community newspaper.

4. In the periodical room of your church or Christian college library, check to see if the subjects you selected for Research item 3 have been written about in your three favorite evangelical magazines during the last year.

5. Look up and take notes on articles about feature writing that have appeared in *Writer* or *Writer's Digest* during the past year.

PRACTICE

1. Select one subject from the list you completed for Research item 3 and write an article overview (subject, purpose, sources, readership, slant or focus, and intended publications).

2. Construct a topic outline with thesis.

3. Write the first draft of the article based on the overview and outline completed for Practice items 1 and 2.

4. Before revising your rough draft, ask a writer friend or any person you respect to read your manuscript. Ask your friend to comment specifically on the clarity of topic explanation in the article.

5. If you are pleased with the final revision, submit it to the primary publication you had in mind when you wrote the expository piece.

DISCUSSION

1. In her critique, Marilyn Kunz cites several examples of excellent diction in "The Price of Praise." Look for other illustrations of fresh word choice in Owens's article and explain why each one is effective.

2. Look for examples of description through the senses in Owens's article and discuss why these add to the article's effectiveness. Why did

Owens select the people she quoted in her article? Explain each one of these.

3. What two or three key words in Monte Unger's introduction could be changed to disguise even more the suburban subject?

4. Attempt to compose a thesis for each article that tells in one sentence what the author is explaining.

5. Compare the organization of the two articles in this chapter noting especially how the introduction, body, and conclusion are used in each.

9
The Editorial

Most editorials in Christian magazines are staff-written, but there has been a recent trend to include guest editorials. This provides excellent opportunities for the free-lancer.

The past reluctance to include guest editorials probably arose in part from the difficulty in writing the editorial. The editorial is not merely an expression of an opinion or a position. The viewpoint must be solidly based on facts and some of this data must be included in the editorial. The reader is probably not as familiar with the topic as the writer and therefore needs to be given the basic information so that he can agree, disagree, or continue to withhold judgment on the editorial writer's opinion.

Again, as with other types of journalistic writing, the free-lancer will benefit from studying editorials everywhere they can be found: daily newspapers, newsmagazines, and favorite Christian periodicals.

Editorials are written to explain, persuade, state positions, interpret, stimulate people to act, evaluate, inform, and occasionally, to change a mood and to entertain.

Editorials often contain two main sections. The first and briefer section is the statement of the subject and the editorial position and the second and longer segment is the explanation of the opening statement. The editorial writer should strive for accuracy in the presentation of facts and fairness in the portrayal of opposing views.

The editorial possesses an awesome potential for guiding the thinking of large numbers of people. With this responsibility in mind, Dr. Sherwood Wirt, founding editor of *Decision* magazine, has suggested that every editorial writer should keep two audiences in mind. "The primary target is the small portion of readers who will be in a position to do something about the matter. . . . The secondary target is the readership whom the editor wants to be aware that he is writing to the primary audience."[1] The editorial writer's accuracy of aim often determines how many people are influenced by the editorial.

Wesley Hartzell, veteran reporter and editor for the *Chicago Tribune*, made these observations about the editorial entries in the 1978 EPA contest:

> A good many, if not a majority, turned out to be sermons or homilies rather than editorials. Sermons and gospel messages, of course, are good any time. Editorials differ in that for the most part they deal with temporary issues, problems and situations.
>
> Most of the editorials were far too long. They will provide more impact if shorter. For one thing the reader might get to the end of the editorial to learn what the editor would like him to do or what the editor plans to do about a given issue. For another, the reader might remember it longer.

Most Christian writers could improve their editorials by periodically reviewing Hartzell's observations.

[1]Sherwood E. Wirt with Ruth McKinney, *Getting Into Print* (Nashville: Thomas Nelson, 1977), pp. 50–51.

Unmentionables

John Stapert, Ph.D.

Certain items of clothing used to be "unmentionable" in polite conversation. Unmentionables were always packed in the bottom of the vacation suitcase. Men didn't often wander into unmentionable departments at Penney's. Although everyone knew unmentionables existed, they were seldom seen except on the laundry line.

Most of that is changed now. The former unmentionables are modeled and lauded on TV. And this year the fashion industry seems to be concentrating its attention on showy undergarments.

There are still unmentionable subjects, of course. They're just different subjects from the former unmentionables. We have unmentionable subjects in the church, too. Almost everyone knows they're there; but you don't see them except when the laundry hangs on the line.

Some of the Reformed Church's laundry has recently come out on the line. It's the financial debacle at Valley Community Drive-In Church of San Dimas, California, that came to light near the beginning of 1974. It might not have come to anyone's attention in January 1974 had it not been for a surprising and accusational letter mailed by Robert Collins—a member of the fund-raising staff for the church—to the church's 800 promissory noteholders. Collins asserted that his employers had mismanaged funds, deceived creditors and distorted financial reports. It is not yet clear how accurate his letter was. That letter went out more than three years ago and prompted a reaction from noteholders. After that the financial condition of the church deteriorated rapidly. The story broke into front-page coverage in the Kalamazoo, Michigan *Gazette* last month as the anger and frustration of a group known as the San Dimas Noteholders Association surfaced at a meeting. That story, picked up by the Associated Press, was published in various forms around the country.

San Dimas is a fine-looking city in southern California. Interstate 10 runs right by it from San Bernardino to Pasadena. It's up against the mountains, with Los Angeles an hour's drive to the southwest. There's been tremendous population growth in and around San Dimas, and more is expected. Its location, attractiveness and growing population made it the choice for a new Reformed church some 10 years ago.

The San Dimas ministry was begun by David Ray, a seminary student in southern California and an admirer of Garden Grove's Dr. Robert Schuller. Like Schuller, and initially inspired by him, Ray began his ministry in a drive-in theater, then moved to a walk-in, drive-in facility whose design is a near-copy of the Garden Grove Church. In time there were a television program and several books by David Ray, again with marked similarities to those produced by Schuller. Additional staff were added, both in ministry and in finance.

From the beginning there was a strong emphasis on financial development. Browsing through some old *Church Heralds,* I noted San Dimas advertisements for promissory notes as early as 1966. Some of the later ads referred to Inspiration City and the Association for Inspirational Living. Most notes, however, were issued in the church's name. It became an aggressive program, too. In 1967 the notes were advertised at 7½ percent interest. That same year the Classis of California[2] was offering notes at 5½ percent to 6½ percent, depending on term, and the Reformed Church in America's Extension Foundation was offering 5 percent.

Interest rates have varied considerably over the past decade. In some years 7½ percent would have been high; in others, low. But from 1968 to 1973 the San Dimas Church consistently offered more than most other issuers. The peak seems to have been in late 1972 and early 1973 when San Dimas offered 9 percent, the Classis of California 7 percent and the Extension Foundation 6 percent.

Over a period of time some $5 million was attracted by the San Dimas church and its associated enterprises by means of promissory notes and trust agreements. What happened to that money is an interesting, but sad, story. The land, sanctuary and nursery school building took about $1¼ million. The rest went for other projects and some went into volatile mutual funds in the stock market.

According to the church $875,000 of the note money was loaned to Inspiration City, a retirement complex which, it was hoped, would more than pay for itself in the long run. Although scheduled for occupancy in 1974, Inspiration City, a seven-story building, now stands among weeds, uninhabited and unfinished. Inspiration City has been declared bankrupt by the courts. The $875,000, plus interest (for a total of more than $1 million), was lost there.

According to the late Joe Whipple, stockbroker and construction manager at San Dimas, the stock investments were made in mutual funds

[2] A *classis* is a denominational governing body composed of ministers and laity—Editor.

that were expected to rise quickly. The stocks were used as collateral for bank loans and the bank's money was used for interest on notes. Eventually the stocks dropped in value and were sold by the bank to satisfy the loan.

Some of the note money was used to pay interest on other notes and accounts. Much of it apparently was used to support the staff and operational costs, since offerings from the congregation fell short of those expenses. Other money, about $115,000, was loaned to the separately incorporated TV programming venture, the Association for Inspirational Living. Prospects for recovering it seem small.

What's the situation now? Robert Collins was fired (or resigned—accounts differ) as soon as his letter went out. David Ray left in 1974. He is presently in Jackson, Mississippi. Joe Whipple died. Bill Wagner, financial manager at San Dimas in the early seventies, has left the staff. That amounts to a complete departure of the principal staff members that got into the multi-faceted ministry and the accompanying financial situation.

In October 1974 the Reverend Melvin De Vries assumed the pastorate of the church, hoping to salvage what he could of the congregation and, as he put it, "praying for a miracle" to save the situation financially. From the standpoint of ministry, there are currently some bright spots. About 2,000 people attended services on Easter weekend this year. Between 30 and 35 new families were added during the past year. The average attendance on Sundays is between 500 and 600.

Most of the congregation seems not to have known about the financial situation that was developing a few years ago. Nor did the Classis of California have much clear information. Records show that classis approved borrowing up to $800,000 at one point, but there's apparently no record of permission to go beyond that. The financial leadership of the church apparently went ahead and sold promissory notes at will. In a 1974 conversation, Mr. Wagner told me that he hoped to gather $12 million eventually through promissory notes and trust agreements.

There seems to be no question that 800 noteholders have been wronged. And even though the wrong took place under previous leadership at the church, the noteholders want the Reformed Church in America to face this situation squarely at some level.

The Noteholders Association calls for full repayment of all notes. It has rejected a partial settlement offer from the church. (Other offers have been made since January 1974.) Legal action has been threatened. In addition, at least two overtures to General Synod call for denominational attention to the San Dimas situation, and General Synod President Dr. Louis Benes has received numerous letters requesting him to do something about it. The General Program Council's $5 million Church Growth Fund Drive has met some opposition from those who are tying the two matters together.

The question of legal responsibility for the indebtedness beyond that of the local church seems doubtful. Whether the Classis of California or the denomination generally has a moral responsibility to the noteholders is a question on which responsible people can differ. Surely, higher judicatories have a stake in the denomination's reputation, even if they didn't have a direct role in creating the problem. It's also apparent that investors could have chosen classis or denominational securities (although at lower interest) rather than the San Dimas notes. That means there are two sides to the morality question—one that asserts denominational responsibility for local church actions and another that asserts creditor responsibility for selecting premium interest rates for investing in church work.

It should not go unnoticed that some of the investors are people who could ill afford to lose anything, and others face a difficult retirement because of what's happened. Christians must care about the poor, regardless of the cause. No matter how the legal and moral questions are ultimately answered, the establishment of a Christian aid fund would meet some severe needs. I hope that can happen.

One thing seems certain: A large and emotional issue at this year's General Synod will be the San Dimas situation and what, if anything, to do about it. This will be a difficult test of the church's ability to deal with a complex issue in an honest and considerate manner. I hope for that too.

CRITIQUE OF
"Unmentionables"

This is an editorial worthy enough to rank among even the best in the secular press. It uses simple language to tell a complex story, is well researched as to the facts in the case, spares no one who may have had some responsibility in the financial debacle which is the editorial's subject, and concludes with a recommendation on what denominational leaders ought to do about it.

One has to admire the courage of an editor who recognizes that a full explanation is owed to denominational members, no matter how painful to church leaders, and proceeds to provide it in a double-page spread.

Until editors of religious publications feel free to examine all aspects of their churches and denominations, they will lack a full maturity.

I liked the way the author undertook to familiarize the reader with San Dimas, where the financial debacle occurred. A short history of the local church and its founding and a history of the financial failure is also included.

In a paragraph the present status of the debacle and some of the actors in this drama are summed up.

These inclusions enable the reader to become fully informed about the complex affair.

Paying these compliments, however, does not mean the editorial is without flaws.

One of the largest is its length. It could have done well without an opening three paragraphs about "unmentionable" articles of clothing. A perfunctory glance at the editorial could cause the reader to conclude that the writer is complaining about ladies' underwear rather than a serious matter involving church finances.

Despite these flaws, however, the editorial remains a refreshing, even a landmark, discussion in a religious publication.

[*Ed. note:* Mr. Hartzell rated this editorial "outstanding" in the criteria of timeliness of issue, breadth of issue, clarity, and writing style. He classified it "good" in cogency of arguments.]

—Wesley Hartzell, judge
Veteran editor, journalist
Currently on the staff of the *Chicago Tribune*
Chicago, Illinois

Climbing on Course

Bernie May

One of the hardest things to teach new pilots about landing on short, hazardous airstrips is to keep their eyes on the good part of the strip, rather than on the hazard. The natural tendency is to concentrate on the obstacle, the danger, the thing we are trying to avoid. But experience teaches us that the pilot who keeps his eye on the hazard will sooner or later hit it dead center.

If he keeps looking at the ditch at the side of the strip, inevitably he'll run into it. If he focuses on the stump near the roll-out area, he'll likely bang his prop against it. The experienced pilot focuses his attention solidly on the track he wants the plane to follow, keeping the hazards in his peripheral vision only.

Pilots aren't the only ones who have this problem of focus. Anyone who majors on minors, who constantly talks about his problems, who always fears the worst or who habitually points out reasons why a thing won't work, will get what he is trying to avoid. The Bible says a man is what he thinks. And poor Job indicates what he had been thinking about all along when he said, "For the thing which I greatly feared is come upon me."

Take demons and evil spirits. They're very real hazards. But get over-concerned about them and pretty soon they'll be all over you like a swarm of bees. The wise man focuses on the Holy Spirit.

And what about those dangerous doctrinal differences looming up at the end of the strip as you try to take off? Concentrate on division and you'll wind up in the middle of a split. But focus on unity, on the things that unite rather than the things that divide, and you'll clear those obstacles with room to spare.

On my first assignment as a pilot in Peru, more years ago than I care to remember, I was dispatched to fly three businessmen to a mountain town high in the Andes. The men had previously flown with some of our older, more experienced pilots, and were apprehensive about being piloted by a twenty-two-year-old who was busy plotting his course on a wrinkled old map.

As I loaded their baggage they stood to one side, talking in anxious tones. Finally one of them asked, "Captain, how long have you flown in Peru?"

"About a year," I answered.

They were increasingly nervous.

"Captain, are you sure you know where all the mountain ridges and peaks are between here and Tingo Maria?"

"No, sir," I answered. "But I know where they're not. And that's the course we're going to fly."

They looked at each other, smiled, and climbed aboard.

There are a lot of dangers on each side. But Jesus has gone before and prepared the way. I know it sounds simplistic, but all we have to do is focus on him and pretty soon we will be wheels up, and climbing on course.

Reprinted by permission of the publisher, *Beyond,* December–January 1976-77.

CRITIQUE OF "Climbing on Course"

My reason for selecting "Climbing on Course" to be the winner of the 1977 Higher Goals competition was that it best exemplified the criteria given me by the Evangelical Press Association by which to measure editorial quality.

Timeliness. The subject matter (flying) made the editorial immediately interesting to the twentieth-century reader, while the basic premise retained a certain timelessness about it. References to demons and evil spirits, church divisions and unity show that the author was aware of the current issues facing the church. Obviously he was not writing in a tunnel.

Breadth of appeal. There is something here for everyone. Paragraphs three, four, and five apply to all believers, as do the closing two sentences. Read and digested, this editorial will not fail to help the reader as he seeks to live the Christian life. The author accents the appeal by the use of dialogue and by including the adventurous element involved in the flying of small aircraft over hazardous territory.

Clarity. Not a single word is beyond ordinary understanding. To accent the positive, to focus on the good and the true, to follow Jesus — these points are made without obfuscation. Ernst Kirschten once said, "Write not that you may be understood, but that you may not be misunderstood." Bernie May meets that requirement.

Cogency. The illustration of the author's experience in Peru lifts the editorial out of the category of straight preaching without dominating the thought. Truth is underscored rather than sidetracked. "Concentrate on the track, not on the stumps and ditches." The author's expertise gives him authenticity as he makes his point.

Writing Style. Notice that the author does not feel the need to use humor, but that his seriousness of purpose is lightened by the flying incident. The flyer's constant acquaintance with the possibility of death is accented by the terseness of style. Atmosphere is contributed by such expressions as "bang his prop," "wheels up," and "a wrinkled old map." We don't feel that we are encountering a writer so much as a skilled professional who knows his field thoroughly, and who is giving us his Christian philosophy based on years of experience—which he draws upon to illustrate his point.

Not being a professional in the same field, I hesitate to suggest improvements. The writing itself sold me. The editorial neither "points with pride" nor "views with alarm," but it adapts biblical truth to our day and serves the Lord in this generation.

—Sherwood E. Wirt, judge
Editor emeritus
Decision Magazine

RESEARCH

1. Read as many newspaper editorials as you can in a thirty-minute period looking for similarities of structure. The *New York Times, Wall Street Journal*, and your daily newspaper will probably be the best sources.
2. Attempt to determine the intended thesis of each editorial contained in three recent issues of three different Christian magazines.
3. Attempt to determine the intended purpose of each of the editorials selected for Research item 2.
4. Using the same editorials collected for Research item 2, try to determine the primary and secondary audiences that the editorial writer had in mind.
5. For your collection of editorials, find one from a Christian magazine and one from a secular publication that are both excellent examples of editorials packed with relevant facts as well as opinion.

PRACTICE

1. Make a list of community or campus issues in which you have a strong interest.
2. Write a letter to the editor or a short guest editorial for your local newspaper based on one of the subjects listed in Practice item 1.
3. Write a letter to an evangelical publication expressing your opinion regarding an article in a recent issue.
4. Write an editorial taking the opposite position of one of the editorials you collected.
5. Begin a collection of well-written secular and Christian editorials for your personal files.

DISCUSSION

1. Discuss the wisdom or appropriateness of using what some may call "scandals within Christian groups" as editorial subjects in evangelical publications.
2. Should such subjects as the one in "Unmentionables" be reported and evaluated in the Christian press before the secular media cover them?
3. What types of reader reactions do you think John Stapert considered as he published "Unmentionables" in his denominational magazine, *The Church Herald?*
4. Professional editors often agree that a good writing style is one that does not call attention to itself. Explain how Bernie May achieved this type of style in "Climbing on Course."
5. How did May use visualization to communicate his thesis?

10
The Critical Review

The review sections of Christian magazines are designed generally to provide the reader with insights into books, records, cassettes, and the arts. This type of writing has a stewardship ministry by providing selection criteria for the readers, helping them become better trustees of the precious time God has given them to manage. *Critical* is used in the literary sense of evaluation.

The book review is the type editors use most regularly. William J. Peterson, editor of *Eternity* magazine, lists some basic guidelines for book reviewing. These originally appeared in a research report circulated by the Evangelical Press Association.

SUGGESTIONS FOR EFFECTIVE BOOK REVIEWING

It is impossible to teach the art of book reviewing in a few paragraphs, but here are a few points of guidance.

1. Good book reviewing is basically good writing. What makes a good editorial or a good short story? The same elements make a good review.

Good writing always goes out and grabs the reader by the hand and leads him where you want him to go. Too many reviews and reviewers assume that their entire readership is already vitally concerned with trichotomy, epistemology and ecumenics. Maybe they should be, but they aren't.

So, first you have to capture the interest of the reader. Then you must interest him in the subject of the book. Then, and only then, can you get him interested in the book. This is a good rule: sell the subject before you sell the book.

2. Book reviews must be simple and succinct. Knowledge should not be

paraded before the reader. Words must not be wasted; verbosity is no trait of the angels. Unless the average reader understands the words of a review, he won't bother to read either the review or the book.

3. Book reviews should grapple with issues. A good story always presents a major problem in an early paragraph. A good book review also deals with major problems.

4. Book reviews should not be picayunish. It is inane to speak of a misspelled word on page 179 or a misplaced comma on page 321. Even errors of fact should be overlooked unless they affect the overall aim of the book. The reviewer should be concerned about beams, not motes.

5. Book reviews should be slanted for a particular readership. In other words, a review in *Bibliotheca Sacra* should be different from a review in *Christian Parent.* Reviewers must bear their audience in mind when they write.

6. Book reviews should disperse necessary facts innocuously. How many book reviews have you seen that went like this?

> The author is professor of philosophy of religion and systematic theology at Tuscaloosa Institute of Theology and received his doctor's degree from Punsatawney University of Biblical Instruction. The chapters are entitled, "The Trinity of God," "The Humanity of Man," "The Beastliness of Beasts," "The Angelicalness of Angels," and "The Devilishness of Satan." Every pastor, future minister and interested layman should have this book in his library. The author says something that needs to be said.

Facts are necessary. Certainly the author should be identified and the nature of the contents should be divulged. But, if you study good book reviews, you will see that there are many painless ways of presenting these facts, without giving a "Who's Who" on the author and a complete Table of Contents.

7. Study good book reviews. You will find some in such publications as *The New York Times, The Book of the Month Club News, Harper's, The New Yorker, Saturday Review* and *The Atlantic.*

These important suggestions for book reviewing can also be applied in part to critiques of the arts, cassettes, and records. Some free-lancers have trotted into an editor's stable of regular writers through the gate marked "Reviews." A well-written review may make an editor take special notice of the author. A conscientious reviewer may have queries examined more carefully and positively because editors know his work from the review section of the magazine.

A free-lancer's letter to a review editor indicating a willingness to write reviews may produce a long-term relationship with that publication.

Review of *The Late Great Planet Earth*

Andrew Kuyvenhoven

Hal Lindsey, with C. C. Carlson, *The Late Great Planet Earth*. Zondervan, 1970.

The future is big business says author Hal Lindsey in his book by the above title (written with C. C. Carlson, Zondervan, 1970) and Lindsey is right. Not only are charlatans and stargazers cashing in on people's fears and curiosity, but books on Bible prophecy are a close second.

If you want to sell religious books today, you should write for the successful-living-line ("This is the hottest item in my store," says George J. Jensen of Coon Rapids, Minnesota), or you should predict future events with references to the Bible. *The Late Great Planet* sold 650,000 copies in nineteen months and "the entire prophetic line is going very strong" says John Bass, an executive of the Christian Booksellers Association.

The sales are not limited to the Bible belts in the Southern States and the Canadian prairies: I saw people reading the *Great Planet* during breaks in a PTA meeting of the Sylvan Christian school in Grand Rapids, and it is said that groups of Christian Reformed Church members are using the 32-page manual, which has been published separately, for their discussion circles.

Nevertheless, the *Late Great Planet* is a bad book.

Seven-Year Period—the Finale of World History?

The content of the book may be summarized as follows: In our Age of Anxiety and Aquarius most people are looking for a clue to the future. Instead of banking on new and old forms of clairvoyance, people should listen to the Bible prophets. After all, their predictions of the future have proved to be reliable since no less than three hundred of their predictions were literally fulfilled in the work of Jesus the Messiah.

The major part of the remaining, as yet unfulfilled, prophecies refer to a seven-year period that will constitute the finale of world history. It is not exactly certain when the countdown of these ultimate seven years may begin. But we are very near the climax: the physical restoration of Israel has found a place on May 14, 1948, and the same generation that has seen this event will also witness the revelation of the Lord (p. 54). That would give us until 1988.

However, one more thing must happen before the last seven years can be counted off: the temple must be rebuilt. Otherwise all signs are shaping up.

The Jews are back in Palestine and they are there to stay. But the King of the South (Egypt and Black Africa) is not going to like it and there will be an attack on Israel. When the Jews and the Afro-Arabs are engaged in mortal combat, the King of the North, Gog, or Russia is going to use its opportunity to overrun the countries of the Middle East and occupy Egypt as well as Israel.

Meanwhile the old Roman empire will have been restored (the European NATO countries are a stepping-stone in this process) and their leader will be the Antichrist, ruling from Rome. When Russia hears that the Roman Fuehrer is preparing for war and when, at the same time, the Chinese army (which is now building a road through Tibet) sends off an army of 200 million people, the Red Army will retreat from Egypt and make its headquarters in the temple area on Mount Moriah (p. 160).

At that point there will be either a nuclear war or some direct act of God as the result of which Russia and the whole Red Army will be annihilated. (Also all major cities of the world, p. 166). Then the Red Chinese and the Europeans (reinforced by the U.S. and Canada) will meet in the strip of land, North of Jerusalem, a valley that runs from the Mediterranean to the Jordan: Armageddon. This will be an unsurpassed bloodbath: the blood will be as deep as the horses' bridles over a distance of four hundred miles.

At the very moment when it seems that no life will be left on earth, Christ will return. Instantly, the Lord will wipe out all the enemies of Israel, and with Jerusalem as His residence, will reign for a thousand years over a faithful people and a land as good and peaceful as paradise. At the end of the thousand years an insurrection will occur, but the Lord will put that down. And then comes the end of human history.

Exit All Christians

All of the above events will be compressed in the seven years of tribulation that constitute the climax of history. Christians do not have to fear any of these events, because they will not be around to witness them. The rapture will occur when the countdown of the seven years begins. On that morning, day, or night the born-again bus driver, quarterback, and schoolteacher will disappear to meet the Lord in the air.

When they disappear, the world will be left in the claws of the Antichrist and the false prophet, his economic adviser. This fuehrer will be worshiped as God and the whole world will be united in a religious system (the harlot) of drugs and astrology, for which the present drug-cult and the ecumenical movement (pp. 116, 130–133) form the stage of preparation.

The Antichrist cannot get at the Christians, because they will be in heaven. But when the Christians are gone, 144,000 Jews will be converted and they will start the greatest crusade for Christ the world has ever seen—"144,000 Jewish Billy Grahams turned loose. . ." (p. 111). The wrath of the beast will be turned on them.

The whole issue of the seven years of tribulation will revolve around this Jewish remnant that has accepted Jesus as Messiah. But they will be somewhat different Christians than we are, because they will have rebuilt the old temple and restored the ancient worship in Jerusalem. Christ's coming at the end of the seven years will be on their behalf and for the establishment of his thousand-year reign in Jerusalem.

I do not call this a bad book because it seems to do violence to certain biblical texts. After all, the prophecies with which this book is most directly concerned pose so many difficult questions and the answers are so varied, that even Hal Lindsey's facile exegesis should not be called bad even if it is weak. He should be admonished for being shoddy, poorly documented, and in general for not studying more carefully that Bible which he exalts so highly.

But . . . the Focus of the Bible Changes

But all these shortcomings for which I would like to schoolmaster him do not make his book a bad book. This book is bad because it changes the whole focus of the Bible. God, who spoke in the Old Testament to the fathers by prophets and seers and who has in these last days spoken to us in His Son, is not allowed to say anything to us through the Son. The appearance of Jesus Christ in the flesh serves no other purpose, in this book, than to prove that the prophets are reliable foretellers of the future.

The author, who prides himself on being a literalist, does not literally believe that all authority has now been given to Christ *and that Jesus is Lord today*. If he believes this most ancient Christian confession, it has no influence whatever on his Bible reading.

Neither is his Bible reading affected by what Christ did to races and nations. We understand the New Testament to say that these old divisions of mankind are overcome in Christ. The proclamation of one God over all, one Mediator for all, and one way of salvation for all men is a concept nothing less than revolutionary for anyone who turns from the Old Testament to the Book of Acts and the Epistle to the Ephesians. But Lindsey continues to think in terms of races and nations—unaffected by what happened in Christ.

In fact, the whole New Testament message is for him a mere interim, a period of history that can be placed in brackets. It ends with the rapture—that is, the day on which the fruits of Christ's work are soundlessly removed from this world—and then the real history of the world and the unfolding of God's plan will find a place. The message of the New Testament is not connected with history, and history does not profit from the work of Christ.

What Does Salvation Mean?

The whole point of the Bible message has subtly changed direction in this book. I am sure that the author did not mean to do this. Probably he thinks it makes no difference if the children of God confess their hope in the words "Jesus is coming" or "We are going." In effect, there is a sharp difference between these two. One becomes aware of this difference especially when one asks the question: What does evangelism and what does salvation mean in this book?

The author is supposed to be a traveling speaker for Campus Crusade for Christ. This organization has done much good work already, especially in giving Christians the courage and know-how to reach their neighbors with the gospel. But what kind of gospel has Hal Lindsey to offer? Between discourses on prophecy he will insert a paragraph now and then (pp. 80, 138, 186) inviting his readers to come to terms with God: "It's so simple. Ask Christ to come into your life. . . ." ". . . the decision concerning your presence during this last seven-year period in history is entirely up to you." "Right at this moment in your own way. . . ."

The tone is familiar. Within the context of this book the invitation is hardly relevant, it seems, and salvation can mean nothing else but getting out of the mess called world through the right door. Believe in Jesus, take the "Ultimate Trip" to the skies (Chapter 11) and let the rest go to hell.

It is probably not intentional, yet oddly consistent with his narrow outlook, that the writer closes his book with an exhortation for the readers to reach (not the world but) "our family, our friends, and our acquaintances with the gospel!" (p. 188). Getting saved is a matter of getting off before the ship sinks.

A Jewish Millennium, a Jewish King?

Mr. Lindsey's book is in a premillennialist tradition. He believes that Jesus will rule over the restored nation of Israel for one thousand years, before He will judge the living and the dead. Lindsey is not the first one to claim this belief and he acknowledges his indebtedness in some footnotes.

Although the general teaching of the Christian Reformed Church does not favor belief in a Jewish millennium with Jesus as a Jewish king, we have always been hospitable to Christians who do hold such views. After reading the *Late Planet,* I wonder if we should tolerate such teaching.

Within the Christian church we can live with different opinions. We should honor the freedom of exegesis and the liberty of the prophets. We must also admit that there are Bible passages that confront us with astounding difficulties and we are humble enough to admit that others may understand better.

But there are certain boundaries to the Christian community within which we can respect the conclusions of Bible students. When the focus of the Word of Prophecy is shifted from the Lord Jesus Christ to the Jewish race and a piece of land near the Mediterranean Sea, it is time to draw the line. When the Lord is said to honor a kingdom notion that He rejected while He was on earth, it is time to decide who is in error, Matthew or Lindsey.

This book is disturbing also because it can be read easily by many people who read little. And since it approaches the Bible so emphatically as the inerrant Word of God, the book may gain the confidence of many of God's children. Time and again the writer says that he takes the Bible literally. That's his "golden rule" (p. 50) of interpretation.

Many people will not be in a position to realize that this golden rule is in fact a nonsensical statement. And Lindsey's contention that those who do not agree with him hold to an "allegorical" interpretation of prophecy is equal to nonsense. The question just isn't whether one is interpreting "literally" or "allegorically." The question is: Are we reading God's Word as God Himself would have it read?

Strict Literalism or a Case of Absurdity?

Mr. Lindsey cannot and does not stick to his golden rule of literalism: the beast whose mortal wound was healed (Rev. 13:12) represents (!) a man who may return from death, at least from fatal illness (p. 108). But the harlot (Rev. 17:4) represents a religious *system,* "splendid on the outside, but corrupt to the core" (p. 133).

And if Lindsey means by "literal interpretation" that the text should be taken at face value, would you try to read I Corinthians 15:51–58 and see if you can discover—without any inside or outside information—that it reveals the mystery of the rapture at the end of the pre-tribulation period (pp. 138–141)? Or do you think that an ordinary Bible reader would ever surmise that the clause "Fallen, fallen is Babylon the great" (Rev. 18:2) speaks of two falls: the first "fallen" refers to the destruction of Rome, three and one-half years later (pp. 133, 134)?

Moreover, should we chide those early Christians that they were not taking Bible prophecy literally when they recited Psalm 2 in a prayer meeting (Acts 4:23–31)? They thought that Herod, Pontius Pilate, and the Sanhedrin were the kings and rulers of Psalm 2 who were making war against God and King Jesus. And the Holy Spirit seemed to agree with this interpretation (Acts 4:31). But author Lindsey says that Psalm 2 must be fulfilled when Jesus has become a real earthly King on the real hill of Zion (p. 170).

And yet, according to Lindsey, you don't have to believe that Jesus will come on a literal cloud, as I always thought. Amazingly, the cloud is spiritualized into the raptured saints with whom King Jesus will descend on Jerusalem (p. 172). But a lake of blood, six feet deep and four hundred miles long must be projected in the heart of Palestine, as a gruesome sign that the author takes the Bible literally.

Instead of doing theology with the help of military strategists (p. 157), instead of drawing strategy maps (155, 159) and having beaches tested for the invasion of amphibious tanks (164) or quoting Chinese military convictions to support Joel's prophecies (165), the writer should have consulted some more books on Bible prophecy written by people who take the Bible seriously.

Our Hope: the Good News of the Kingdom

Recently another book was published, a book few people will read because it is tough and serious. It is called *The Puritan Hope*, by Iain Murray, and the subtitle is A Study in Revival and the Interpretation of Prophecy. The book shows that the Puritans expected the millennium, including the conversion of the Jews, as the result of faithful preaching of the gospel. Dr. DeKoster made some editorial remarks on Murray's book in *The Banner* of October 22, 1972.

The Puritans were for a good deal "post-millennialists," which is a point of view that "no self-respecting scholar" can hold today, according to Lindsey (p. 176). The post-millennialist view holds that, as the result of the preaching of the gospel, a mass-conversion of the world and of the Jews will come before the return of the Lord.

This is, of course, a difficult topic. It centers around the interpretation of

Romans 11:15 and 26 and it involves a study of the question if there is a biblical basis for a special dealing of God with Israel in the New Testament dispensation. If Mr. Lindsey had read the Puritans, perhaps he would not have met the "self-respecting scholars" for whom he is looking, but he would have found unhurried Bible students who would have shied away from the breezy prophecies of the *Late Planet* out of respect for the Bible as well as love for the planet.

Even if I would have to come to the conclusion that there is no solid and ultimate ground for this particular hope of the Puritans, I would much rather join their ranks than the crusade of Lindsey. Because with the Puritans the gospel preaching is still God's tender way of bringing the indestructible Kingdom. But Lindsey has made the proclamation of the gospel a futile ambulance service of plucking brands out of the fire. That's because he fails to see that the present Kingship of Christ is the only solid ground for doing the Master's work on the planet:

"All authority has been given to me . . . *therefore*, make disciples of all the nations."

CRITIQUE OF
"Review of *The Late Great Planet Earth*"

Clyde Kilby, Professor of English at Wheaton College, selected this review as the first-place winner in the Critical Review category of the 1973 EPA Awards Contest. The criteria for this category include basic information about the subject, critical perceptivity, validity of the reviewer's criteria, writing style, and reviewer's subjective response.

Kuyvenhoven gave his readers the basic facts about the subject. Early in the review (paragraph two), he recalls the phenomenal sales of the book that became a multimillion seller. Before Lindsey became a household word in evangelical family rooms, the reviewer properly supplied his readers with some background data relative to Lindsey's view of the Scriptures (paragraph seventeen) and a hint as to his vocation (paragraph twenty-one). Some readers also might have appreciated information about C. C. Carlson, the co-author.

This review was an important one in 1973, because even then hundreds of thousands of Christians and non-Christians were reading Lindsey's book (paragraphs two and three). Kuyvenhoven's specific audience was a part of the growing number of Christian readers: the members of the Christian Reformed Church.

The reviewer cannot be condemned for lack of subjective response. His purpose was to warn. He stated his thesis in a single-sentence paragraph (four). His strong reactions and analyses were evident in paragraphs fifteen through twenty-nine, among others. He can be commended for specific documentation as he cited page numbers throughout his analysis, enabling readers to look up the passage and come to their own conclusions.

The length of this review hindered its effectiveness. I wonder how many of the *Banner* readers made it through the ten-paragraph summary of *Late Great Planet Earth*. Surely that could have been said in fewer words.

The review could also have started faster and more forcefully if the thesis, "The *Late Great Planet Earth* is a bad book" (paragraph four) and its explanation (paragraphs fifteen and sixteen) had been used as the lead. During the book's first months of rocketing sales and enthusiastic acclaim, placing it on the "not-recommended shelf" would have drawn many into this evaluation.

The reviewer's writing is clear but uncreative.

Even though Kuyvenhoven vigorously attacks the book's focus, scholarship, and premise, the tone still rings of servanthood. He wrote to a specific denominational audience with a distinctive theological heritage. He reminded them at key places (paragraphs 3, 25, 28, 35) that the review was intended to help them evaluate the book for themselves.

—The Editor

We Need the Eggs

Jon Pott

Annie Hall. Directed by Woody Allen. Written by Woody Allen and Marshall Brickman. Starring Woody Allen and Diane Keaton. Cinematography by Gordon Willis. MPAA rating: PG.

For a man who defines his position as somewhere between atheism and agnosticism, comedian Woody Allen has gotten his share of attention from the religious press since *The Wittenburg Door*, only partly unhinged, proclaimed him Theologian of the Year for 1974. The reason, of course, is that his wit is a provocative wit and the questions which vex him are many of them religious: "If only God would give me some clear sign! Like making a large deposit in my name at a Swiss bank."

The devout must find in *Annie Hall*, his latest and most serious film, the usual things to offend—from bedhopping to that glib profanity which serves as so large a part of language on the contemporary screen. And yet, to peer beyond the wisecracks is to discern clearly none other than that anxious, ambivalent member of the "now" generation struggling to hold his own precisely against glibness, delusion, and the pain of transient relationships.

Annie Hall is Woody Allen at his uproarious best; it is also a wistful, affecting love story—of Alvy Singer, well-known Jewish comedian from Brooklyn (played by Allen himself) and Annie Hall (Diane Keaton), beautiful, hilariously flaky WASP from mid-America, come to New York in search of a career as a pop singer. This bittersweet experiment in the new morality never really has much chance. Long on self-depreciating charm but short on the gift for genuine intimacy, Alvy has mastered the art of using his wit to keep his psychic distance. His tics are the stuff of virtuosic monologues for college audiences, but he squirms in misery and ineptitude at closer quarters, surviving only through evasion and droll elan. He doesn't like mellow evenings at parties, he jokes uncomfortably. He gets ripe and rots: Dragged by his second wife to a fashionable gathering of New York literati, including her publisher, he sneaks off to a bedroom to watch the Knicks on television. Put upon to sniff cocaine among a group of friends, he sneezes explosively into the snuffbox and several thousand dollars' worth of powder go up in a cloud. He cringes at autograph seekers; he avoids showering at the tennis club ("I don't like to appear naked in front of males of the same gender"); after twelve years of visiting his psychiatrist, he still is unable to let go emotionally, and the doctor makes no progress.

Annie fares little better with his self-centered, suffocating compulsions. He refuses to enter a movie theater two minutes into the film when she meets him late. When she gives up her own apartment to move in with him, he immediately feels cramped by the threat of permanence ("Your apartment is our raft of freedom"). His idea of celebrating *her* birthday is to haul her out on a pilgrimage to his boyhood haunts, the very spawning grounds, we realize, of his neuroses. To compensate for his deficiencies outside the bedroom, he bathes the interior—only half in jest—in the cheap, erotic glow of a red lightbulb.

"*Annie Hall,*" writes one critic, "is a perverse self-help manual about How To Be Your Own Worst Enemy." Fair enough. Still, in all his antic vulnerability Alvy not only has our sympathy but our respect. His quirks and flaws are ironically the measure of his depth, for an atmosphere slick, glossy, and pragmatically turned out, he prowls persistently among the big questions. Or rather, the questions stalk him. Death is an obsession with him, he admits to Annie as they browse in a bookstore, and he insists on buying her two weighty books on the subject. He is haunted by the poetry of Sylvia Plath, who gassed herself at thirty-one. Life he can see only as "divided between the horrible and the miserable." The horrible is the life of the blind and the crippled ("I don't know how they make it"); the miserable is the life of the rest of us. What's the use of studying? he asks glumly in a flashback as a precocious school kid (played by Jonathan Munk). The universe is going to blow up anyway.

Notwithstanding his metaphysical bent, he has a healthy distaste for intellectual pretentiousness. "What I wouldn't do for a large sock filled with horse manure," he seethes as he stands in line at a movie theater in front of an insufferable Columbia academic pontificating about Fellini and Marshall McLuhan. Then, in the delicious enactment of a fantasy, he steps behind a pole and produces McLuhan himself to deflate the guy: "You know *nothing* of my work." "If only life were like that," laments Alvy to the camera.

His robust cynicism extends to leftist cant and the cult of feeling. He is hardly an ascetic himself, but his barbed tongue spares neither the chic morality of *The New York Review of Books* nor the visceral mindlessness of a long-haired actor emoting about acting as a religious experience. The years he's blown at his analyst have left him woefully disillusioned: "I'm going to give him one more year and then I'm going to Lourdes."

True, he is unwilling—at least until near the end—to commit himself fully to a relationship with Annie. It is equally true that he longs for something more. Her ritualistic pot-smoking before they bed down is a constant affront to his sensibility. He wants the "whole thing," he complains, not a zombie with artificially aroused nerve endings. Finally he takes her joint away—whereupon in an arresting filmic technique Allen splits her image in two, one body remaining in bed as an indifferent lover and the other getting up and walking across the room to a chair to observe the scene. "Now that's what I call removed," Alvy protests.

The romance ends as a kind of tale of two cities. Annie opts for Los Angeles and the West Coast, wooed there by the promises of an established singer with clout (played by Paul Simon) who caught her act in New York. She loves the scene for its glamour and manicured cleanliness. He is nauseated by its hedonism and plastic phoniness—a place where at Christmas Santa's sleigh prances across a plush green lawn with nary a snowflake in sight; where pretty-boy actors wear sun masks to stave off aging; where the canned laughter of a comedy show is manipulated in the control room to the precise satisfaction of the star. Alvy much prefers the tribulations of New York, where garbage litters the streets and anti-Semites—so his paranoia tells him—infest City Hall, but where illusion is less pervasive and one has half a chance of confronting the truth.

Annie Hall is a marvelously crafted film, making deft and altogether convincing use of a variety of techniques: narrative asides spoken directly to the audience; double images, allowing characters to wander into and observe earlier scenes involving themselves; a split screen, juxtaposing separate but related events; subtitles, to convey what characters are really thinking as they prattle on. The structure is episodic, with the episodes presented contrapuntally, but without confusion, out of order. As for the acting, Woody Allen as the diminutive, irreverent, endearingly flawed Alvy is splendid in what is undoubtedly a semi-autobiographical role. Diane Keaton, by now a regular in Allen movies, is sensational as the somehow savvy scatterbrain perpetually fluttering over an idea without ever quite touching down.

Those who found in Allen's earlier films a tendency toward madcap over-ingenuity and deepthink will find little to complain about here. *Annie Hall* is enormously funny, but the jokes hang brilliantly together to shape a coherent vision. A part of that vision is neatly encapsulated in the final, familiar gag Alvy relates. Why do people of so little constancy and commitment expose themselves to the anxiety of relationships which therefore have so little hope of permanence? A man goes to a psychiatrist to complain about a friend who thinks he is a chicken. "Why don't you bring him in for treatment?" asks the doctor. "I would, but we need the eggs."

Not the most hopeful wisdom by which to live—but a penetrating and poignant look at secular life and loves.

CRITIQUE OF "We Need the Eggs"

A reviewer or critic of any work of art has certain specific responsibilities not only to his reader but also to the artist and the work under scrutiny.

The reviewer must inform his reader as to the nature of the work, providing sufficient background or setting and giving an overview of the novel, play, film, exhibition, or whatever, without at the same time reducing his critique to a plot rehash. The reviewer should also educate the reader by telling him what to look for in the work—its subtleties, flaws, ambiguities, banalities.

A review ought to illumine the work it treats. Upon finishing the review, a reader should be able to see a work more clearly and understand its structure, form, themes, and motifs because of the light brought by the reviewer's commentary. This requires the reviewer to meet the work on its own terms, offering the reader reasonable comparison and contrast.

For example, those who admire Fitzgerald's novel *The Great Gatsby* may have been dissatisfied with the recent motion picture, especially if they call it a "version" of the novel. However, in fairness to the filmmaker we can't compare books and movies; they exist in different media. We can contrast the making of books with the making of films, but that's a topic all its own.

A reviewer must avoid competing with the artist. Some notorious reviewers have built reputations for their bitter personal attacks. They establish arenas of power, then assail anyone who dares to enter the particular province the reviewer calls his own. Their reviews become a means of getting even for such sacrilege! But a reviewer must, above everything else, be fair, criticizing what *is* rather than what he might have preferred to see or read. In other words, a reviewer must allow the artist his own vision and purpose and show respect for them.

To do all of this well means the reviewer must possess three gifts. He must be able to *analyze* —to take a work apart and show the interdependence of its themes. He must also be able to *synthesize*—to put the pieces back together again and show how they attain structural unity. Lastly, he must be able to *express* these insights in language so clear and effective that his reader is moved to act upon his advice. In short, a review is a recommendation either to spend time and money with this work or to spare oneself the waste.

In reviewing *Annie Hall,* Mr. Pott has met all these criteria. But he has done one thing more. Too often Christian periodicals—and those who write for them—have assumed that criticism must be preachy; that to justify devoting space in their hallowed pages to something as worldly as a movie review, the critic must turn the commentary into a theological discussion. Here instead we have a first-rate example of a truly integrated Christian perspective, accepting the film and its values and allowing these to speak for themselves.

—D. Bruce Lockerbie, judge
Chairman, Fine Arts Department
The Stony Brook School
Stony Brook, N.Y.

The Omen

A Review by Thomas Howard, Ph.D.

Two years ago, Hollywood convinced us we wanted to see *The Exorcist*. This was a whole new direction, it said. The ads were understated: you saw the silhouette of a solitary man in a homburg, casting an ominous shadow. You did not know who he was. He looked very much like an approaching strangler or medium, and the darker side of your imagination stirred in anticipation. As it happened, he was a priest, and a saintly one at that. He was the exorcist.

Now, most cinema-goers had never, Hollywood knew, come across exorcism. So it all had to be explained. The film did an excellent job of corralling everyone into this dark and straitened defile, and by the time the action got round to the exorcism itself, you knew what was going on. You knew that this was something more thrilling than counseling or surgery or psychoanalysis. When you were up against the wall, and the situation defied all the craft of science, you turned to the Church and her ancient wisdom and powers.

The shrewd thing about *The Exorcist* was that it didn't turn to witchcraft or necromancy or any other form of the occult for its thrills. It used rare stuffs that lie, not in the dens of the warlocks, but in the sacristies of the Church. It was not heterodoxy you saw but orthodoxy, all splayed out across the bloody screen.

The confusing and horrifying thing about the film to the orthodox imagination was, of course, that it was *Hollywood* that was doing this. The entertainment industry had reached its long hairy arm into the sacristy and had pulled out the most recondite things it could find. It had no more idea about the taboos that surround the use of these things than it had about the splendors of the City of God. It was like a baboon that had found communion wafers in the pyx, squeaking and gibbering and playing tiddly-winks and shove-ha'penny with the little discs. Even for Protestant Christians, who, if they believe in exorcism at all, would tend to try to accomplish it by prayer alone, the spectacle was obscene.

Hollywood is very astute. Its barometers still show The Violent and The Bizarre to be drifting about in the atmosphere. But another build-up of cloud has clearly showed up on the gauge. It is The Prophetic.

As far as the film-makers are concerned, this reading is just another subdivision of the bigger category Box Office. They have picked up exciting low-pressure indications like Planet Earth and Armageddon and Anti-Christ. "Now what's all this?" they ask themselves. "What's this that people are buying now? What? Prophecy? The Bible? Now wait—tell us more. Where's a Bible? What page? Revelation? Where's that? At the end? Oh. Right. Let's see now [flip, flip, flip] . . . oh . . . is this it—this about the Beast, and the battle, and signs in heaven and on earth? Hey, that's pretty good. Now are you *sure* that this stuff is selling? I mean, is anyone beside Billy Graham talking about it?" And so forth.

So they have made us a film about that now. Oh no—you won't see St. Michael in armor flying on Pegasus through the air over Palestine, or the hosts of Gog and Magog and the Chief Prince of Meshech and Tubal surging towards Esdraelon. You will see Gregory Peck as the American ambassador to the Court of St. James, Lee Remick as his wife, and their five-year-old "son" (there was a hugger-mugger birth-exchange, actually), who turns out to be the agent through whom the Devil proposes to begin his End-time moves. (The producers have made a pretty muddle of prophecy, so do not imagine that you will need the theologians to help you sort it out: it is pre-Sunday-school stuff.) With this scenario, they can do almost anything, and they do. There is a black dog, example, with glittering eyes and red mouth, who growls menacingly when anything awful is about to happen, the way Peter Lorre whistled "In the Hall of the Mountain King" in the movie "M" just before he murdered his child-victims.

I had an odd experience with this nefarious dog as I sat in the nearly empty theater at the shopping mall in Manchester, New Hampshire, at a 3 p.m. showing. A menacing panting and snuffing began to sound just under a seat nearby. No one was near me; there were only about six people in the whole theater. I thought at first it was the stereophonic sound, arranged under our seats to frighten us. But it wasn't. Then I thought perhaps it was someone who had fainted during the 1 p.m. showing and was now coming to life. But I could find no body. I thought of a stray dog skulking about, but there was none. Finally I tried out my own breathing: perhaps I was puffing asthmatically and the acoustics of the theater were bringing it back to me from a few feet away. But I could not get it to synchronize with the noises. So I did what you do when you find yourself alone with the unmanageable: I sought company. I moved back to where two boys and an old man were sitting. I thought that if some miserable and blackguardly ghost were going to use this tawdry scene for an entry (and for any Christian this is never completely ruled out), he'd have to cope with more than one person.

In any event, there is a black dog, and there are prophecies (all higgledy-piggledy), and strange people who know things, and then a sequence of increasingly sinister events that takes you from London to Rome to the excavations at Megiddo, and that finally leads to the violent death of every single character in the film.

I do not think I am spoiling a good story for you by letting the cat (the dog?) out of the bag like this. The first thing to be said about the film is that it is not worth anyone's two hours or two dollars. For a start, Hollywood and its actors have no resources, emotional, dramatic, or intellectual, to draw on for this sort of subject matter, and hence have to draw on their usual bag of melodrama, sentimentalism, and sham-horror, evoked for the audience by stuttering, brimming eyes, jutting jaws, gritted teeth, and mad dashes up and down stairs. Gregory Peck may have talent, but he is miscast here.

Besides this, the "special effects" are not nearly so stunning as they were in *The Exorcist*. (If it is objected that I am spending too much time in comparison with that film, the rejoinder is that the makers of this film have invited, nay forced, such comparisons, by patently trying to cash in on the *Exorcist* market. They will have to live with the comparisons they have purchased.) In *The Omen,* you have people dangling from ropes and crashing through high windows to the street below, and one man's head being sheared neatly off by a huge pane of glass that slips from a truck, and a priest impaled with a toppling lightning rod at the door of a church, and so forth. The unnerving thing about all this is that the producers are apparently correct in supposing that you can mix biblical prophecy and this sort of jejune carrying-on, and get the public to buy it. It is like trying to dramatize the Ascension by using the Pink Panther: it is bad enough to find it done at all, but infinitely more dismaying to discover that it is selling.

But there is more than film criticism to be done here. Two points need to be made. First, a film like this *is,* alas, a yardstick. You *can* tell something about a civilization from its artifacts. If they are made of enameled gold, that indicates something. If they are made of polystyrene foam, that suggests something else. If you find copies of Sophocles buried in the rubble, you can make some guesses about what the people liked. If you find cans full of celluloid strips with spectacles like *The Omen* recorded on them, you can guess what *they* liked.

When a civilization has jettisoned the platitudes of plain, ancient, moral truth that are the very guardians and guarantors of its people's real freedom and joy, then it sets itself on the feverish quest for excitements to replace that moral truth. This quest leads with depressing predictability straight through from the diverting to the odd to the bizarre to the grotesque to the bestial to the demonic. With increasing stimulus, boredom sets in, and at the same time the threshold of people's capacity for being aroused goes up and up. This is why pornography, orgies, violence, gladiatorial combats, and jiggery-pokery crop up in rotting civilizations: people are bored with ordinariness and don't know what to do, and it takes more and more to rouse them from their ennui. I was amazed, for example, at the sheer force of the sounds and colors used for the screen announcements that told us we could smoke only in the rest rooms, could rent the theater auditorium, and so on. These items were accompanied by crashing Sousa-type fanfares over the PA system and whirling kaleidoscopic and stroboscopic effects on the screen. Clearly we are a people who need to be assaulted if we are to be budged at all. *The Omen* was made for the likes of us.

Secondly, the film is a disquieting reflection of the vocabulary and preoccupations of contemporary pop Christianity, and the evangelical church is not without guilt here. Biblical hucksters in the last seventy-five years have made Daniel, the Gospels, and Revelation their toys, giving us wild and vivid pictures and graphs as to what it was all about. Evangelicalism bought a great deal of this trinketry and helped to bruit it abroad, and Hollywood has heard the sound thereof. In so doing, this wing of the Church departed from the ancient stream of catholic orthodoxy that has always affirmed, "We believe that Thou shalt come to be our Judge," but has at the same time been reluctant to nail a given prophetic text down to a given historic event of either the past or the future. Dragons and phials and bowls and horsemen and falling stars and splitting mountains—what do they all mean? They mean something, surely, but it is something infinitely more dread and real than what our charts depict for us. And it will all be recognizable when the time comes. The recognition will not come from alchemists and grizzled hermits with their retorts and their cabala, or even from shouting stump-preachers with their flapping Bibles. It will come, rather, from holy souls who have lived faithfully in obedience to those ancient platitudes of moral truth found, not by picking the Scriptures to bits and Scotch-taping them back together into a scrapbook, but by submitting their entire imagination to the whole counsel of God.

CRITIQUE OF "The Omen"

Dwight Baker, teaching assistant at Purdue University, selected Thomas Howard's review of the film, *The Omen,* as the first-prize winner in the 1977 EPA Awards Contest. Five criteria have been established for evaluating critical reviews in the EPA contest: communication of basic information about the subject (i.e., basic facts and artist's goals); critical perceptivity; validity of reviewer's criteria; writing style; and reviewer's subjective comments.

In his lead, Howard puts *The Omen* into perspective in relation to its predecessor *The Exorcist*. Using the editorial "we," Howard immediately places himself and his readers within the target audience of Hollywood producers. A common identity is swiftly established.

Our reviewer could have given us a few more facts about the film, such as production costs and the names of producers, directors, and cast. But if the main purposes of a review include illumination, analysis, and insight, then Howard has provided an excellent service for the readers of *Christianity Today*. They could make an informed decision about expending time and money on this film.

Paragraphs three through seven help the reader to see the film from Hollywood's perspective. Howard notes the film's lack of resources in paragraph ten and its poor special effects are cited in paragraph eleven.

As we have come to expect from Howard, his style stimulates. The diction is extremely refreshing: "bloody screen" (paragraph three—might be considered vulgar by some), "higgledy-piggledy (paragraph nine), and "jiggery-pokery" (paragraph thirteen). Much of the word choice comes naturally from the subject of the occult: "necromancy," "dens," and "warlocks" (paragraph three). He uses powerful verbs and their variations: "corralling everyone" (paragraph two) and "a civilization has jettisoned" (paragraph thirteen).

I loved the humorous anecdote about the dog sounds that hounded Howard as he viewed the film. The colorful and multi-sense narration of that incident lets the reader know the reviewer is also human.

Most importantly, Howard concludes this review in prophetic style by analyzing the film's role as a mirror of society and the church (paragraphs twelve through fourteen). Whenever a Christian reviewer renders this type of ministry, his readers are indebted for insights that will help them to be more sensitive to the culture they are to be salting.

—The Editor

RESEARCH

1. Begin your collection of critical reviews. From both Christian and secular publications, find at least three examples of the book review. Do the same for records, music, and drama.

2. Find four book reviews (two Christian and two secular) that do an effective job of pulling the reader into the review.

3. Locate four drama reviews (two Christian and two secular) that do the best job of telling the reader about the main message of the play or film.

4. Look through the book review section of a Christian magazine and try to determine the type of readership each reviewer had in mind.

5. Write to the book editor of one of your favorite Christian magazines, list your reading interests, and ask if you could be given the opportunity to write a book review on a trial basis. You may wish to suggest some specific books that you would like to review.

PRACTICE

1. Write a critique of a book review you have selected. Compare your review against four of the suggestions made by William Peterson at the beginning of this chapter.

2. Write a book review for your local church paper.

3. If you get approval from the editor, write a book or film review for your weekly community newspaper. Select a recent book, film, or play that is especially relevant to the interests and needs of the people in your locale.

4. Start your collection of outstanding reviews. Look in newspapers, newsmagazines, literary magazines, educational journals, and evangelical publications. Mark the strengths and weaknesses of each for quick restudy in the future.

5. Locate six advertisements for Christian books in recent issues of your favorite evangelical magazines. Write a creative title that would accompany a review of each of these books. Note that the most effective reviews have a heading or title that is not merely a restatement of the book's title.

DISCUSSION

1. A critical review should provide the reader with the basic information

about the work or subject being evaluated. How well did each of the three reviews in this chapter accomplish that goal?

2. How do you rank these three reviews in their grappling with the basic issues?

3. How effective is each of these reviews in grabbing the reader's attention in the lead?

4. Would a discussion of the theological implications of *Annie Hall* have strengthened that review?

5. Have any of these reviewers used words that probably are not in the recognition vocabularies of most evangelical leaders? If so, cite these examples and suggest word choices that would reduce the fog level.

11
The Column

The Higher Goals division of the Evangelical Press Association's annual Awards Contest has a category called, "Standing Feature." Entries in this specialized category must be a section of a periodical that appears regularly under the same title. The column is an example of this type of entry.

A free-lancer must earn the job of being a columnist. In many cases, dozens or even hundreds of reviews, articles, and editorials have to be written before an editor will trust a regular column to an author.

In May of 1968 at *Decision* Magazine's School of Christian Writing, Joseph Bayly, Vice President of David C. Cook Publishing Company, gave the following insights and advice about writing a column:

> A column is a regular feature, usually appearing in each issue of a periodical publication.
>
> The writer's by-line usually is carried. The one exception is the Eutychus column in *Christianity Today,* where the columnist's anonymity probably adds interest.
>
> The nature of columns is as varied as the publications in which they appear. Christian magazines have columns on a wide range of subjects, from book and record reviews to personal advice, theology and opinion.
>
> Increasingly Christian writers are finding opportunities in local newspapers where the most frequent is probably the religion or church column. However, I am aware of Christians who have been responsible for society, theater, travel, interviews with visiting personalities and homemaking columns.
>
> A column usually, but not always, reflects the personal opinion of the writer. In doing so, it provides a regular, recurring exposure to a particular audience. Over a period of time the impact of this exposure builds up.

From an editor's standpoint, the dependability of a column is a plus in planning his/her periodical. One urgent necessity for a columnist is to meet deadlines.

From a writer's own viewpoint, the recurring deadlines are the greatest encouragement to writing. What he will say next week or next month is never far from his thoughts. Over a period of time, the column provides a storehouse of the writer's expressed opinion. The experience of writing a column tends to sharpen one's skill.

Don't automatically assume that your columns can be collected in book form, however. There is usually little interest in such a collection today.

The recurring nature of the column has some important implications as far as style is concerned.

Over the long haul, I believe the columnist must adopt a conversational tone. He cannot maintain tension, or, ordinarily, be "now hear this" in what he writes. The column is in one sense conversational, and must be written as if the columnist were actually talking to a person.

One trap that a column can fall into is a deadly sameness of ideas and expression. Here as everywhere else, variety is necessary. Occasionally the columnist should surprise readers by a break of pace. The question, "What's he talking about this month?" may make people turn to your column first, and this shows up well on reader surveys.

While the overall column title is helpful (in my case, "Out Of My Mind," the title I've used in *Eternity* for 18 years), current usage seems to be to subordinate this title to a larger caption that tells about the specific column contents.

How do you get to write a column?

First cultivate an editor whose periodical carries the sort of material you are capable of writing. Get other articles published before you broach the idea of a column.

Let this editor know you would like to try to handle an existing column if he ever has an emergency need. But meanwhile submit articles to this and other periodicals so that your by-line will become familiar to readers.

If you have a fresh idea for a column, ask the editor about it. It's always helpful to send several samples of what you are talking about.

Be patient. You may have to wait until you're better known as a writer.

Where do you get ideas for a column each month when a deadline rolls around?

When I first began to be published every month (in *HIS* magazine, before *Eternity*), I used to worry a lot about whether I would have a fresh idea the following month. I began to pray for creativity and ideas at that time and have never stopped.

Like all other kinds of writing, the ideas for a column come from everywhere and every possible type of situation. Try to learn something new from everyone you talk to. Read a lot, especially periodical literature.

If an idea occurs, write it down and set it aside for the time when you will actually be writing the column. Ideas are among the most perishable commodities, so never think that you will remember and write the idea down later.

Like most Christian writing, a column arises out of a person's life. The columnist's lifestyle and experiences will have a great deal to do with sustaining interest in a column of opinion.

Janet Lewis, Stanford poet and novelist, expressed it this way: "I never thought the writing was more important than the living. A writer writes out of his or her deepest experiences. The imagination itself comes out of life. My writing would have been very shallow and empty without the life I lived."

Cultivate the habit of asking, "What are its Christian implications?"

Don't let frequent writing make you careless with your facts.

Don't be afraid to adopt a light approach, even to laugh at yourself at times.

Perhaps of greatest importance, be yourself.

Don't get caught up in a crusade. Try to avoid being typecasted. Charles Haddon Spurgeon once commented about another preacher, "Strange how a harp of ten thousand strings should strum on one so long." Watch out that you don't give this impression: it's very easy when you come to people month after month, even more so in a weekly or daily column.

One responsibility of a columnist in a Christian periodical, in my opinion, is to answer letters that come to him. Sometimes people object to what the columnist has said, sometimes they misunderstand, sometimes they have found light on the subject, sometimes they want help in an area that the columnist has dealt with. Whatever the reason they write, I believe that we have a responsibility to respond.

As readers come to know a columnist, a sort of old-shoe familiarity is established, even though they may never have met him.

I became aware of this after I had been writing my column ("Out of My Mind") in *Eternity* for several years. I was speaking in California and an elderly man came up afterward, introducing himself with these words: "I told the wife I wanted to come tonight to hear you speak, because I already know you and I want you to meet me."

This is the highest compliment a columnist can receive.

"No Halo, Please, We're Human"

Gene Bertolet

The Korean peninsula dangles from the Asian mainland like a tattered Christmas stocking, its toe jutting westward into the Yellow Sea. After November, color it brown, except for January's blizzards. That's more of an off-white, streaked with gray and flecked with the black soot of a million *yunton* fires.

It's no time to venture down country by commercial transportation. But plans were made for me to travel with Paul Haines from Seoul to Mokpo, some 200 miles south, at the very toe of this sock. Paul would be mapping Every Creature Crusade strategy with church leaders and I was to tag along with my trusty Minolta and sketch pad. We would work together on developing brochures to convey the drama of Korea's church planting ministry to our homeland constituency.

Our Monday morning departure from Seoul was perfect. The bus was on schedule, had not been overbooked—at least for us, and the air was crisp and cold without a hint of precipitation. The brown landscape and frozen paddies were indeed a promising sight for this late January excursion. And we would be safely back in Seoul come Saturday evening.

Five cities and as many days later found Paul and me well off schedule. Warm Korean floors and farewells are difficult to get away from on brisk winter days. Consequently, Friday's dusk overtook us as we approached Mokpo. And it was beginning to snow. Paul was tilted back in his reclining bus seat, hat over his eyes, listening to a Korean newscast. A weather alert must have been issued because out from under Paul's furry hat came " 'Heavy snow warning.' Hope we don't get snowbound on that express train tomorrow." I didn't take up dialogue on the subject, but mentally exploring such a trauma, I shared Paul's hope.

It took all of Saturday to complete the Mokpo survey. Our host was the district superintendent of the Korea Evangelical Church. He and Paul chattered incessantly while I blew on my numb fingers and brushed snow off my Minolta.

Finally about dark Paul announced that more snow was predicted and we were too late for the night train. So we would stay overnight, attend morning worship services, and attempt the eight-hour trip back to Seoul on the afternoon express.

What is best about blizzards in Korea are steamy restaurants with the pungent aroma of spicy meat over a charcoal fire. The superintendent knew of just such a place. And as we settled onto the warm *ondol*-heated floor, sliding our stiff legs under the low table, I prepared to savor the remaining hours in Mokpo as an unpretentious observer.

Paul, the superintendent, and one of his elders talked for some time, I presume about church planting strategy. Occasionally the superintendent looked my way and asked typical English language textbook questions like, "From where do you come in the United States?" I gave textbook answers. "I came from the state of Indiana. . . ."

The conversation in Korean continued while I passively picked up a few words here and there. Paul abruptly turned to me and said, "I'll be preaching in a small church in the morning and the superintendent wants you to preach in his church; how about it?"

My response was quick. "If you're preaching somewhere else, who'll interpret for me?"

Before Paul could respond, the superintendent across the table said, "I will interpret for you." He had not missed a word.

Obviously that was not from a textbook. And Paul assured me the pastor was fluent in English, though he made no attempt to impress me with his ability. He chose rather to direct questions through Paul, and I would answer him in English.

I accepted the invitation to preach and then lapsed into meditation on possibilities for a three-point sermon outline.

Then it happened. The warmness around the table became as hostile as the blizzard outside. The conversation had stopped and Paul was asking a question to which he already knew the answer. "The pastor wants to know what denomination ordained you."

What had I gotten myself and this pastor into? I was aware of the historical and cultural importance placed upon ordination. There is in Korea a great gulf fixed between the laity and the clergy. Though there is mutual appreciation for abilities and gifts, the *moksa* (pastor) commands a kind of respect afforded few. In reverence for both the Word of God and the man trained to preach it, the pulpit is usually enormous and elevated above the congregation. A podium is reserved for the layman. It stands floor level with the pews and is shared with the women of the church. I thought of the dozens of times I had "preached" in America, just to be funded as a missionary to Korea. And I probably had as much formal Bible training in Bible college as many Korean pastors get in seminary. I could sense resentment for the system creeping past my collar on the way to turn my ears red. It was scarcely slowed by the brief remembrance of something I had noted from a prefield orientation seminar. "Some things in other cultures are neither right nor wrong; they're just different." The attitude toward laymen was certainly different from America, and to me it was wrong.

The inward explosion of emotion finally emerged as a subdued apology. "I've never been ordained, but only because. . . ." My defense trailed off as I noted the superintendent's shock. He was totally engulfed in a swirling sea of Oriental custom, Christian ethic, and respect for Paul and me as foreigners. He had offered his pulpit to a layman. There was no way to save face. And my feeble attempt to decline on the basis that I hadn't brought a Sunday suit only worsened the situation. Not only was a layman going to preach in the biggest church in Mokpo, but he would be dressed like a sporty American tourist.

I pondered the awkwardness both the pastor and I would share the next morning. I had no idea how he would cope with his cultural dilemma. But I felt duty bound to put together a sermon that would forever settle his doubts about the preaching abilities of the laity. I spent a restless night shaping the verbiage that would indict the narrowness of the Korean clergy.

The snow had stopped during the night and the sun rose upon a beautiful Sunday. Not at all what had been predicted. Nor was the message still taking shape in my thoughts. Somehow the Lord got through to me that I hadn't come to impress, but to serve. I asked Him to forgive me for my intentions and do with the morning as He saw best.

We arrived at the church to find the tiny oil heater in the huge auditorium was not functioning. Early worshipers sat bundled in their pews, some bowed in prayer while others curiously watched my every move. In response to the pastor's gesture, I followed him down the side aisle to the elevated platform, trying not to notice the spindly lectern on the main floor. We paused at the steps to remove our shoes and he said, "It is much too cold, we will leave our overcoats on this morning."

"How interesting," I thought, "No one will even know I'm wearing a corduroy sport coat with leather lapels." I thanked God for a faulty heater and the bitter cold gnawing at my toes as I sat stocking-footed on the platform.

The opening part of the service was brief, and suddenly I was introduced to the congregation below me. It was an awesome sight, the sunlight streaming through the tall eastern windows, illuminating the puffs of vapor from the two or three hundred huddled worshipers.

I slipped my notes from my Testament and placed them on the massive pulpit. It was my testimony as a layman. How God had made a promise to me in Acts 1:8 and kept it to the "uttermost." It was over in 20 minutes and from my lofty perch I could detect tears glistening in the sun drenched sanctuary.

The pastor shook my hand and said, "Thank you, Mr. Bertolet, I have been moved. My people have been moved."

I thought the shortness of my sharing would allow the pastor time to preach. But he announced to the congregation and then to me in English that he had forgotten this was Communion Sunday. I had "preached" the morning message. Communion would conclude the service.

It was the most meaningful sharing of the Lord's Supper I have ever known. Our oneness in Christ transcended language and culture.

With the service over, the pastor hustled me into a taxi for a quick trip to the train station where I was to rejoin Paul. There remained a few moments to exchange traditional farewell phrases with bows and handshakes. As I turned to pass through the boarding gate the pastor captured my hand in both of his for a final time and said, "The next time you come to Mokpo. . ." and then pausing as to weigh the full magnitude of what he was about to say, concluded with, "I want you to preach in my church."

CRITIQUE OF "No Halo, Please, We're Human"

Many strengths combine to make "No Halo, Please, We're Human" a successful standing feature. The very idea that prompted the series is its initial and crucial strength. The headline catches the reader off guard, exposing and refuting a common, yet usually unuttered, misconception about missionaries. The choice of words, "no halo" and "we're human" evoke abrupt surprise, drawing the reader in, enlisting his confidence and interest.

Having caught the reader's interest through this device of surprise, the original subtitle of this column further promises a valuable service: "this series of confessions by missionaries should change your prayers." The real merit of this standing feature, thus, lies in the service it offers. This service is at once eminently needed and refreshingly different in approach, compelling the casual browser to push further into the article itself.

Immediately the style engages the eye. Vivid nouns and strong verbs combine in the colorful image of the Korean peninsula as a tattered Christmas stocking, its toe jutting into the Yellow Sea. Even the adjectives are derived frequently from verbs, further strengthening the style. The arresting command, "After November, color it brown," secures the reader's involvement. The tone color (browns, off-white blizzards streaked with gray, and black soot) prepares the setting as the narrative begins to move. Paragraph two swiftly introduces the action, "It's no time to venture down country by commercial transportation." The reader is further drawn in by the transitional conjunction, "But . . . " and the missionary trek from Seoul to Mokpo is at once introduced. No time wasted, the narrative is underway. The introductory style has been very tight.

The progress of the narrative sequence itself is enhanced by freedom from clichés, from the expected phrases of other missionary articles. Instead, the writer uses fresh details to keep the scene itself always before the reader's eye, as in paragraph five, "I blew on my numb fingers and brushed the snow from my Minolta," or paragraph seven, "Steamy restaurants with the pungent aroma of spicy meat," or "the puffs of vapor from the two or three hundred huddled worshipers" (paragraph twenty-one).

Toward the conclusion the writer skillfully draws the spiritual application from the narrative, still avoiding the standard phrases and using powerful understatement instead: "Thank you, Mr. Bertolet, I have been moved. My people have been moved" (paragraph twenty-three). Or, "Somehow the Lord got through to me that I hadn't come to impress, but to serve. . ." (paragraph seventeen). The simplicity of these statements gives them added power when they appear, letting the full weight of implication carry its own force. Only the phrase, "It was the most meaningful sharing of. . ." (paragraph 25) borders on the commonplace. The writer, however, has saved the phrase for the end of the article rather than sprinkling such phrases throughout.

The only significant weakness here is the match between the headline, "No Halo, Please. . ." and the point of the article, which comes very late. Perhaps the narrative takes too long to let the reader know what its point is going to be. Some early hint or foreshadowing could allow a tighter fit between the concept governing this standing feature and the entry for this particular month.

Nevertheless, the standing feature idea here is unique and fresh, highly meritorious. Further, the style of the article itself could well serve as a model for many other missionary articles, for it is peopled by lively humans whose movements are described in well-chosen nouns and verbs and clear, unpretentious language.

[*Ed. note:* Dr. Barcus judged the writing style, the opinions expressed, and the uniqueness factor as "outstanding" for this standing feature entry.]

—Nancy B. Barcus, judge
Assistant Professor of English
Houghton College
Houghton, N.Y.

Rebirth

A Review by Wesley G. Pippert

Charles W. Colson, *Born Again*, published by Chosen Books, distributed by Fleming H. Revell. Old Tappan, N.J., 1976, 351 pp., $8.95.

I. GENUINENESS

About the time of publication of *Born Again*, Charles W. Colson spoke at the University of Michigan under the sponsorship of Inter-Varsity, Campus Crusade, the Word of God charismatic community, and the black United Students for Christ.

A couple of representatives of the organizations, at a preliminary planning session, had revealed some doubts about the authenticity of the conversion of the man who was President Richard M. Nixon's political operative and confidant. Somewhat skeptically, they read *Born Again*. At the next planning meeting they reported their reaction. They were totally convinced of the genuineness of Colson's conversion, and even exuberant about the clarity and depth with which he juxtaposed his new life in Christ and his old life in a Watergate Washington.

Other persons have had similar reactions. In her review of *Born Again*, Mary McGrory, who won a Pulitzer Prize for her biting Watergate columns, asked, "Was he?" She answered her own question, "Yes, he was." (She said, however, "But if he has been washed in the blood of the Lamb, there still are signs of ring around the collar." She cited Colson's referring to the 1972 mining of Haiphong harbor as "one of Richard Nixon's finest hours," Colson's rigging of public opinion polls at that time, his secret taping of a damning telephone call from Watergate burglar E. Howard Hunt.) Edmund Fuller, in the *Wall Street Journal*, said he moved from skepticism to a belief in the book's honesty—"it is indeed an encouraging witness about misjudgment, misdeeds, suffering and the redeeming of lives."

I also had doubts in late 1973 and early 1974, not about the genuineness of Colson's conversion but about the depth of his spiritual understanding, as he pursued every legal maneuver to avoid conviction in the Watergate cover-up and Ellsberg break in cases. Since then, in my view, Colson's life has removed all doubt; he pleaded guilty to a charge he himself offered to the prosecutors in full knowledge it meant prison and the end of his $200,000 a year law practice; he served one of the longest of all Watergate sentences, seeking no favors while in prison; he cooperated with the Watergate prosecutors and the House impeachment inquiry; his lifestyle changed from that notorious toughness to even a gentleness; he has thrown his awesome energies and skill into service for a group for whom Jesus himself had special concern, prisoners.

Colson's book may be the best yet written about Watergate. Paradoxically, Watergate is not the most moving part of *Born Again*. Rather, his description of life in prison is the most vivid, the most stark part of the book.

It is impossible to read *Born Again,* or to hear Colson speak, or to observe him, without being convinced of his new life.

II. NIXON

Colson has not turned on Nixon as did some Watergate figures. He treats him with more sorrow than anger. The two men continued a close relationship throughout the Watergate unraveling and resignation period. On the day Colson pleaded guilty, Nixon sent him a handwritten note saying, "it is equally a sad day for me."

The day after the plea, Nixon phoned. "Near the end of the conversation I told him that regardless of any mistakes he had made, it was because of his presidency that my son would not have to go to war," Colson writes. "That to me outweighed the pain, even of prison. I meant it, too; his moral judgment had been blurred, yet I couldn't forget the courageous longviewed way in which he set out to create a moral stable order in the world. I did not know then that among the miles of magnetic tape stashed away in the bowels of the White House was the proof of deceptions that would soon mean the end for this man and his dreams."

Their relationship continues to this day. Colson writes with regret at missed opportunities to witness to Nixon during the dismal days of 1973 and 1974. Knowing Colson's zeal and aggressiveness, it is safe to believe that Colson has no longer passed up opportunities.

III. PERSONAL GUILT

Shortly after his conversion became public knowledge in late 1973, Colson told me that "arrogance" was the great sin of Watergate. At the time he was no longer Nixon's Special Council but he was in continuing contact with the White House. In that interview, however, Colson refused to draw any relation between his new beliefs and Watergate.

He came to see there was a connection. In *Born Again,* he elaborates on his belief that arrogance was the basic wrong of Watergate. Pride. Hubris. A Holy War against opponents. These were the traits the Nixon administration exalted.

"Pride. Richard Nixon's deep sense of pride in his office was the quality which I most admired," Colson says. "In fact, pride was at the heart of the Nixon presidency in its reach for historical importance and greatness."

On the night of a breakthrough in the strategic arms talks with the Soviet Union, aboard the presidential yacht *Sequoia,* Nixon talked to Henry Kissinger, H. R. Haldeman, John Erlichman, and Colson about treatment of opponents—"get them on the floor and step on them, crush them, show them no mercy." Colson writes, "and so . . . a Holy War was declared against the enemy—those who opposed the noble goals we sought. . . . *They* who differed with us, whatever their motives, must be vanquished. The seeds of destruction were by now already sown—not in them but in us."

And again: "In our small White House circle, machismo and toughness were equated with trust and loyalty. . . . *Hubris* became the mark of the Nixon man because *hubris* was the quality Nixon admired most."

In all of this, Colson perceives and describes more clearly than any other Watergate chronicler the flawed nature of the Nixon administration. Sinful men had succumbed to the lust for power; they had betrayed the people's trust. Colson also states forthrightly what he feels is needed to bring the American people together as one nation under God: "It can come in only one way—as each of us bows in submission to Him and as the Almighty leads us from darkness into light."

In his Ann Arbor speech, Colson said this must happen just as a flu epidemic spreads, one by one. "God deals with us as individuals and we come together as individuals," he said. "The revival of American spirit begins with each of us." That, he said, is God's secret plan for the nations.

Born Again is an eloquent, from-the-heart witness to the need for every one of us, lofty and lowly, to repent and believe.

IV. GOD AND THE NATIONS

Yet, there is a profound incompleteness in Colson's statements. It is not enough for a nation's leaders merely to make a personal commitment to Christ. If the men in the Nixon administration had been believers, would they still have bombed Haiphong harbor? Would they have pursued different policies toward America's poor and oppressed? Colson doesn't tell us—and, in fact, is silent about the whole area of a biblical integration of personal faith and public policy.

The Bible is not silent, however. The prophets and Jesus Christ himself declare that God will judge the nations not merely on the basis of the personal morality of their leaders but on how they treat the widow, the fatherless, the stranger, the wage-earner. In fact, God frequently used ungodly men to accomplish his objectives for a nation.

Scripture seems to declare that God was at least as interested in how the Nixon administration treated the disadvantaged and meted out justice and mercy as how immoral it was in Watergate.

Colson's closest spiritual brother is former Senator Harold Hughes, a liberal Democrat who is opposed to capital punishment, involvement in Vietnam, and other social injustices. Presumably they talk about these things, too. One would like to listen in on such discussions, and as Colson's faith continues to deepen and broaden, one wonders whether and how his political beliefs will change, too.

CRITIQUE OF "Rebirth"

Rich Pauley, who in 1977 was on the staff of the Fort Wayne *News-Sentinel*, selected Wesley Pippert's review of *Born Again* by Charles Colson as the best entry in the Standing Feature category of the EPA Awards Contest. A review column qualifies for this category if it is "a section of a periodical that appears regularly under the same title." Pippert's review appeared in the "Journal Review" section in the *Reformed Journal* (May–June, 1976).

The three editorial criteria used for judging this category are writing style, well-expressed opinions, and uniqueness of contribution. Pippert scored "outstanding" on the rating scale for each of these three criteria. The solid, clear prose is what a reader would expect from a veteran United Press International reporter. Pippert gives his opinions about Colson, Nixon, *Born Again*, and related subjects effectively without being offensive.

The *Reformed Journal* obtained one of the most qualified persons in the United States to write this review, thereby making it unique. Pippert covered Watergate for UPI, and two full-sized filing cabinets in the

National Press Building in Washington, D.C., testify to the thoroughness of his investigation. A two-page index taped to one of these cabinets lists two sections under the category "Colson." Pippert was the first reporter to interview Colson after the former Nixon aide accepted Christ.

It's encouraging to see a writer identify the main points of his article through the use of headings. "Genuineness," "Nixon," "Personal Guilt," and "God and the Nations." This arrangement divides the review into the main subjects that the author wants to emphasize, provides digestible segments for the reader, and gives the editor another element for page layout.

Pippert's anecdotal lead quickly involves the reader with the subject of the review and attempts to reduce skepticism of those who are not Colson's fans.

The reporter's experience with specific detail can be seen in the direct quotations, dates, numbers, and the name of the presidential yacht.

Following William Peterson's advice, this review concludes by raising questions about the larger issues involved, such as a Christian politician's moral responsibilities toward "the widow, the fatherless, the stranger, the wage-earner."

—The Editor

RESEARCH

1. Study your favorite newspaper or magazine columnist for two weeks. List the different structures or styles used during that time.

2. What examples can you find in the columns studied for Research item 1 that reveal the columnist's knowledge of his readers?

3. If possible, try to interview a columnist from your weekly paper. Find out how he got started, how he gets his ideas, and what methods he uses to write the column.

4. Examine three of your favorite general Christian magazines to see how many different literary types are used within their columns.

5. Start your file of effective columns by finding three from daily newspapers and secular magazines and three from Christian magazines. Mark their strengths and weaknesses for future reference.

PRACTICE

1. Keeping in mind the needs and interests of your readership, write a guest column for your church newspaper or weekly newspaper. See if the editor is interested.

2. Compose a title for the new column that you think should appear in a Christian magazine. List the first six topics that you would use in this new standing feature.

3. Make a list of the personality traits you can note by reading several columns by your favorite columnist. Remember that a writer's style is his personality in print.

4. Rewrite the introduction of an effective column aiming at a different readership.

5. If you have written several general articles for your campus, church, or weekly newspaper, ask the editor if you could write a column on a trial basis. Submit a working title for the column and a list of subjects. If possible, also submit one or two sample columns.

DISCUSSION

1. "No Halo, Please, We're Human" is essentially a column in narrative form. What characteristics of the narrative are observable in this column?

2. The annual Evangelical Press Association Awards Contest lists the following three criteria as part of the basis for judging standing features or columns: writing style, well-expressed opinion, and uniqueness of contribution. Using these criteria, evaluate the two columns included in this chapter.

3. Someone has said that a good column is written by an author who cares. To what extent is this characteristic evident in the two columns reprinted in this chapter?

4. Look for examples of specific detail that heighten the sensory impact of "No Halo, Please, We're Human."

5. What single sentence within the column could be cited as a thesis for Wesley Pippert's review of Colson's *Born Again?*

12
The Humorous Article

Humorous writing is often the most appreciated by readers, the most neglected by editors, and the hardest to produce for writers. Richard Armour says that "it is as hard to make readers laugh as it is to make them cry."[1]

The Eighth New Collegiate Dictionary by Merriam-Webster gives two of its definitions for humor: "(3a) that quality which appeals to a sense of the ludicrous or absurdly incongruous . . . (3c) something that is or is designed to be comical or amusing."

In the nineteenth century, Richard Milnes defined a sense of humor as "the just balance of all the faculties of man, the best security against the pride of knowledge and the conceits of the imagination, the strongest inducement to submit with a wise and pious patience to vicissitudes of human existence" (*Memoir of Thomas Hood*).

A Dictionary of Modern English Usage contains some valuable observations about the purposes, provinces, techniques, and readership of humor, with and without satire.[2] Fowler suggests that humor attempts to make a new discovery for a sympathetic audience by observing human nature. Wit tries to throw light on a subject by surprising an intelligent audience through the clever use of words and ideas. He also says that satire deals with morals and lifestyle and uses exaggeration to jolt the self-satisfied into reform.

[1]"Yes, Humor is Publishable," *The Writer* (June 1976), p. 17.

[2]H. W. Fowler, *A Dictionary of Modern English Usage*, 2nd ed. rev. (New York: Oxford University Press, 1965), pp. 252–53.

In an article in *Spectrum,* Denny Rydberg, editor of *The Wittenburg Door,* gave his views on the place of humor in evangelical magazines:

> There is a lot to laugh about in the church. I think you've got to have a sense of humor if you're going to exist, especially in the evangelical church. We [*Wittenburg Door* editors] are convinced that there are also serious issues in the church and that people respond and listen and maybe change a little bit if we get them to laugh along with us rather than pound them over the head in a kind of preachy fashion. We think if we can get people's attention by laughing and asking questions, it's much better than coming on with the old hard-sell approach.
>
> We feel that humor helps people get a proper perspective of themselves.
>
> Is there a place for humor in a Christian magazine? Granted the Apostle Paul was not your greatest comedian. He had very few humorous passages. It's hard to develop his theology of humor, and you don't see Jesus sharing a lot of one-liners. But according to some Hebrew scholars, Hebrews were very interested in word pictures. When Jesus would say it's as difficult for a rich man to enter heaven as it is for a camel to go through the eye of a needle, that was a side-splitter. Also, calling Pharisees whitewashed tombs when they were very concerned about touching dead bodies was really very funny. Not to the Pharisees, but to the rest of the audience.
>
> We have tried to concentrate on reform and renewal within the church, using humor and satire as our vehicle.[3]

Basically, to write humorous copy a writer must be a sensitive and careful observer of people; their foibles, mistakes, and inconsistencies. These observations can be used as humorous anecdotes in articles of almost every type. The humorous anecdote can help a reader see that the author also realizes he is human, with all the attendant struggles.

The humorous article or anecdote ministers to readers by encouraging them to unwind emotionally. This will help them avoid immobilization caused by the tautness of inner springs. Readers can be blessed through the judicious use of humor carefully wrapped in Christian love.

A practical motto for Christian writers, editors, and readers might be this: "Take our God and ministries seriously, but not ourselves." Humor helps many accomplish that goal.

[3]"The Subtle Prophet in Christian Humor," *Christian Communications Spectrum* (Fall 1978).

Life Among the Nacirema

F. F. Throckmorton, Ph.D. with Steve Lawhead

The following is taken from the notebooks of Dr. Fenwick Fishmeal Throckmorton, noted anthropologist and lecturer. It is a rather graphic and disturbing account of a vanished people whose bizarre, if not frightening behavior will long remain shrouded in mystery.

The most alarming aspect of this strange culture was the nearly total absorption with physical appearance. Much like primitive peoples everywhere, the Nacirema valued self-image above all else. Nowhere can this be seen more clearly than in their courtship ritual.

The Nacirema were an ancient wandering people that lived in the broad expanse of land just south of what is now called Canada, and north of the Central American regions of what is known today as Mexico.

Although these unusual people seemed to possess a quaint native intelligence, they immersed themselves in meaningless symbolic ritual practices. And although they developed a highly complex society, their social interaction—even between individuals of the same tribal village—was shot through with primitive magic and superstition. This is clearly evident in the courtship ritual of the young Nacirema.

Before courtship could begin, a strange series of private rites had to be performed by both members of the courting couple. These rites were carried out in secrecy within small chambers built for just this purpose within the walls of Nacirema dwellings. For both the male and female, the rite began with filling the ceremonial basin with water. This water was believed to have the power to remove unattractive qualities from the face, thus making it ready to be seen by the other party. The water was aided by rubbing a small bar of perfumed animal fat on a ceremonial cloth which was drawn back and forth over the face.

The young male's ritual may or may not have included the frightening practice of scraping the face and neck with an extremely sharp instrument in an effort to remove any natural hair from the face. Facial hair was considered unattractive unless it was arranged in certain stylized shapes. Once this was accomplished, the often bleeding face was dried and perfumed.

The female ritual included a bizarre custom of great antiquity: the application of pigmented creams to the face. These creams were thought to lend an enchanting quality to the female's appearance. The unnatural colors were expected to charm the male, who generally used no color on his face. Her face was also perfumed, although it is to be presumed other body parts were perfumed as well. Often the female would extract stray hairs from the area near her eyes by pulling them suddenly with a two-pronged instrument.

Another fascinating and wholly meaningless practice was a meditation rite performed by every young Nacirema. The meditation consisted of focusing all one's attention upon a specific part of the body (usually the face, but sometimes the stomach or backside), in an effort to "will away" any imperfection to be found there. For example, a nose considered too big would be agonized over for long periods of time before a mirror.

Slight red protrusions, called pimples, which every Nacirema was subject to, fell under this treatment as well. Although we know that pimples are a natural part of growing up, the Nacirema culture deeply resented them. Tribal shamans produced special unguents and magic ointments to make the pimples disappear. The unguents never worked, but had a psychological calming effect on the primitive mind. Sometimes these pimples were even attacked with sharp torture implements, or pressed violently between the fingers.

The Nacirema, and especially the young, were very superstitious about their bodies. They held to a veritably impossible standard of bodily perfection. Anyone judged too fat or too thin, too tall or too short, or any of a thousand variations, was ostracized and made the object of public mockery. This is perhaps the most barbaric feature of the race—the extremely cruel capacity for ridiculing another of their tribe for physical appearance, something he could do nothing about. It passes all understanding.

The last item in the ceremony was a mouth ritual practiced by both members of the courting pair. It involved the application of a special, magical powder or paste (made white in color by ground-up oyster shells) onto a slender bundle of hog bristles. Then this bundle, along with the paste, was inserted into the mouth and lashed against the teeth in what best could be described as a controlled frenzy. This grotesque display, like the others, was supposed to enhance the appearance.

Once this ceremony was completed, the young male would emerge from the ceremonial chamber to procure a means of transportation for himself from his own male parent. In a playful drama full of symbolic "threats," adult agreement was reluctantly granted, often not without formal bartering for future services of the young male.

When the male arrived at the female's ancestral dwelling place, he was made to remain waiting uncomfortably under the intense scrutiny of the female's family members. This was to purge the soul of the visitor and secure satisfaction or approval on which to base further courtship proceedings.

The female then left her dwelling in the company of the courting male. For some unknown reason this action was called a "date." Any meaning which might have been gleaned from the word is completely lost now; however, it is known what constituted a "date" for many young Nacirema.

Young Nacirema would gather outside a communal lodge house forming into single lines for the privilege of obtaining entrance into the lodge house. Admission into the lodge house was considered highly desirable. Therefore, the young males would attempt to gain favor with the lodge keeper by giving small gifts, which, if judged worthy, would allow the pair inside.

This practice was commonly accepted as a natural part of community behavior. In fact, the process was speeded up by arbitrarily standardizing the value of the gift. Thus anyone with a special-sized green gift was allowed inside.

Once inside, the courting pairs took up places in formally arranged sitting devices. It was usually quite dark inside the lodge house. After a brief time of meditation, visual thought projections were displayed for the amusement of the courting pairs. These were magical in origin, based on local folk tales or fantasies. It has only lately been discovered that the lodge housekeeper in reality employed elaborate (but primitive) machinery to accomplish his magic effects. The young Nacirema were not usually aware of this.

After the visual stimulus or "picture show" there would be a time of mutual refreshment. Here again a communal lodge house located near the village marketplace would be approached and the keeper offered gifts. The male would use these gifts to trade or barter some provision—usually a little bread and meat with potato and sweet-tasting liquid. This meal was of very little consequence; it was only symbolic of the male's ability to provide nourishment for the female.

The sweet-tasting drink is another matter. It was made from crushed leaves of the kola-nut tree and mixed with sugar water. This herbal drink held a significant place in this primitive culture—almost sacred. Large quantities of this bittersweet beverage were consumed with great frequency. It was believed to have been a life-giving stimulant. The words "Cola increases being" or "Coke adds life" have been deciphered in ancient writings.

After the symbolic meal the male returned the female to her ancestral dwelling place. It was then that he sought a judgment of approval for his part in the courtship ritual. This was not directly requested, for that would have been socially unacceptable. Instead he was made to endure all manner of embarrassment by waiting for the judgment. In the end, if the female considered him attractive and worthy of favor, she would give him a ceremonial sign. This was demonstrated in a most absurd way. The female "pooched up" her lips and placed them up against the male's lips: an almost meaningless exchange, but one held in great respect and awe, and not without a great emotional significance attached to it.

The male would then return to his ancestral dwelling to await the completion of another seven-day cycle when he could again begin the courtship ritual.

It is hard, rather impossible, to imagine the sense of well-being these people searched for through this practice. This was something greater than life itself to them. Just being seen by other members of the tribe with an attractive suitor was enough to propel young Nacirema into a higher status within the tribe. This artificial status, or the lack of it, greatly affected self-esteem, worth, value of life and many other things. Those with increased status would then become "popular" or "in demand" by their peers.

It would be misleading to leave one with the impression that every member of the tribe participated in this courtship ritual. That is not true. Many Nacirema youths, for one reason or another, participated rarely or not at all. They were known as "Citetomes." There was nothing appreciably different about these young people—merely the fact that they did not have enough status within the tribe to ask for or accept a partner in the courtship ritual.

There are those who would decry the study of anthropology, calling it a complete waste of time. However, it should be pointed out that in learning about even such a frivolous people as the Nacirema, we learn a lot about ourselves.

CRITIQUE OF
"Life Among the Nacirema"

Soren Kierkegaard described comedy as a "transparency through which we see the serious." At its best, comedy makes us think and reexamine our values. Abe Burrows states, "I claim with comedy we make much more serious points than we do with anything that's supposed to be serious. A laugh is one of the most profound things that can happen to a human being. When you make a man laugh, you have evidently hit him right where he lives—deep. You've done something universal. You've moved him in an area that he probably didn't even dare think about, and he laughs."[4]

There are many things that the best of Christians are noted for: compassion, discipline, wholesomeness, integrity, to name a few. Humor is seldom if ever on a list of Christian attributes. Yet the ability to laugh at ourselves is very often a key to both health and insight.

Campus Life's "Life Among the Nacirema" was first-place winner in the 1977 Evangelical Press Association awards contest because it so delightfully followed in a contemporary style the classic form for humor. The object of humor (as contrasted with satire, farce, or burlesque), is to understand and reveal human nature. The method is merely observation of behavior. The ironic tone is gentle and sympathetic.

Fowler's *Concise Oxford Dictionary* defines "perception" as the "intuitive recognition of truth." Since from time immemorial parents have been smiling at the desperate preoccupation of their young people with physical appearance and its alteration, the article is not outstanding in perception. It is in the imaginative handling of the subject that the author's creative genius shines. Teen-agers as an ancient wandering people, developing a highly complex society shot through with magic and superstition? That's fun. And if a reader, unsure of the genre, begins to flag in interest, the reference in paragraph two to the courtship ritual is sure to intrigue.

Phrasing, if we mean choice and arrangement of words, is excellent. The wit of the writer to create tongue-in-cheek "anthropological" descriptions of common household objects is admirable—a sink becomes a "ceremonial basin" in paragraph five, a toothbrush a "slender bundle of hog bristles" in paragraph eleven. The style itself keeps the reader amused

[4]Larry Wilde, "The Genesis of Comedy," *Television Quarterly* 13, no. 4 (Winter 1976-77), pp. 67–70.

because by necessity he must engage in running interpretation of the description and as he succeeds, it is funny.

And the humor *is* the impact. We laugh, and yet we see at the same time the absurdity of preoccupation with the ever-changing phenomena of our physical appearance.

Perhaps it is at the end that the article is weakened. There seems to be a failure of confidence on the part of the author that the reader can actually make the application. "In learning about even such a frivolous people as the Nacirema, we learn a lot about ourselves," he writes. Of course we know by now the article is about ourselves! Must such a pompous end be tacked on?

The humor of "Life Among the Nacirema" *is* transparent. We can see the serious. That's what makes the article so good. The impact of comedy is always deflated when the writer indulges in explanation or application.

—Myrna Grant, judge
Coordinator of Broadcasting
Wheaton Graduate School
Wheaton, Illinois

"Current Religious Thought"

Ducking the Mailed Fist

James D. Douglas

Soon after leaving seminary, I applied for a post as chaplain to a military school, and through some oversight I was put on the short list. Confidently I boned up on questions I expected to be asked. Never was disillusion more utter. Came the day, and I was ushered before a formidable array of top brass. I promptly discovered that the martial mind roves along lines decidedly unfair.

For starters, a brigadier sent down a curly one. "Do you," he demanded balefully, "consider yourself a supporter of lost causes?" (Gentle reader of the current, religious, and thoughtful, how would you have responded?) Mercifully I have no recollection of how I coped with the situation. By the time all other candidates had presumably withdrawn and they got around to offering me the job, I had already committed myself to another area where Lost Causemanship was not regarded as a burning issue.

Many years later, a not dissimilar matter arose during my candidacy for a key post in my own denomination. This was admittedly something of a kite-flying ploy, for while the establishment encouraged a nodding acquaintance with the Scarlet Woman, I was known to be in league with her detractors. Again, however, I made the short list.

The selection committee was courteous, friendly, and (like the earlier chaplain-seekers) tactful enough during a lengthy interview to raise not a single theological or religious question. Only on one point did they come close to it. "Are you," I was asked, "likely to take a strong stand on anything?" This was honesty indeed. Strong stands, it was implied, were definitely Out. I did not get the job, and I could appreciate the wisdom of its not being offered to one with my suspect antecedents.

Now this should be the cue for jumping on my theological steed and rushing madly off in all directions, but today I am resolved on low-keyed, feet-on-the-ground stuff. My fellow columnists on this page can, I know, be relied on to redress the balance toward controversial divinity and spiritual uplift. I want to take a strong stand on lost causes.

I am not referring to those that are irreclaimably lost, like that of the unfortunate ladies who were condemned to carry water in a sieve, or of Sisyphus the veteran stone-roller (though he got a lot of exercise on the side). Nor am I a professional espouser of lost causes, like Dean Burgon, Norman Thomas, and E. M. Forster, who almost seemed to make a career out of it.

Most of us do, however, have our list of incorrigibles. Mine includes chatterers in church before the service begins; unthoughtful hymn-singers expressing a preference for an "oldtime religion" with which they simply could not cope; Christian publishers who do not pay their contributors and rely on their goodness not to hie them before the magistrate; drivers who discuss sanctification while doing forty-five in a thirty-mile zone on the basis that they are "no longer under the law." The latter tendency genuinely mystifies me, and once I summoned up courage to say so to one totally committed to the authority of Scripture. I mentioned First Peter 2:13. "Ah," he said breezily, "I always add to that one the postscript, 'provided the ordinance is reasonable.' " The theological implications are staggering.

But that is a diversion. My friend Eutychus V has been squeezing impressive mileage out of asking readers what they would do if they were editing this journal. Eut should have known better, and thoroughly deserved the answers he got.

Nevertheless I am not too proud to learn from him. Let me take reader participation a step further, and seek advice on how to get evangelicals to meet literary deadlines solemnly undertaken. Evangelicals, I said deliberately, because piety and procrastination are often found in bizarre affinity. I know that this is a lost cause, and that there will be muttered maledictions on my bringing it up at all; but as the organizer of sundry literary projects past and present, I am determined to strike a blow on behalf of editors and publishers everywhere—a much maligned and misunderstood breed.

It is fourteen years since I jauntily accepted my first encyclopedic assignment, one from which men wiser in their generation had recoiled in alarm. Now, a little grayer and considerably less trusting (no editor can have serious doubts about original sin), I would give some advice to those who are rashly contemplating a similar type of work: Don't do it.

If you disregard this, note the following:

1. No man is a hero to his editor; indeed, many a scholar's reputation for piety depends upon the editorial silence. The preacher-scribe is very susceptible to the double-think. Will Rogers used to say that no nation should go to war till it had paid for the last one; he might have agreed that no minister should hold forth on moral turpitude till he has fulfilled his own

ethical commitments to others. It would be tempting to emulate one Thai radio station and broadcast a list of public delinquents.

2. Theological conservatives are the worst offenders; thus in order to keep the statistics favorable I regularly sneak into the ranks a platoon of those whose theological unorthodoxy is more than offset by their meticulous attention to deadlines.

3. The ideal editor, like the ideal school principal, ought to be slightly unpopular. Coping with a couple of hundred scholars, including the normal quota of the idiosyncratic, I often think of myself in terms of Father O'Flynn, the Irish cleric famed in song and story, given to

Checkin' the crazy ones
Coaxin' onaisy ones
Liftin' the lazy ones
On wid the stick.

4. When sweet reasonableness fails, I try firmness, but the mailed fist tends to be ignored, or brings back reproachful tales of obscure ailments, unparalleled domestic calamities ("my bookcase fell on me"), strange emergencies ("I had to go to Jerusalem"), or faculty in-fighting of gory and disabling dimensions. One brash young professor said I didn't know that no writer took an editor seriously unless subjected to merciless harassment. He'd caught me out, for I *didn't* know that, me with a touching addiction to Robert W. Service ("a promise made is a debt unpaid").

5. So we come to sneaky and unscrupulous tactics, and I offer a piece of counsel gratis to the longsuffering who have read thus far: The most effective way to get a long overdue article out of a laggard is to *write to his wife*. And make it poignant. "But that's fiendish!" commented a young Episcopalian on whom I tried it last week. That may be so, but it shows a gratifying success rate. In the case of one wifeless scholar, I addressed a plain postcard in capital letters to his dog; his tail will forever wag in my heart, for I had the material within a week.

The trouble is, by the time I get around to *editing* I have been exhausted by the preliminaries. There's a lesson in that somewhere if I could just lay my finger on it.

CRITIQUE OF
"Ducking the Mailed Fist"

Did you read J. D. Douglas's piece more than twice and still find yourself wondering just what he was saying?

This is the product of a man guilty of the very writing sins he exposes. I'm only guessing, mind you, but could it be that Douglas procrastinated and then had to force himself to write his column? Surely this is off-the-top-of-the-head stuff; you see no evidence of research or even outlining.

So why is something that would probably fail as a college paper (because it has little to say and goes "round the barn" a time or two) judged a winner by the Evangelical Press Association and reprinted here as a model to budding writers?

Because humor is the category, and this is funny.

To be funny on paper you must break rules. Anything truly funny that you have ever read broke the rules of composition. Test that and see if it's so.

Douglas begins with paragraph after paragraph of throat-clearing. It's flip and throwaway style, like that of an old man who knows there's as much fun in the telling as in the story. It doesn't make it any more relevant to the piece, and we find ourselves wondering why in the world he's telling us all this.

He hints at a more serious reason — espousing lost causes — and then wants us to accept that one such burning matter is chatterers in church!

Can you see the writer at the typewriter, imagining you the reader with the frozen smile and glazed eyes of one who doesn't "get" it? Douglas hesitates and considers adding, "You had to be there."

So here is a man with a deadline—probably already past—and space to fill. He's bright. He's funny. He has a reputation. He can pull this off and get away with it.

A new writer wouldn't submit it. But a man with an audience can break every rule, lay down his points — insignificant and hard to recognize though they may be (directionless too, while we're at it)—and then polish the flippancy and the irreverence. And there you have it. Humor.

What's funny about it besides the way he words it? What's funny about a comedian who exaggerates, "Excuse me!" Or another who talks about leaving crumbs in the bottom of the water bottle in the refrigerator?

It's funny because you've been there. You don't have to identify with every detail of Douglas's projects or experiences. There are enough similarities in your life to make this work for you.

It made me laugh because I can identify with it. I still don't know what his job interviews had to do with anything else in the piece, but when he got around to whatever it was he was trying to get around to, I was with him.

I was procrastinating even in writing this critique. It was late. I was getting reminders. I had space to fill. Lucky for me, Douglas had done his job so *I* had something to work with. Something to say.

You had to be there.

Jerry B. Jenkins
Executive Editor
Moody Monthly

RESEARCH

1. Take notes on three articles on humorous writing that have appeared in *Writer* and *Writer's Digest* during the last three years.

2. Study three humorous articles in the last six issues of *Reader's Digest*. What humor techniques have the authors used?

3. Examine several Christian magazines to see how often humorous articles are being published.

4. What techniques, approaches, slants, and structures has Eutychus used in *Christianity Today* during the last six months?

5. Start your collection of humorous articles from both Christian and secular publications—including your daily newspaper.

PRACTICE

1. Make a list of six subjects that would be appropriate for a humorous article. Look for the absurd and ridiculous aspects of life.

2. Construct three article overviews based on the six subjects selected for Practice item 1 (i.e., subject, purpose, sources, slant or focus, readership, and intended publications).

3. Write a topic outline with a thesis from the overview you like the best. Ask one or two friends for their opinions.

4. Write the article. While revising, check carefully to see if the thesis and purpose come through clearly and forcefully.

5. Submit the article to the editor of the target publication. Always keep a copy of what you submit.

DISCUSSION

1. In light of Fowler's observation that the purpose of humor is discovery, what insights about human nature are presented in the two articles in this chapter?

2. Do you agree with Myrna Grant that the conclusion of "Life Among the Nacirema" diminishes the impact of the article?

3. In addition to the examples noted by Grant, cite more illustrations of creative diction as used by Steve Lawhead in his *Campus Life* article.

4. Are there British expressions in "Ducking the Mailed Fist" that might be unclear to some American readers of *Christianity Today?* If so, cite some examples and suggest some American synonyms.

5. Are evangelical magazines using enough humor? Is the quality good? Is the impact effective?

Appendix

Doctrinal Statement of the Evangelical Press Association

a. We believe the Bible to be the inspired, the only infallible, authoritative Word of God.
b. We believe that there is one God, eternally existent in three persons: Father, Son and Holy Spirit.
c. We believe in the deity of our Lord Jesus Christ, in His virgin birth, in His sinless life, in His shed blood, in His bodily resurrection, in His ascension to the right hand of the Father, and in His personal return in power and glory.
d. We believe that for the salvation of lost and sinful man, regeneration by the Holy Spirit is absolutely essential.
e. We believe in the present ministry of the Holy Spirit by whose indwelling the Christian is enabled to live a godly life.
f. We believe in the resurrection of both the saved and the lost: of them that are saved unto the resurrection of life, and of them that are lost unto the resurrection of damnation.
g. We believe in the spiritual unity of believers in our Lord Jesus Christ.

Code of Ethics of the Evangelical Press Association

The primary function of Christian publications is to advance the work and witness of Jesus Christ in the world. Our first responsibility is faithfulness to the truth and will of God, as it is expressed in the Bible, which we accept as the infallible revelation of God, our only authority for faith and conduct. This dedicates Christian journalism to serve the highest welfare of mankind.

As our secondary responsibility we recognize our duty to serve the "principles, purposes, and policies" of the cause or organization our publications represent.

I

The freedom of Christian publications to publish the truth and to set forth the principles contained in the Word of God must be zealously guarded. Christian publications should be honest and courageous in all their presentations. Sincerity, truthfulness and accuracy should characterize all Christian publications.

II

Readers of Christian publications have the right to expect that news items and articles published are written truthfully. Those responsible for the publication must exercise the utmost care that nothing contrary to the truth is published. It is the privilege, as it is the duty, of a Christian publication to make prompt and complete correction of its own serious mistakes of fact or opinion, whatever their origin.

III

Christian publications are conscious of their duty to protect the good name and reputation of others. Should it become necessary at any time to engage in controversy for the defense and maintenance of the truth, care should be taken to present opposing views honestly and fairly.

IV

Christian publications do not publish any material except with consent of the authors or owner. The editing of the articles should not change the thoughts expressed by the author, without consultation with, and permission of, the author. Articles published in other magazines should not be reproduced without first receiving permission. Such articles should receive proper acknowledgment. Whenever previously published material is used, care should be taken to ascertain and acknowledge—if possible—authorship and source.

Glossary of Writing and Allied Terms

Anecdote
A short narrative that tells of one incident; usually illustrates a point in an article.

Article Type
A specialized kind of feature article (e.g., expository, interview, personality).

Associated Church Press (ACP)
321 James, Geneva, IL 60134, (312) 323-1055. A religious press organization and fellowship of the editors of publications in the mainline Protestant denominations.

Author Intrusion
A writer's inclusion of his reactions in a feature article, often detracting from the article's main subject, thesis, and impact.

Biographical Article
A feature article that attempts to give an overview of the subject's entire life.

Body
The main section of a news or feature article, usually constituting eighty–eighty-five percent of the article, subdivided into two to five main points.

Build-up
The systematic presentation of documentation in a story that leads to the next main point; in fiction and narrative writing, the rising action leading to the climax.

By-line
The author's name, usually placed under the title in the printed version of the article.

Cliché

An overused word, phrase, or expression that does not cause the reader to visualize the subject (e.g., "clear as crystal").

Climax

A term used in fiction to indicate the place in the plot when the reader can tell if the leading character will succeed or fail; also used in reference to to similar experience of the main personality in narrative, first-person, and personality articles.

Column

A regularly appearing feature, section, or department in a periodical using the same heading; usually written by the same person each time with a new title for each new column.

Conflict

The struggle of two opposing forces, people, or movements; an important element in both fiction and nonfiction to attract and maintain reader interest.

Critical Review

An evaluation of a book, article, record, cassette, play, film, musical presentation, or work of art designed to help the reader make a selection.

Critique

An evaluation of a piece of writing.

Dialogue

The directly quoted speech of two or more people.

Diction

A writer's selection of words, especially nouns and verbs.

Display Window

The title, subtitle, and lead of a feature article.

Documentation

Giving support or evidence to a generalized statement by the use of one or more of the following: quotations, anecdotes, dialogue, illustrations, and description.

Editorial

An opinion piece designed to influence public opinion that states the position of the editor, publisher, or guest editorialist.

Editorial *We*

Use of the first-person plural pronoun *we*, often creating ambiguity concerning which or how many people the writer means.

Editorial Well
The section of a magazine in which the main feature articles appear.

Euphemism
An indirect method of expression (e.g., "passing away" instead of 'dying"): robs standard English prose of its natural impact.

Evangelical
A person who believes that one receives God's forgiveness for sins and His eternal life through a personal act of faith in His Son, Jesus Christ, and who believes that the Bible is an authoritative guide for daily living.

Evangelical Press Association (EPA)
The professional organization for publishers and editors of evangelical periodicals; headquartered in Overland Park, Kansas; Mr. Gary Warner, executive secretary, P. O. Box 4550, Overland Park, KS 66204 (913) 381-2017.

EP News Service
The news service of the Evangelical Press Association; sent to member editors and publishers.

Expository Article
A feature article whose main purpose is to explain a subject to the reader.

Expository Writing
Writing whose main purpose is to explain.

Feature Article
A special treatment of a subject that goes deeper than the reporting level, usually focusing on a person, event, process, organization, movement, trend, or issue; written to explain, encourage, help, analyze, challenge, motivate, warn, or entertain—as well as to inform.

Flashback
An insertion, usually in anecdotal form, in the chronology of a narrative that recalls or recreates a previous occurrence.

Focus
A part of the subject of an article that has special significance for the intended readership.

Free-lancer
A writer who submits manuscripts to a publication, usually as a result of a query letter or an assignment from an editor; not a staff member of a magazine.

How-It-Was-Done Article
The process or utility article written from the third-person perspective and in the past tense.

How-To-Do-It Article
A process or utility article that is written from the first- or second-pronoun perspective and in the present tense.

Humor
The amusing or comical aspects of life that often add warmth and color to a feature article when placed strategically.

Humorous Article
An article designed to entertain, explain, or inform that uses humor as the device to attract the reader's interest.

Interrogatives
The basic news questions that should be answered in a news story or feature article: who, what, why, when, where, and how.

Interview Article
A feature article that emphasizes the significant statements made by a person of interest to a specific readership.

Inverted Pyramid or Triangle
The standard structure for a news story with the lead followed by the body of facts developed in descending order of importance.

Lead
The introduction of an article; it can be the first sentence, first paragraph, or the first three or four paragraphs depending on the length of the article, usually five–ten percent of the total article.

Liaison
The official publication of the Evangelical Press Association.

Multi-Sense Description
Writing that attempts to recreate as many of the sensory reactions as are inherent in a scene (seeing, hearing, smelling, touching, and tasting).

Narrative
The recreation of an event or series of incidents or experiences, usually in chronological order; written from first-person or third-person pronoun perspective.

National Association of Evangelicals (NAE)
A voluntary association of evangelical denominations, churches, schools,

organizations, and individuals based on a seven-point statement of faith; composed of 3.5 million members in 35,000 churches (38 complete denominations and individual churches from 31 other groups); Box 28, Wheaton, IL 60187.

News Article
An article structured in the inverted pyramid pattern and designed to answer the basic interrogative questions: who, what, when, where, why, and how.

Over-The-Transom Manuscript
An unassigned manuscript submitted to an editor; an unsolicited article.

Overview
One of the first steps in planning an article; a listing of the article's subject, purpose, possible sources, intended readership, slant or focus, and potential markets (three or more periodicals).

Personality Article
A feature article that highlights one person's character and his significant accomplishments.

Perspective
The angle from which the writer views an incident or scene: It can be spatial (from different locations), chronological (at different times), or grammatical (first-person pronoun, "I" or "we"; second-person, "you"; or third-person, "he, she, it, or they").

Publication, Intended
The periodical, journal, or magazine the free-lancer aims at while writing the article.

Purpose
The specific objective the author has for each article. (e.g., to explain, to exhort, to amplify, to illuminate, to challenge, to stimulate, to entertain, to inform, to encourage, to warn, to motivate).

Query letter
A free-lancer's letter to an editor outlining an article idea.

Q-and-A
Question-and-answer format for an interview article.

Readership
The individual or group of individuals a writer keeps in mind as the potential audience while he plans, researches, and writes the feature article.

Relevance
The quality of writing that touches the needs and interests of the readers.

Religious News Service (RNS)
An organization in New York City that supplies daily news reports on the world of religion to periodicals, radio and television stations, and individuals who subscribe to the service. 43 W. 57th St., New York, N.Y. 10019.

S.A.S.E.
A self-addressed, stamped envelope that a free-lancer should include when submitting a query or manuscript to an editor.

Satire
Ridicule that aims at reform.

Selection
The part of research that involves choosing the facts most relevant to the article's thesis and that are most significant and relevant to the reader.

Show, Don't Tell, Principle
Letting the reader see the subject of an article through anecdotes, quotations, and description.

Side Bar
A small article that accompanies a main article; it usually provides background or another angle on the subject of the full-length feature.

Significance
The element of importance in a subject as viewed from the reader's perspective; usually, the higher the significance level, the higher the reader interest.

Slant
Approaching a subject from a perspective that has high appeal for the intended readership; also used to refer to an angle of a story.

Sobriquet
A hackneyed nickname used in place of a proper noun (e.g., "Windy City" for Chicago).

Standing Feature
A term used in the EPA Awards Contest to refer to a column or other magazine content (such as news) which is one of a series appearing under a recurring head and which appears regularly in the periodical.

Style
A writer's personality as seen in his writing.

Subtitle
An expansion and further explanation of an article's title.

Suspense
The anticipation of a crucial happening in a story; an effective technique in maintaining reader interest is the conflict element of a story or article.

Tautology
Unnecessary repetition.

Thesis
A one-sentence statement of the main idea of an article.

Title
The headline of an article.

Tone
An author's attitude toward his subject and his readership (e.g., respectful, satirical, questioning).

Topic Outline
The structure of a feature article, usually including two to five main points expressed in short phrases or single words; should be preceded by the thesis for the article.

Transition
The smooth movement from one point of writing to another (word to word, sentence to sentence, paragraph to paragraph, section to section); often accomplished by pronouns and synonyms; a mark of the conscientious writer.

Wit
Surprising the reader through the imaginative use of words and ideas.

The Evangelical Free-Lancer's Library

The editor has found the following sources helpful in free-lance writing. Most of the reference works can be found in college and public libraries. Most writers will probably want to purchase books for a personal library during a period of months or years.

I. REFERENCES

Angione, Howard. *The Associated Press Stylebook and Libel Manual.* New York: The Associated Press, 1977.

Bartlett, John. comp. *Familiar Quotations*. Emily Monison Beck, ed. 14th ed. Boston: Little, Brown, and Company, 1968.

Bernstein, Theodore M. *Careful Writer: A Modern Guide to English Usage.* New York: Atheneum, 1965.

The Bible (as many different translations, versions, and paraphrases as the writer can obtain).

Burack, A. S., ed. *The Writer's Handbook.* Boston: The Writer, 1971.

Copperud, Roy H. *A Dictionary of Usage and Style.* New York: Hawthorn Books, 1964.

Evans, Bergen and Evans, Cornelia. *A Dictionary of Contemporary American Usage*. New York: Random House, 1957.

Fowler, Henry W. *A Dictionary of Modern English Usage*. 2nd ed. Gowers, Ernest, ed. Oxford University Press, 1966.

Literary Market Place: With Names and Numbers. New York and London: R. R. Bowker Company (published annually).

A Manual of Style: For Authors, Editors, and Copywriters. 12th rev. ed. Chicago: The University of Chicago Press, 1969.

The Misspeller's Dictionary. Peter and Craig Norback, eds. New York: Quadrangle, The New York Times Book Company, 1974.

New Bible Commentary. rev. ed. Donald Guthrie, ed. Grand Rapids: William B. Eerdmans, 1970.

New Bible Dictionary. James D. Douglas, ed. Grand Rapids: Wm. B. Eerdmans, 1962.

The New Roget's Thesaurus in Dictionary Form. new ed. Norman Lewis. New York: G. P. Putnam's Sons, 1978.

Strong's Exhaustive Concordance of the Bible. Nashville: Thomas Nelson, 1977.

Webster's Biographical Dictionary. Springfield, Mass.: G. and C. Merriam, 1976.

Webster's Collegiate Thesaurus. Springfield, Mass.: G. and C. Merriam, 1976.

Webster's New Collegiate Dictionary. 8th ed. Springfield, Mass.: G. and C. Merriam, 1973 (based on *Webster's Third New International Dictionary*, 1966).

Webster's New Geographical Dictionary. rev. ed. Springfield, Mass.: G. and C. Merriam, 1977.

Writer's Market. Cincinnati: *Writer's Digest* (published annually).

II. BOOKS

Anderson, Margaret J. *The Christian Writer's Handbook*. New York: Harper and Row, 1977.

Copperud, Roy H. *Words on Paper*. New York: Hawthorn Books, 1960.

Engel, James. *Contemporary Christian Communications*. Nashville: Thomas Nelson, 1979.

Gunning, Robert. *How to Take Fog Out of Writing*. Chicago: Dartnell Corporation, 1964.

Gunning, Robert. *Technique of Clear Writing*. rev. ed. New York: McGraw-Hill, 1964.

Hodges, John C. and Whitten, Mary E. *Harbrace College Handbook*. 8th ed. New York: Harcourt, Brace, Jovanovich, 1977.

Holmes, Marjorie. *Writing the Creative Article*. rev. ed. Boston: The Writer, 1973.

Hough, George A. 3rd. *News Writing*. Boston: Houghton Mifflin, 1975.

Nichols, Sue. *Words on Target: For Better Christian Communication*. Atlanta: John Knox Press, 1963.

Patterson, Helen M. *Writing and Selling Feature Articles*. 3rd ed. Englewood Cliffs, N. J.: Prentice-Hall, 1965.

Schapper, Beatrice. *How to Make Money Writing Articles*. New York: Arco, 1974.

Schell, Mildred. *Wanted: Writers for the Christian Market*. Valley Forge: Judson Press, 1975.

Strunk, W., Jr. and White, E. B. *The Elements of Style*. 3rd ed. New York: Macmillan, 1979.

Successful Writers and Editors Guidebook. ed. by Christian Writers Institute. Carol Stream, Illinois: Creation House, 1977.

Williamson, Daniel R. *Feature Writing for Newspapers*. New York: Hastings House, 1975.

Wirt, Sherwood Eliot. *Getting Into Print: Solid Help for Christian Writers*. Nashville: Thomas Nelson, 1977.

Wirt, Sherwood Eliot. *You Can Tell The World: New Directions For Christian Writers*. Minneapolis: Augsburg, 1975.

III. MAGAZINES

Columbia Journalism Review
Quill
Writer
Writer's Digest

Evangelical Press Association Market Guide

INTRODUCTION

The query is a letter written by a free-lancer to an editor suggesting an article idea.

The query letter is one of the most important pieces a free-lancer writes. This special letter tells the editor volumes about the prospective writer: his word craftmanship, conscientiousness, desire to be published, organizational and logic abilities, knowledge of the magazine, and intended readership.

Several years ago, the editors of *Moody Monthly* assembled the following suggestions for writing the query letter:

SUCCESSFUL QUERY-LETTER WRITING

Perhaps you're an old pro on queries. Relax. Do it your way. We do not hold out for a specific form or method, but we do need specifics. Be sure your approach includes:

1. *A working title* which will help us grab your idea quickly—not only the subject but the slant or direction.
2. *A backup statement* suggesting why you think the proposed article would be appreciated by our kind of readers.
3. *Some indication of proposed treatment or approach* — anecdotal, reportorial, personal experience, message, etc. In some cases it may help to include main points as you foresee them.

4. *If you foresee problems* in handling a touchy subject, reassure us by telling us so and tell us how you intend to get around them.
5. *Don't forget mechanical details:* suggested length, availability of pictures, how soon you could do it.

On certain articles, it may be easier to take the précis route. This may include:

An opening paragraph or two or three, followed by
A listing of main points in sequence, and
A wrapup statement of what the article would do for readers, treatment, proposed length, available pictures, etc.

Please keep queries concise.

Unless we have worked with you a few times before, a statement of your familiarity with the proposed subject (or available sources) together with a word about your writing experience would be helpful.

Allow us about three weeks to let our editors circulate and confer on what you are suggesting.

* * *

Always address a query to a specific editor listed in the following guide or in the magazine itself. Check the "EPA Market Guide" to see what types of manuscripts the editor wants or to see if that publication prefers completed manuscripts or queries.

Study your proposed publication carefully before submitting any manuscripts.

The periodicals listed in the "EPA Market Guide" are all members of EPA and have given their permission to be included.

EPA MARKET GUIDE

Advance

1445 Boonville Avenue, Springfield, MO 65802. (417) 862-2781, ext. 1462. Editor: Gwen Jones. Circulation: 23,500. Monthly. Readership: Assemblies of God ministers and church leaders. Purpose: To provide the ministers and local churches with promotion and program materials, church administration aids, and ministerial helps. Manuscript needs: Limited amount of free-lance material accepted: articles 800-1,000 words on preaching, doctrine, practice; sermon ideas (brief thought-starters or developed outlines); and how-to-do-it features.

Advent Christian Witness

P.O. Box 23152, Charlotte, NC 28212. (704) 545-6161. Editor: C. William Bailey. Circulation: 6,500. Monthly. Readership: members and friends of the Advent Christian Church—Families, from teens up. Purpose: Official organ of the Advent Christian General Conference. Manuscript needs: Doctrinal, inspirational and devotional, personal Christian experience; usual limit 1,000 words; would consider longer outstanding articles to be used in a series. Query first. Enclose S.A.S.E.

Alliance Witness, The

Box C, Nyack, NY 10960. (914) 353-0750. Editor: H. Robert Coles. Circulation: 52,000. Biweekly. Readership: Members and adherents of The Christian and Missionary Alliance; evangelical Christians of all denominations. Purpose: A magazine of Christian life and missions. Manuscript needs: Bible exposition, teen-age-oriented material, home and family articles, first-person testimonies of significant spiritual transformation or development. 1,200-1,500 words.

Arkenstone

P.O. Box 12926, St. Louis, MO 63141. (314) 752-3983. Editor: Kathleen Thro. Circulation: 1,000. Bimonthly. Readership: Christians interested in arts and culture. Purpose: To use arts for God's glory—a forum of discussion for problems related to the arts, Christ and the world in which we live; also as an outlet for creativity. Manuscript needs: Studies, observation, essays, on topics related to literature, painting, photography, music, dance, from a Christian perspective. Fiction and poetry also. 2,000-5,000 words. S.A.S.E.

Baptist Herald

1 South 210 Summit Ave., Oakbrook Terrace, IL 60181. (312) 495-2000. Editor: Dr. Reinhold J. Kerstan. Circulation: about 10,000. Monthly. Readership: Mainly adult readers with religious interests (North American Baptist Conference). Purpose: To inform, edify, and instruct religiously. Manuscript needs: Personal experience, interviews, inspirational, human interest. 1,000-2,000 words. Enclose S.A.S.E.

Bread

6401 The Paseo, Kansas City, MO 64131. (816) 333-7000. Editor: Debbie Salter. Circulation: 50,000. Monthly. Readership: Junior-high and Senior-high who are members of a Nazarene church or part of the outreach ministry. Purpose: To feature personal growth articles that will minister to felt needs of a teenager and inspire application. Manuscript needs: First-person experiences as a disciple—500-1,200 words; As-told-to articles dealing with teenage themes—1,000-1,700 words; Bible study insights—100-500 words; Minor emphasis on fiction (not over 3,500 words) and poetry (10-30 lines with a specific life application message). Query first. Enclose S.A.S.E.

Brethren Evangelist, The

524 College Ave., Ashland, OH 44805. (419) 389-2611. Editor: Richard Winfield, Circulation: 3,800. Monthly. Readership: Members and friends of the Brethren Church. Purpose: To help our readers become effective disciples of Jesus Christ and responsible, active participants in the life and ministry of the Brethren Church. Manuscript needs: We will *consider* any subject, spiritually significant and interesting and vital to our readers. Biblical themes if heavy on application, Christian home and family, contemporary issues, personal instruction and Christian growth, church administration and methods of Christian work. 1,500 words, max. prefer 1,000 or less. Enclose S.A.S.E.

Calvinist Contact

99 Niagara Street, St. Catharines, Ontario, Canada L2R 4L3. (416) 682-5614. Editor: Keith Knight. Circulation: 10,200. Weekly. Readership: Reformed (Calvinistic) Christians with a Dutch historic background; education from elementary to post-graduate school. Purpose: To provide a weekly forum of world and national events from a Christian perspective. Manuscript needs: "Newsy" events such as interviews with well-known Christians, reports of action by Christian organizations, etc. Maximum length: five pages, double-spaced. Query first. Enclose S.A.S.E.

Campus Life Magazine

Box 419, Wheaton, IL 60187. (312) 668-6600. Editor: Steve Lawhead. Circulation: 225,000. Ten times per year. Readership: Ages 15-22 (high school and college readers). Manuscript needs: Short fiction, personal stories, weird or off-beat sports or activities (ex: bathtub ski race, snurfing, dog-sledding, dog frisbee, human-powered vehicle race)—anything a high-school reader is likely to be interested in. Enclose S.A.S.E.

Challenger

P.O. Box 617, Petaluma, CA 94952. (707) 762-1314. Editor: Reverend Wally Yew. Circulation: 10,000. Monthly. Readership: Mostly Chinese Christians. Young intellectuals. Purpose: To educate and challenge Christians on the needs of the Chinese. Manuscript needs: 500-1,500 words. Content: evangelistic, contemporary issues related to Christians in general and Chinese Christians in particular, and missions. Enclose S.A.S.E.

Christ for the Nations

Box 24910, Dallas, TX 75224. (214) 376-1711. Editor: Mrs. Gordon Lindsay. Circulation: 130,000. Monthly. Readership: Pentecostals, Charismatics. Purpose: An in-house organ of the larger missionary service organization. Manuscript needs: MSS that inspire, teach, train, and appeal. Some poetry. Some photography. Do not use denominational and doctrinal slanted articles. Query first. Enclose S.A.S.E.

Christian Athlete, The

1125 Grand, Suite 812, Traders Bank Bldg., Kansas City, MO 64106. (816) 842-3908. Editor: Skip Stogsdill. Circulation: 50,000. Monthly except May–October. Readership: Predominantly high school and college athletes and coaches, plus interested adults. Purpose: To present Jesus' alternative lifestyle to the sport/faith community. Manuscript needs: Profiles/articles no more than 1,000 words built around the topic for each issue. Query first to get list of topics for the year. Enclose S.A.S.E.

Christian Courier, The

915 W. Wisconsin Ave., Suite 214. Milwaukee, WI 53233. (414) 271-6400. Editor: Robin Kaczmarek. Circulation: 15,000. Monthly. Readership: Christian and non-Christian. Purpose: To reach the city with a Christian message. Manuscript needs: Any and all. Enclose S.A.S.E.

Christian Herald

40 Overlook Drive, Chappaqua, NY 10514. (914) 769-9000. Editor: David Kucharsky. Circulation: 270,000. Monthly. Readership: evangelical Christian families. Purpose: To glorify God by giving people a fuller understanding of biblical truth. Manuscript needs: Those that are provocative, positive, informative, and inspiring. We want articles that answer questions and problems, and we also are looking for lots of material on Christian people. The personality profiles must be highly readable; cliché-ridden superficial testimonies will not do. Up to 3,500 words (shorter preferred). Query first. Enclose S.A.S.E.

Christian Home and School

865 28th Street, S.E., Grand Rapids, MI 49508. (616) 245-8618. Editor: Philip Elve, Ph.D. Circulation: 15,000. Ten times a year. Readership: Professional educators; families; pastors; all those interested in Christian day schools. Purpose: A magazine devoted to the cause of education in the Christian home and in the parentally controlled Christian day school. Query first.

Christian Life

Gundersen and Schmale Roads, Wheaton, IL 60187. (312) 653-4200. Editor: Robert Walker. Circulation: 100,000. Monthly. Readership: Mostly born-again Christians from a cross-section of denominations: Baptists, Catholics, Lutherans, Methodists, Pentecostals, Presbyterians, C&MA, etc. Purpose: To show God at work in our world today. Manuscript needs: We are looking for well-researched articles on subjects of significance to Christians. They should be anecdotal in approach. Length: 1,500 to 2,500 words. Enclose S.A.S.E.

Christian Living

850 N. Grove, Elgin, IL 60120. (312) 741-2400. Editor: Larry Brook. Circulation: Not available. Quarterly. Readership: High school students involved in Sunday school. Purpose: To aid in group and individual Bible study. To illustrate how biblical principles are fleshed out by young people and adult models. Manuscript needs: Well-researched, contemporary, interesting articles on topics of interest to senior highs. Features on teens working in community and church, especially unusual projects. Teens doing unusual things which may serve as idea-starters for readers. For example, one Chicago group came up with unique ways to earn money to send a teen missionary from their church on a summer short term. Young people who have unusual experiences or accomplishments which would be an encouragement to other readers. Slides appreciated with each article. Query non-fiction. Prefer completed articles for fiction. Enclose S.A.S.E.

Christianity Today

465 Gundersen Drive, Carol Stream, IL 60187. (312) 682-3020. Editor: Kenneth S. Kantzer. Circulation: 155,000. Fortnightly. Readership: ministers, church leaders, thinkers. Purpose: To propagate and provide fundamental truths of Scriptures . . . strengthen and promote Christian faith, perpetuate and defend historic Christianity, promote fundamental religious training and education. Manuscript needs: Primarily concerned with topics of contemporary interest which relate theological insights to these topics in a timely and readable way. We like articles to encourage thoughtfulness in our readers. We rarely use fiction, biographical features, sermons, picture stories, technical works, or others that require more than incidental documentation, or articles advocating a particular denominational or confessional distinctive within the Christian faith. Enclose S.A.S.E.

Church Herald, The

1324 Lake Drive, S.E., Grand Rapids, MI 49506. (616) 458-5156. Editor: John Stapert. Circulation: 74,000. Biweekly. Readership: Official magazine of the Reformed Church in America. Purpose: The *Church Herald* seeks to present the Gospel of Christ and set forth the great truths in the Scriptures, to present the life and work of the Reformed Church at home and abroad, and to keep its readers informed concerning religious news and events of interest and significance in the Christian world, all that they may become more fully committed to Christ and more actively involved in the work of his Kingdom. Manuscript needs: Non-fiction—400 to 1,500 words; fiction—up to 1,500 words; children's material—short stories and articles up to 750 words; also puzzles and fillers. Poetry—preferably no more than 30 lines. Enclose S.A.S.E.

Co-Laborer

P.O. Box 1088 Nashville, TN 37202 (1134 Murfreesboro Rd.) (615) 361-1010. Editor-in-Chief: Cleo Pursell. Editor: Donna Carr. Circulation: 17,000. Quarterly. Readership: Christian women. Especially members of the Women's National Auxiliary Convention of Free Will Baptists. Purpose: Magazine and program book for Woman's Auxiliaries. Articles on missions and some inspirational or devotional materials slanted for women. Does not pay.

Connect (formerly Teen Power)

Box 513, Glen Ellyn, IL 60137. (312) 668-6000. Editor: Susan Zitzman. Exec. Ed.: Don W. Crawford. Circulation: 140,000. Quarterly in weekly parts. Readership: Teens, 12–17 (especially young teens). Purpose: Sunday school take-home paper. Manuscript needs: Stories, true and fiction, that show the teen how God's power is available to him in Jesus Christ. True stories presented in the first person, as if told by teens. Also stories about older youth or adults with experiences of interest or help to teens. Good black-and-white photos a plus. 1,000-1,500 words. Fiction should deal with teen problems of today. Short features; photo features; informative articles.

CBMC Contact

Editorial: P.O. Box 2728, Glen Ellyn, IL 60137. (312) 653-4588. Circulation: P.O. Box 3380, Chattanooga, TN 37404. (615) 698-4444. Editor: Phil Landrum. Circulation: 15,000. Bimonthly. Readership: Businessmen (mostly executives and owners). Purpose: Outreach tool to uncommitted businessmen.

Contact

P.O. Box 1088, Nashville, TN 37202. (615) 361-1010. Editor: Jack L. Williams. Circulation: 8,000. Monthly. Readership: Almost exclusively denominational. Free Will Baptist pastors and laypersons. Purpose: To provide reading material that will inform, instruct, and inspire Free Will Baptists. Manuscript needs: Major articles of 800-1,200 words. Variety of subject matter acceptable if it is practical and of current interest. Query first. Enclose S.A.S.E.

Conviction

657 W. 18th St., Los Angeles, CA 90015. (213) 748-2041. Editor: Paul Zettersten. Circulation: 4,200. Monthly. Readership: Basically Charismatic. Most are attending churches affiliated with the Fellowship of Christian Assemblies. Purpose: In the interest of New Testament faith and fellowship. Manuscript needs: Evangelistic (700 words); teen-oriented (800 words); mission-oriented (1,200 words); season- and holiday-related (600-1,500 words); and articles dealing with spiritual gifts and experiences (600-1,500 words). Enclose S.A.S.E.

Covenant Companion, The

5101 N. Francisco Avenue, Chicago, IL 60625. (312) 784-3000. Editor: James R. Hawkinson. Circulation: 28,000. Twice monthly except monthly in July and

August. Readership: Official organ of the Evangelical Covenant Church of America. Purpose: To gather, enlighten, and stimulate the people we serve and promote our common mission for Jesus Christ. Manuscript needs: MSS with Christian impact—on themes relating to daily life. Generally 1,000 words or less. Enclose S.A.S.E.

Crusader Magazine

Box 7244, Grand Rapids, MI 49510. (616) 241-5616. Editor: David J. Koetje. Circulation: 12,700. Seven times a year. Readership: Boys (ages 9–14). Purpose: To help boys discover how God is at work in their lives and in the world around them. Manuscript needs: Short story fiction approximately 1,500 words. Minority-related stories. Enclose S.A.S.E.

Decision

1300 Harmon Place, Minneapolis, MN 55403. (612) 338-0500. Editor: Roger C. Palms. Circulation: 3,093,000. Monthly. Readership: Adult evangelical Christians. Purpose: To present the gospel of Jesus Christ. Manuscript needs: (1) Non-fiction articles, preferably testimonies or "as-told-to" accounts, written in the first person, that convey what Christ has done. In length the article should be approximately 1,600-1,800 words. (2) Short devotional thoughts and poems for the "The Quiet Heart" column. (3) Poems in divided stanza or single-stanza form written in free verse or rhyme form. (4) Concise narratives (800 words) written in fresh style with spiritual application. (5) Fresh illustrative and narrative material (up to 200 words) for our "Reflections" column. Enclose S.A.S.E.

Deeper Life

P.O. Box 700, San Diego, CA 92138. (714) 278-4160 ext. 73. Editor: Kirt Salisbury. Circulation: 400,000. Ten times a year. Readership: Christians of all denominations including Jewish who are interested in this ministry. Purpose: Personal ministry and news of current ministry outreaches. Manuscripts needed: Contributing editorials used only after assignment or if based on world evangelism outreaches.

Doorways

International Students, Inc., P.O. Box C, Star Ranch; Colorado Springs, CO 80901. (303) 475-9500. Editor: Hal W. Guffey; Linda M. Twedt, Assistant Editor. Circulation: 20,000. Quarterly. Readership: Mission executives (particularly those involved or interested in Muslim evangelization), Christian families across America, campus student workers, foreign student advisers, Christian internationals, missionaries who have had to return to U.S. Purpose: To inform ISI's supporters and friends of mission outreach to international visitors; to instruct and encourage American Christians to make disciples of all nations; to create an interest in ISI's missions strategy. Manuscript needs: First-person, third-person ("as-told-to") conversion stories of foreigners who found Christ in America (250-1,500 words); Book-length MSS will be considered. Also true accounts of the home as a mission field (entertaining internationals, befriending them, and sharing Christ); training materials for helping develop such a local ministry. Enclose S.A.S.E.

Eternity

1716 Spruce Street, Philadelphia, PA 19103. (215) 546-3696. Editor: William J. Petersen; Executive editor: Steve Board. Circulation: 55,000. Monthly. Readership: Informed Christians (evangelical Protestants). One-quarter are religious professionals. 85 percent college educated. National distribution. Purpose: To represent evangelical thought, inform and discuss issues of interest to evangelicals. Manuscript needs: MSS are usually less than 3,000 words. We are interested in carefully researched and skillfully written articles on matters of biblical knowledge, personal development, church issues, and ethical problems. Prefer journalistic treatment over essay type. Devotional, fiction, and poetry material accepted very sparingly. Satire welcomed. Enclose S.A.S.E.

Evangel

999 College Avenue, Winona Lake, IN 46590. (219) 267-7161. Editor: Vera Bethel. Circulation: 35,000. Weekly. Readership: Young adult (ages 25–35), urban, married. Purpose: To inspire, challenge, and inform. Manuscript needs: Personal experience non-fiction (1,000-1,500 words). Fiction on contemporary themes (1,500-2,000 words). Inspirational fillers, 200-500 words. Enclose S.A.S.E.

Evangelical Beacon, The

1515 East 66th Street, Minneapolis, MN 55423. (612) 866-3343. Editor: George M. Keck. Circulation: 35,000. Biweekly. Readership: Members, pastors, friends, constituents of the Evangelical Free Church of America. Purpose: Official publication of EFCA—information, inspiration, evangelism. Manuscript needs: Personal testimonies (EFCA connection helpful), articles on Christian life and conduct, how Scripture has been applied to a situation or need, biblical approaches to social problems, short devotionals, humor, etc. (100 to 2,000 words). Enclose S.A.S.E.

Evangelical Review

2751 Buford Highway, N.E., Atlanta, GA 30324. (404) 325-7857. Editor: Robert Hill. Circulation: 225,000. Quarterly. Readership: Those interested in missions, education, evangelism. Manuscript needs: Current news items among evangelicals.

Evangelizing Today's Child

6136 W. Roxbury Place, Littleton, CO 80123. (303) 979-3313. Editor: B. Milton Bryan. Circulation: 38,000. Bimonthly. Readership: Sunday school teachers, Good News Club teachers from evangelical churches. Purpose: To equip Christians to win and disciple children today. Manuscript needs: Christian education re: children (2,000-3,000 words). Especially interested in feature and first-person accounts about childhood conversion and evangelism of children. Query first. Enclose S.A.S.E.

Faith Aflame

P.O. Box 1111, Lynchburg, VA 24505. (804) 528-4112. Editor: Dr. Elmer Towns. Circulation: 1,000,000. Bimonthly. Readership: General Christian audience. Purpose: (1) To inspire Christians to live a consistent Christian life, (2) to challenge churches to soulwinning, and (3) to publicize the ministry of The Old-Time Gospel Hour. Manuscript needs: Only one article per issue is accepted from writers (600-1,200 words). Article must challenge readers to a specific aspect of the Christian life. Do not submit general articles. Enclose S.A.S.E.

Family Life Today

Gospel Light Publications, 110 W. Broadway, Glendale, CA 91204. (213) 247-2330. Editor: Georgiana Walker. Circulation: 40,000. Monthly. Readership: Christian families with children from ages 0–15. Manuscript needs: Articles focused on specific aspects of Christian marriage, parenting, and family relationships. First-person features on living, coping, and serving Christ as a family. Enclose S.A.S.E.

Free Way

Box 513, Glen Ellyn, IL 60137. (312) 668-6000. Editor: Michael Sigler. Executive Editor: Don W. Crawford. Circulation: 90,000. Quarterly in weekly parts. Readership: High-schoolers and young adults. Purpose: Sunday school take-home paper—reaches unchurched also. Manuscript needs: True stories (1,000-1,500 words) showing how God has worked in a young person's life through exciting or trying circumstances. Anecdotes showing individual's humanity. Also short features (300-500 words), i.e., satire, a tip (not a sermon), insight on a Bible verse, etc. Some fiction—exception, not the rule. Photo features. Some poetry. Enclose S.A.S.E.

Group

Box 481, Loveland, CO 80537. (303) 669-3836. Editor: Thom Schultz. Circulation: 25,000. Eight times a year. Readership: Members and leaders of high-school age Christian youth groups. Purpose: To help young Christians and their youth groups become everything they can become. Manuscript needs: Articles that tell the story of successful youth groups or group projects. Groups involved in music, drama, art, helping others, missionary work, etc. are regularly spotlighted; how-to articles for fund-raising, membership building, worship planning, games, and ice breakers; scripts for original skits and mini-plays; personal growth articles are often used, especially those including exercises for the group. Also stimulation games; some articles of general interest are used—but should relate to Christian young people of high-school age (up to 2,000 words). No fiction. "Try This One" section uses short ideas for group use. These include games, ice breakers, discussion starters, role-plays, etc. (up to 500 words). Enclose S.A.S.E.

Helping Hand

P.O. Box 12609, Oklahoma City, OK 73157. (405) 787-7110, ext. 141. Editor: Alfreda Flowers. Circulation 7,500. Readership: Women. Manuscript needs: Short stories 1,200 words or less; essays 650 words; poetry; feature 1,200 words or less. Enclose S.A.S.E.

Herald of Holiness

6401 The Paseo, Kansas City, MO 64131. (816) 333-7000. Editor: W. E. McCumber. Circulation: 187,000. Semi-monthly. Readership: Protestant, evangelical, Wesleyan largely. (Official organ of the Church of the Nazarene.) Purpose: To inform and inspire effective Christian living. Manuscript needs: Doctrinal, practical, inspirational, with high human interest quotient, non-technical in language, 800-1,200 words. Enclose S.A.S.E.

High Adventure

1445 Boonville Avenue, Springfield, MO 65802. (417) 862-2781, ext. 1497. Editor: Johnnie Barnes. Circulation: 36,000. Quarterly. Readership: Adolescent boys. Purpose: To provide boys with worthwhile, enjoyable leisurely reading. To challenge them in narrative form to higher ideals and greater spiritual dedication. To perpetuate the spirit of the Royal Rangers program through stories, ideas, and illustrations. Manuscript needs: Adventure stories (1,200 words), western and pioneer adventure type stories (1,200 words), nature study features (500 words), campcraft features (500 words), special devotions. Query first. Enclose S.A.S.E.

HIS Magazine

5206 Main Street, Downers Grove, IL 60515. (312) 964-5700. Editor: Linda Doll. Circulation: 30,000. Monthly—Oct.–June. Readership: HIS is edited primarily for the Christian student on the secular campus. Purpose: HIS seeks to help the Christian student deepen his knowledge of the Christian faith. Manuscript needs: Brief articles written from a biblical perspective and aimed at students in areas such as personal relationships, small groups, love-sex-marriage, adjusting to college, Bible exposition, relations to parents, personal testimonies of Christians who have had crises, prayer, group Bible study, unity and division, a lifestyle that's Christian, areas of public morality and social concern, a Christian's humor, satire, and fantasy. Enclose S.A.S.E.

His People

Penthouse 5, Radisson Denver Hotel, 1790 Grant Street, Denver, CO 80203. (303) 861-2040. Editor: Dick Reynolds. Circulation: 15,000. Monthly. Readership: Primarily Christian-evangelical. Purpose: To share news of what's happening in Christian work in region. Manuscript needs: Personal interview with Christians—1. Known personalities; 2. Christian-next-door types with good personal story to tell; 3. Christian organizations not heavily covered by press—good works. Query first. Enclose S.A.S.E.

Impact

Conservative Baptist Foreign Mission Society (CBFMS), Box 5, Wheaton, IL 60187. (312) 665-1200. Editor: Lynda Johnson. Circulation: 35,000. Six times per year. Readership: Conservative Baptist constituency. PurposeTo present a realistic, challenging picture of missions today. Poems, photos, or articles related to missions (the biblical basis, the need for missions, one's experience overseas—preferably those who served with CBFMS). Up to 2,400 words. Query first. Enclose S.A.S.E.

Insight

P.O. Box 7244, Grand Rapids, MI 49510. (616) 241-5616. Editor: James C. Lont. Assistant Editor: Denise A. Goff. Circulation: 22,000. Ten times per year. Readership: Primarily high-school age young people who are members of youth groups. Purpose: A Calvinistic youth magazine for young people ages 15–19 years old. Manuscript needs: Most *Insight* readers are well-exposed to the Christian faith. We are constantly looking for articles and poems that are fresh and that present the Christian life realistically. MSS. must not use religious clichés or solve problems with simplistic spiritualized answers that don't really take the struggle into account. Enclose S.A.S.E.

Interlit

820 N. Grove, Elgin, IL 60120. (312) 741-2400. Editor: Gladys J. Peterson. Circulation: 8,000. Quarterly. Readership: Missionaries, nationals, publishers, academic personnel, and others involved in a Christian communication ministry. Purpose: News bulletin for those engaged in Christian publishing, literacy, communication training, and mass media around the world. Manuscript needs: Articles dealing with literature, literacy, communication training, and the mass media. Almost all articles are assigned. Query first. Enclose S.A.S.E.

Journal of Christian Camping

P.O. Box 400, Somonauk, IL 60552. (815) 786-8453. Editor: Bob Kerstetter. Circulation: 3,600. Bimonthly. Readership: Professionals and others interested in organized youth and adult camping. Purpose: To improve the overall quality of camping ministry. Manuscript needs: 1,000-3,000 words on any single aspect of camping. Study publication first. Will send sample copy for $1.00; writer's guidelines free. No first-person writing at all. Query first. Enclose S.A.S.E.

Kids!

Box 2000, Marion, IN 46952. (317) 674-3301, ext. 147. Editor: Virginia Jeffries. Circulation: 11,000. Ten times per year. Readership: Children, grades 1–6. Purpose: To build Christian character. Manuscript needs: Arts, crafts, projects, games, action-oriented stories, true-life adventures, inspirational (children overcoming problems), humor (family life, school, church), church history, informational (current issues) 500-750 words. Enclose S.A.S.E.

Light and Life

999 College Avenue, Winona Lake, IN 46590. (219) 267-7161. Editor: G. Roger Schoenhals. Circulation: 58,000. Five times quarterly. Readership: *Light and Life* is the denominational organ of the Free Methodist Church. Yet, over half of the readers are not Free Methodists. This indicates the outreach dimension of our editorial philosophy. All ages, but primarily college and up. Purpose: To proclaim the good news of Jesus Christ; to serve the needs of persons; to draw persons to Christ and the church; to stimulate Christian growth and responsible Christian living; to present the message, ministries, and happenings of the Free Methodist Church. Manuscripts needed: First-person lead pieces: 1,500 word first-person account of God's help in time of personal crisis. Practical how-to pieces on Christian discipleship (750 words). Devotional articles with touch of humor (750 words). Enclose S.A.S.E.

Lighted Pathway

1080 Montgomery Avenue, Cleveland, TN 37311. (616) 474-4512. Editor: Hoyt E. Stone. Monthly. Readership: Youth emphasis/Family. Purpose: Inspiration. Manuscript needs: Short stories, human interest articles, showing how young people, especially teens and collegians, cope with everyday problems. Mostly 1,000 words, some variation for special occasion issues such as Christmas and Easter. Christ-centered. Enclose S.A.S.E.

Live

1445 Boonville, Springfield, MO 65802 (417) 862-2781, ext. 1209. Editor: Kenneth D. Barney. Circulation: 223,000. Monthly. Readership: Adults. Purpose: To show adults solving realistic problems through Christian principles. Manuscript needs: Fiction—1,200-2,000 words. Non-fiction—up to 1,000 words. Fillers up to 500 words. Use very few serials, but will consider four- to six-part stories if each part conforms to average word length for short stories. All special day material should be sent one year in advance. Enclose S.A.S.E.

Living Today

Scripture Press, 1825 College Avenue, Wheaton, IL 60187. (312) 668-6000. Editor: Roy Irving: Circulation: Over 160,000. Quarterly. Readership: Adult Christians in evangelical churches. Purpose: To help adults gain an understanding of every book of the Bible and to see how the truths of Scripture apply to life today. Manuscript needs: Articles of general interest that will inspire and challenge Christian adults to discover and do God's will for their lives. Articles that will illustrate God's power at work today. Topical, seasonal. Short subjects and features. 600-2,000 words. Query first. Enclose S.A.S.E.

Logos Journal

201 Church Street, Plainfield, NJ 07060. (201) 754-0745. Editor: William Carmichael. Circulation: 59,000. Bimonthly. Readership: Interdenominational, Charismatic-oriented, including a sizeable Catholic renewal audience. Purpose: To teach reconciliation and renewal, to report on the worldwide charismatic renewal. Manuscript needs: Opinion piece each issue—800-1,000 words on some issue of wide relevance to contemporary Christians. Personal story of healing/salvation/renewal—maximum 2,000 words; use one per issue. Reports of renewal in the church, in missions. Occasional personality story of men and women whose lives bring challenge and inspiration. Enclose S.A.S.E.

Looking Ahead For Junior Highs

David C. Cook Publishing Company, 850 N. Grove, Elgin, IL 60120. (312) 741-2400. Editor: Kris Miller Tomasik. Circulation: Not available. Quarterly. Readership: Junior-high students involved in Sunday school. Purpose: To aid in group and individual Bible study. To illustrate how biblical principles are lived by young people and adult models. Manuscript needs: Well-plotted fiction. Well-researched article on topics of interest to junior highs. Features on young people working in their communities and churches, doing special projects. Special interest in up-to-date minority features. Need for sports articles. Color slides or black-and-white photographs encouraged. Query non-fiction. Send completed article for fiction. Enclose S.A.S.E.

Mennonite Brethren Herald

159 Henderson Highway, Winnipeg, Manitoba R2L 1L4 (204) 667-3560. Editor: Harold Jantz. Circulation: 10,000. Fortnightly. Readership: Mainly Mennonite Brethren families, strongly church-oriented, many professional people, housewives, Canadian. Purpose: A church-rooted, family-oriented, Mennonite periodical. Manuscript needs: Welcomes articles that attempt to relate following Jesus to the issues of daily living. Believes that discerning fellowships are the basis of healthy Christian living and wants articles which reflect that approach. Enclose S.A.S.E.

META Magazine

1600 Shattuck Avenue, Berkeley, CA 94709. (415) 548-2476. Editor: Brian Beal. Circulation: 6,300. Monthly. Readership: Young and old. Concerned with contemporary issues. Interested in finding answers to today's problems. Purpose: META endeavors to deal with meeting the needs of people. Manuscript needs: Length—1,500-3,000 words. Content: Articles should be factual and deal with scriptural perspectives. Each month META confronts various modern issues (i.e., rock music, sexual rights. lifestyles, literature, cinema etc.) with open-minded scrutiny and presents relevant biblical truths toward each subject. Query first. Enclose S.A.S.E.

Moody Monthly

2101 W. Howard Street, Chicago, IL 60645. Executive Editor: Jerry Jenkins:

Circulation: 300,000. Monthly. Readership: Conservative, evangelical, fundamental Protestants. Purpose: To encourage, inspire, inform, and broaden. Manuscript needs: Family, biblical, inspirational 1,000-2,500 words. Query first. No unsolicited MSS accepted. Enclose S.A.S.E.

New Wine Magazine

P.O. Box 9199, Ft. Lauderdale, FL 33310 (305) 971-6020. Editor: Don W. Basham. Circulation: 100,000. Monthly. Readership: Nondenominational, mostly charismatic. Purpose: To provide Bible-teaching articles and inspiring testimonies and interviews that promote Christian growth. Manuscript needs: Practical instruction from Scripture and experience, interviews with leaders in the body of Christ, testimonies. Length in double-spaced, typed pages; 5-7 pages. Enclose S.A.S.E.

Pentecostal Evangel

1445 Boonville, Springfield, MO 65802. (417) 862-2781, Ext. 1455. Editor: Robert C. Cunningham. Managing Editor: Richard Champion. Purpose: To inspire readers to live for Christ; to convey significant news of the denomination and encourage readers to participate in its projects. Manuscript needs: Stories of unusual answers to prayer; devotional articles; personal testimonies; articles on home life that convey Christian teaching; seasonal material. It is important that writers be familiar with the doctrinal views of the Assemblies of God. 600-1,500 words. Enclose S.A.S.E.

Pioneer Girls Perspective

Pioneer Girls, Box 788, Wheaton, IL 60187. (312) 293-1600. Editor: Julie Smith. Circulation 18,000. Quarterly. Readership: Lay women who are leaders of Pioneer Girls clubs in local churches. Purpose: To be an educational tool for women leading Pioneer Girls clubs. Manuscript needs: Deal with growth for the woman apart from her club leader role; relationship skills; leadership skills; world of girls 6–18 including social issues; Bible study/devotional pieces. 1,000-2,500 words. Enclose S.A.S.E.

Power for Living

Scripture Press, Box 513, Glen Ellyn, IL 60137. (312) 668-6000. Editor: Anne Harrington DeWolfe. Executive Editor: Don W. Crawford. Circulation: 400,000. Quarterly. Readership: Adults. Purpose: Sunday school take-home paper. Manuscript needs: Personal experience true stories showing how God gives individual Christians power for living. Profiles for unusual or colorful Christians whose lives can be inspirational to others. Stories that offer evidence that Christianity really works (1,000-2,000 words). Shorter pieces 300-500 words needed for "Viewpoint" and "Turning Point" features in PFL. No Fiction. Clear black-and-white photos helpful. Enclose S.A.S.E.

Prayer Line, The

P.O. Box 7032, Seattle, WA 98133. (206) 363-3586. Editor: Reverend

Jonathan Edward Nisbet, Litt.D. Circulation: 3,000. Quarterly. Readership: Various classes. Purpose: To present the gospel of Jesus Christ and help with a prayer life of Christians. Manuscript needs: Salvation messages and messages that help the growth of a prayer life and spiritual life (1,500-2,000 words). Query first. Enclose S.A.S.E.

Presbyterian Journal, The

P.O. Box 3108, Asheville, NC 28802. (704) 254-4015. Reverend G. Aiken Taylor. Circulation: 22,000. Weekly. Readership: Independent—largely Presbyterian constituency scattered throughout all 50 states and some 23 foreign countries. Purpose: Seeking unity of a Presbyterian and Reformed witness in our time. Manuscript needs: Devotional—subjects of current ecclesiastical and theological interest. (Not over 3,000 words.) Enclose S.A.S.E.

Psychology for Living

1409 North Walnut Grove, Box 5,000, Rosemead, CA 91770. (213) 288-7000. Editor: Jeanette Lockerbie. Circulation: 45,000. Monthly except July. Readership: Pastors, school teachers, professional people and homemakers ages 35–55. Purpose: To help people through biblical, psychologically oriented material, cope with everyday problems. Manuscript needs. Must be Christ-centered material up to 1,200 words. Practical articles on real-life problems; steps to take in resolving problems. Abstract, textbook style not desirable. Interested in material for all age groups. Enclose S.A.S.E.

Purpose Magazine

616 Walnut Avenue, Scottdale, PA 15683. (412) 887-8500. Editor: David E. Hostetler. Circulation: 21,000. Monthly. Readership: Young adult and adult. Purpose: To encourage Christian discipleship. Manuscript needs: Articles dealing with Christians at work, serving the Lord in everything they do from recreation to professional employment. Prefer articles that include Christians serving others from within the context of Christian brotherhood and community. Maximum length is 1,200 words. Enclose S.A.S.E.

Railroad Evangelist, The

Route #4, Box 36D, Spencer, IN 47460. (812) 829-4667. Editor: Herman R. Rose. Circulation: 6,000. Monthly. Readership: Railroad employees and their friends. Purpose: To help make contact with non-churched railroad employees. To help all Christians realize all born-again people are in the same family of God. Manuscript needs: Personal testimonies of railroad people who were brought to Jesus Christ by other Christian railroad employees.

Reach

P.O. Box 12609, Oklahoma City, OK 73157. (405) 787-7110, ext. 141. Editor: Alfreda Flowers. Circulation: 5,000. Readership: Youth. Purpose: Denominational—also speaks about different current issues—share the Good News. Manuscript needs: Short stories (1,200 words or less). Enclose S.A.S.E.

Reflection

Pioneer Girls, Inc., Box 788, Wheaton, IL 60187. (312) 293-1600. Editor: Dr. Sara Anne Robertson. Associate Editor: Laura Alden. Circulation: 11,000. Bimonthly. Readership: Girls in grades 7–12 (primarily grades 7–9). Many are in Pioneer Girls clubs, but references to Pioneer Girls are minimal. Purpose: To present Christ and make scriptural truth relevant to daily living. To provide material that will develop individual and relational maturity. Manuscript needs: Non-fiction: How-to (crafts geared to teen-age girls), humor, inspirational, interview, and personal experience (800-1,800 words). Fiction: Adventure, fantasy, historical, humorous, religious, romance, and suspense (800-1,500 words). Fillers: short humor, anecdotes, cartoons, poetry. Enclose S.A.S.E.

Reformed Journal, The

255 Jefferson Avenue SE, Grand Rapids, MI 49503. (616) 459-4591. Editor: Marlin J. VanElderen. Circulation: 3,000. Monthly. Readership: (85 percent college graduates), theologically interested evangelical leaders, largely from Reformed (Calvinist) background. Purpose: To offer comment and opinion on current trends and developments in the churches and society and culture from a Reformed point of view. Manuscript needs: Short comments (2-4 typewritten double-spaced pages), articles (8-11 pages), book reviews (2-6 pages), some poetry and short stories.

Spectrum

Wheaton Graduate School, Wheaton, IL 60187. (312) 682-5000. Editor: James L. Johnson. Circulation: 4,300. Quarterly. Readership: Media students and educators. Purpose: Update on problems in media and communications. Manuscript Needs: 5,000-6,000 words on all phases of media—instructional, documented, "cutting edge" types.

Success

P.O. Box 15337, Denver, CO 80215. (303) 988-5300. Editor: Mrs. Edith Quinlan: Circulation: 15,000. Quarterly. Readership: Christian educators and workers in the local church. Purpose: To help Christian education workers achieve success in their work. Manuscript needs: Length: 300-500 words. Christian education general articles, showing the need for information and help; feature articles, success stories. Articles recounting successful teaching activities in the Sunday school or youth work. Sunday school department articles; subjects of specific aid to departmental superintendents, secretaries, teachers, or other workers. Departments: Cradle Roll; Nursery; Kindergarten; Primary; Junior; Junior-High; High-School; College–Career; Adult. Enclose S.A.S.E.

Sunday School Counselor

1445 Boonville Avenue, Springfield, MO 65802. (417) 862-2781. Editor: Sylvia Lee. Circulation: 45,000. Monthly. Readership: Sunday school teachers and leaders. Purpose: The *Sunday School Counselor* seeks to provide local Sunday school leaders, teachers, and workers with inspiration, information, and practical methods. Manuscript needs: Short, interesting items about a classroom problem and how it was solved; how-to features on such topics as discipline, teaching techniques and methods, handcrafts, Sunday school outreach, audiovisuals, teacher-pupil relationships, inexpensive means of improving facilities, and so on—from 500 to 1,200 words. Enclose S.A.S.E.

Sunday School Digest

David C. Cook Publishing Company, 850 N. Grove Avenue, Elgin, IL 60120. (312) 741-2400. Editor: Darlene McRoberts. Circulation: Not available. Weekly. Readership: Christian adults of all ages and denominations. Purpose: *Sunday School Digest* provides a weekly combination of original articles and reprints, selected to help adult readers better understand the Christian faith, to keep them informed of issues and happenings within the Christian community, and to challenge them to a deeper personal commitment to Christ. Manuscript needs: Non-fiction (with photos if possible): articles applying Christian faith to personal and world problems, personality profiles, articles of family interest, articles about exciting accomplishments of older adults. Fiction: hard-hitting, fast-moving, no preachy endings! Fillers: Anecdotes of inspirational value; jokes and short humor. Queries preferred. Enclose S.A.S.E.

Timepiece

Pendulum Ministries, 8000 East Girard Avenue, Suite 709, Denver, CO 80231. (303) 751-2894. Editor: Rex Allen John. Circulation: 2,000. Quarterly. Readership: Adult; mainly Christian. Purpose: To encourage, uplift, provoke thought and challenge to growth. Manuscript needs: Related directly to Scripture or Christian life; expository; biographical (500-2,000 words). Query first. Enclose S.A.S.E.

Today's Christian Woman

Fleming H. Revell Company, Old Tappan, NJ 07675. Circulation: 75,000. Readership: Christian women from a wide range of denominational backgrounds and interests. Purpose: To give Christian women a women's magazine they can be proud of; one that will inspire and stretch them. Enclose S.A.S.E.

Touch

Box 7244, Grand Rapids, MI 49510. (616) 241-5616. Editor: Joanne Ilbrink: Circulation: 14,500. Ten times a year. Readership: Girls ages 9–14; members of Calvinette clubs. Purpose: To help girls see how God works in their lives and the world around them. Manuscript needs: Non-fiction (How-to's, personality, biography) maximum 1,000 words. Fiction-adventure, real-life with moral implied or spelled out, humorous—maximum 1,500 words. Enclose S.A.S.E.

Trails

Pioneer Girls, Inc., Box 788, Wheaton, IL 60187. (312) 293-1600. Editor: Dr. Sara Anne Robertson. Associate Editor: Laura Alden. Circulation: 23,500. Bimonthly. Readership: Girls in grades 1–6 (primarily grades 4–6); many are in Pioneer Girls clubs, but references to Pioneer Girls are minimal. Purpose: To present Christ and make scriptural truth relevant to daily living. To provide material that will develop individual and relational maturity. Manuscript needs: How-to (crafts and puzzles); humor; informational; inspirational; contemporary issues. (800-1,800 words). Fiction: adventure, fantasy, historical, humorous, mainstream, mystery, religious (800-1,500 words). Fillers: short humor, anecdotes, cartoons, poetry. Enclose S.A.S.E.

Trim Tab

Box 87099, Atlanta, GA 20337. (404) 461-9320. Editor: Janice Barfield. Circulation: 7,000. Monthly. Readership: Airline personnel. Purpose: To lift up Christ in the airlines and to encourage believers. Manuscript needs: Testimonies of airline personnel (800-900 words). Query first. Enclose S.A.S.E.

United Evangelical Action

P.O. Box 28, Wheaton, IL 60187. (312) 665-0500. Editor: Harold B. Smith. Managing Editor: Anita Moreland. Circulation: 9,000. Readership: Evangelical leaders (clergy and active laypeople), all members of the National Association of Evangelicals. Purpose: To stimulate Christian leaders both intellectually and spiritually by confronting issues of concern in American society and the American church; and by examining evangelical Christians' role in relation to those concerns. Manuscript needs: All articles should be about 1,500 words. Topics related to the publication's purpose would include issues of debate among evangelicals, topics related to the vitality of the church in America, specific churches that have unique ministries in their locality or subjects that should be of concern to evangelicals. Enclose S.A.S.E.

Venture

Box 150, Wheaton, IL 60187. (312) 665-0630. Editor: Rick Mould. Circulation: 20,000. Eight times per year. Readership: Boys, ages 12–18 who are active in the Brigade Program of their local church. Purpose: To speak to boys on issues of concern on behalf of Christian men. Fiction and non-fiction (800-1,200 words).

Voices

2045 Half Day Road, Deerfield, IL 60015. (312) 945-6700. Editor: Randy Balmer. Circulation: 30,000. Quarterly. Readership: Friends, including alumni, of Trinity Evangelical Divinity School. Intellectually, our readers represent a broad cross-section of the evangelical community. Purpose: To stimulate thought and encourage creative action on crucial issues. Manuscript needs: Each issue approaches a different topic, and articles generally center on that topic; thus inquiry is essential. We seek thoughtful, carefully written articles that offer insight into the crucial issues facing evangelicals in the twentieth century. Critical book reviews are also welcome. Query first.

Wind

Box 2000, Marion, IN 46952. (317) 674-3301, ext. 146. Editor: Bob Black.

Circulation: 7,000. Monthly. Readership: Teens of the Wesleyan Church, primarily. Purpose: To reach teens with the claims of the gospel in a contemporary manner. Manuscript needs: Topical features, inspirational articles, and humorous pieces aimed at teens and delivered from a spiritual (not preachy-pious) angle. 1,000 words maximum. Enclose S.A.S.E.

Wittenburg Door, The

c/o Youth Specialties, 861 Sixth Avenue, Suite 411, San Diego, CA 92101. (714) 234-6454. Editor: Denny Rydberg. Circulation: 10,000. Bimonthly. Readership: Primarily those who can accept humor and sarcasm as a legitimate form of Christian journalism. Purpose: To encourage church reform and renewal. Manuscript needs. Usually not over 1,500 words. Articles should be punchy and humorous. Enclose S.A.S.E.

Woman's Touch

1445 Boonville Avenue, Springfield, MO 65802. (417) 862-8778. Editor: Elva Hoover. Circulation: 21,000. Bimonthly. Readership: Christian women, various denominations; and women we want to reach for Christ. Purpose: To serve as a vehicle for testimonies and features showing God's grace and work in the lives of women; and to attract other women to Christ. Manuscript needs: First-person stories of crises in the lives of women and families which brought spiritual birth, growth, and/or increased awareness of the needs of others. No sermons. The features should be related to recent (within last 4–5 years) events and also helps with current problems–living alone, the working woman, outreach to the community, coping with a handicap, problems with children, living with an unsaved spouse, winning people to Jesus, preparing for retirement, family life, etc. Enclose S.A.S.E.

Young Ambassador.

Back to the Bible Broadcast, Box 82808, Lincoln, NE 68501. (402) 474-4567. Editor: Melvin A. Jones. Managing Editor: Robert Sink. Circulation: 78,000. Monthly. Readership: Junior-high teens (12–16) who usually attend churches of a conservative, evangelical theological persuasion. Purpose: To help Christian teens live consistently for Christ. To help them grow in their knowledge of the Bible and its principles for living. Manuscript needs: Non-fiction up to 2,000 words. Prefer 800- to 1,500-word articles. Articles on biblical topics affecting teens (i.e., family life, boy-girl relationships, importance of missions, fruit of the Spirit, friends, responsibilities, sins, spiritual growth). Historical or documentary articles about Christian personalities, missions, life in Bible times, etc. Bible-science and apologetics-related articles. Interviews with teens who are demonstrating their faith in Christ in some special way. Biographical articles about teens who have overcome obstacles in their lives or who have served Christ in some unusual way (such as summer mission work). Simplified studies of Bible doctrines. Bible character sketches. Personal experience articles relating to teen-age living. Interviews with well-known Christian sports personalities. Articles about or interviews with missionary kids. "How-to" articles about youth groups, seasonal programs, witnessing, dating, showing appreciation to parents, etc. Short, creative devotional articles of 100- to 800 words. Humorous fillers less than 75 words. Fiction: 1,500-1,800 words. Preference is given to even shorter fiction stories if plot is well developed. Strong, well-developed plot with a definite spiritual tone, but not preachy. A realistic contemporary setting. Offers an answer to problems teens are facing today. Not a "happily-ever-after" ending. A seasonal flavor can help place a story in an issue (submit at least six months in advance of season). A strong spiritual lesson is a must. Need some stories with a strong, clear salvation emphasis. Occasionally accept fantasies with a strong spiritual lesson. Stories should generally revolve around the life of a 13- to 15-year-old character. Enclose S.A.S.E.

Youth Alive!

1445 Boonville Avenue, Springfield, MO 65802. (417) 862-2781. Editor: Carol A. Ball. Circulation: 11,000. Monthly. Readership: High-school teens. Purpose: Encouraging a positive Christian lifestyle—practical Christian living. Manuscript needs: Don't use a lot of fiction; no crafts articles; primarily "how-to-cope" articles—peer group, parent relationships, high-school campus situations, adult authority; use some poetry. Article length: maximum 1,600 words. Enclose S.A.S.E.

Youth and Christian Education Leadership

922 Montgomery Avenue, N.E., Cleveland, TN 37311. (615) 476-4512. Editor: James E. Humbertson. Circulation: 18,000. Monthly. Readership: Christian education workers at the local church level. Purpose: To provide motivational and field-tested aids for C.E. workers. Manuscript needs: Articles up to 1,000 words on promotional ideas for Sunday schools, inspirational articles for teachers, teaching techniques, for each age level of Sunday school and family night classes. Query first.

If interested in EPA membership or further information, write or call:

Gary Warner, Executive Secretary
The Evangelical Press Association, Inc.
P.O. Box 4550
Overland Park, Kansas 66204
(913) 381-2017